Alan W. Brown
Delivering Digital Transformation

Alan W. Brown

Delivering Digital Transformation

A Manager's Guide to the Digital Revolution

DE GRUYTER

ISBN 978-3-11-066008-1

Bibliographic information published by the Deutsche Nationalbibliothek
The Deutsche Nationalbibliothek lists this publication in the Deutsche Nationalbibliografie; detailed
bibliographic data are available on the Internet at http://dnb.dnb.de.

Acknowledgements

The long process of producing a book is both a thrilling and exhausting journey in equal measure. And as with all such endeavors, it would have been impossible without the guidance, help, and support of many people. It is therefore my pleasure to acknowledge their contribution.

Many of the ideas explored in this book have benefited enormously through discussions and interactions with many people at Exeter INDEX, Surrey CoDE, NotBinary, DEfactoED, and elsewhere. In particular, I would like to thank Roger Maull, Mark Thompson, Phil Godsiff, David Lopez, David Plans, Beth Kewell, Carla Bonina, Ben Eaton, Annabelle Gawer, Ben Shenoy, Dave Griffin, James Herbert, Jon Holt, Sacha Rook, David Knight, Tim Field, and many others!

Specific aspects of the book owe a great deal to individuals with whom I have collaborated on various digital transformation projects. They include John Collomosse, Atti Emecz, Jerry Fishenden, Elvin Turner, Stefan Thoma, Tony Grout, and Dave West. Special thanks to Roger Camrass for sharing his deep experiences in business transformation, and for his direct input to several chapters of this book.

Several industry colleagues have been kind enough to devote their time and energy to bring this book to life. They have inspired elements of the content, and helped to shape my understanding of the practical opportunities and challenges of our digital world. My thanks to Charles Cameron, Jonathan Tudor, Graham Scott, Daren Wood, Petrina Steel, and Angus Knowles-Cuttler.

For book production and delivery, my thanks to Steve Hardman at DeGruyter for his guidance and advice. I am particularly indebted to Yin F Lim for her hard work in shaping the format and final content of this book. Her skill, patience, and dedication have been instrumental in getting this book to the finish line.

Finally, none of this would have been possible without the love and support of my family. To Moira, Sean, and Carl, this book is for you.

Contents

Part 3:   building for success

Preface

A revolution is occurring as digital technology becomes embedded in every aspect of our lives. One of the most dramatic impacts is a burgeoning digital economy based on a rapid movement toward commerce conducted online, expanded channels to connect products and service producers with their consumers, business models based on digitized assets and new forms of value capture, dynamic groups of individuals forming communities that quickly influence opinions and buying patterns, emerging digital forms of currency, and much more. Business leaders, industry strategists, academics, and policy makers are all scrambling to make sense of these trends, and to understand the scope and depth of their impact.

More fundamentally, the effects of these disruptive changes can be seen across all industries, with new business models unseating industry incumbents, uncertainty hovering around the future of the workplace, fast collaborative approaches to product and service design driving innovation, and market boundaries being redrawn as supply chains become platform-based ecosystems. So profound are the changes that many now refer to this as the Fourth Industrial Revolution[1], taking us beyond the early Internet age dominated by e-commerce and one-stop information portals toward new forms of value derived from data generated in real time by intelligent interconnected devices at home and on the factory floor, feeding advanced forms of predictive data analytics.

This book provides the background to help the reader understand the context and key themes of the emerging digital economy. It gives a framework for appreciating the critical implications of the drive to adopt digital technologies in business, and offers practical insights to guide the digital transformation being undertaken by today's organizations. In particular, the book explores the fundamental role played by the integration of core infrastructure services (computing power, data, and communication services) to enable this transformation. It highlights the digitization of service delivery as one of the most rapid and compelling trends of the past two decades, spurring not just a technical revolution, but also a cultural shift in what people now expect in service delivery: speed, accuracy, and transparency.

---

1 For an overview of the 4th Industrial Revolution and its impact, see: https://www.weforum.org/agenda/2016/01/the-fourth-industrial-revolution-what-it-means-and-how-to-respond/

Based on a wide variety of examples and success patterns, this book provides today's leaders, managers, and practitioners with the tools for both understanding and leading in the digital world. It offers a broad, accessible point of view on the digital revolution and its impacts in business and society. Central to this are three core themes that lie at the heart of digital transformation: *Agility, Innovation, and Disciplined Management,* for which the book provides a fundamental assessment of current thinking, offers insights through critical analysis of good and bad practices, and illustrates strategies for success using relevant real-life examples. The result is a compelling blend of practical insights underpinned with the latest business and management theory, and supported by a wide range of contemporary examples, best practices, and success patterns.

Consequently, this book is an essential primer and guide for managers and practitioners at every level in organizations finding themselves in need of rethinking their products and services for the digital age. It is also an essential reference for teachers and students in advanced business and management courses seeking a contemporary view of digital technology's impact on strategy and leadership, in the current transformation toward a digital economy.

Structure of the Book

The breadth and scale of its impact means that understanding digital transformation requires considerable effort to assess a wide range of concepts and ideas. Much can be learned through the plethora of books, websites, knowledge portals, reports, and white papers already available. This book aims to draw together many of the key ideas found in these disparate sources in order to arm the reader with a strong practical foundation for effective leadership and strategy in the digital age.

Part 1: Understanding the Context	
1. Digital Dilemmas	2. Foundations of Digital Transformation
3. The Rise of the Machine	4. The Human Dimension
Part 2: Shaping the Path	
5. Agile 6. Innovation	7. Disciplined Management
Part 3: Building for Success	
8. A Case Study	9. Summary and a Look to the Future

Fig. A: An Outline of the Book Structure

Hence, the book is organized into three main parts (see Figure A):
- Part 1, **Understanding the Context**, explores the historical background and essential trends underlying digital transformation.
- Part 2, **Shaping the Path**, expands on the three core themes at the heart of digital transformation and describes the strategies for their adoption.
- Part 3, **Building for Success**, brings together the different threads of digital transformation through a detailed case study, summarizing with a perspective on some of the most significant future directions.

The book can be read in a linear manner, from beginning to end, as a continuous thread of ideas to build your knowledge of digital transformation. Importantly, each chapter has been written a way that allows them to be consumed independent of each other by those with specific interests and concerns.

Finally, for those wanting more information on the themes explored in this book, a website has been set up to provide updates, additional examples, and teaching materials. Please visit www.DigitalHandbook.net or send an email to info@DigitalHandbook.net to find out more, provide your feedback, submit questions, and much more.

Part 1: **understanding the context**

1 Digital Dilemmas

Introduction

Digital transformation initiatives are currently sweeping across all business sectors, and no aspect of business is immune.[1] If anything, the pace of change appears to be picking up,[2] with digital technologies spurring organizations to renew their technology infrastructure, upgrade production processes, and connect with clients through digitally enabled channels.[3] Such initiatives promise to revolutionize traditional business models, optimize the design and delivery of new goods and services, manage production systems more efficiently, redesign working practices and management principles, and much more. But how can we understand the breadth and depth of what is happening? How can we prepare for, and adapt to, its changing form and impact?

What is most visible about this digital transformation revolution is a sea change in the way individuals utilize digital technology. It has become cheap, easy to use, and consumable like a utility. It is mobile, always on, and works seamlessly with the devices in which it is embedded. In just a few years, we have become sophisticated users of such technologies, accustomed to the flexibility and freedoms they enable. But more fundamentally, as Don Tapscott[4] forecast a decade ago, the consequence of a generation of workers and consumers who have 'grown up digital' is a very different set of expectations, working practices, and value models.

The impact in business has been equally as dramatic, if less visible. Initially, industries focused on upgrading digital technologies, media, and delivery channels to open up new ways for connecting with customers, clients, and stakeholders. This resulted in improved efficiencies in areas such as customer service delivery, back office data management, and many forms of management auditing and reporting. Such savings were an essential aim of business strategy during the years of financial austerity experienced in most business sectors following the financial crisis and economic recession of the early 2000s.

However, digital transformation has also led to a more fundamental shift. It has driven organizations to question major assumptions about the users being served, the experiences offered to them, and the most efficient ways to deliver those experiences in a coordinated, consistent and cost-effective way. More recently, digital transformation has come to mean a shift of perspective away from the specific technologies inherent in a digital world and toward the principles on which digital-driven organizations operate. Companies lauded for their digital credentials such as Amazon or Google demonstrate a way of working that differentiates them from their competitors. Their distinguishing features are not specific choices of technology *per se*, but their strategies toward business decision-making and operating excellence in the face of rapid change.[5]

Despite this, the fundamentals of digital transformation are widely misunderstood,[6] and the term appears to be an umbrella for a seemingly endless collection of ideas.[7] McKinsey's global survey in 2015 highlighted that "going digital is quickly becoming common practice, or at least a common mandate, at many companies". The survey recognized, however, that most companies are receiving little value from these initiatives as they struggle to understand and adapt digital technologies to complex, multi-threaded environments.[8] A Gartner CEO survey from 2017 concluded that while CEOs are becoming better at understanding the benefits of a digital business strategy, many of them still align digital transformation with ongoing e-commerce and digital marketing programs rather than viewing it more broadly in terms of digital product design, service innovation, or business model redesign to take advantage of digital platforms and ecosystems.[9]

The scope, significance, and impact of digital transformation on business has become a lightning rod for vigorous discussions on the future of humanity in an increasingly digital world.[10] These include questions about the future of work,[11] the impact of automation on jobs and the economy,[12] the Government's role in a data-driven democracy,[13] and even the very notion of what it means to be "human" in a technologically advanced society.[14] Several dimensions of this debate are particularly worth highlighting here.

The Great Digital Debate

It is impossible to open a newspaper or magazine, explore a technology-oriented website, or read a business-driven blog feed without coming across the issue of digital disruption. Every technological and social commentator has an opinion. Some hold a dystopian view of a world run by computers creating wide-scale unemployment and social unrest; a result of increased machine intelligence powered by data generated from sensors embedded in every street corner, office, and home appliance. For others there awaits a utopian future with humans freed from routine tasks, where increasingly sophisticated computers anticipate our needs to help enrich lives, where multiple data streams are analyzed to remove barriers to improved health, eradicating diseases, and enabling longer lifespans.[15]

Fig. 1.1: Four Key Lenses for Understanding the Digital Debate

The breadth of opinion, and the intensity of the arguments, demonstrate a deep concern not just for the future of business but also for the role of the individual and the shape of our society as a whole. Here we consider four key lenses through which we review the digital debate: globalization, digitization, the dynamic workforce, and consumerization (see Figure 1.1).

Globalization

Human interaction around the world has grown at an astounding rate. In 2018, there was an estimated 3.9 billion people connected via the Internet, over half of the world's population. Only 20 years ago this figure was less than 1%. Amplifying the effect is the growing trend toward urban living. In 2016, 23% of the world's population, or 1.7 billion people, lived in a city with at least 1 million inhabitants. This is expected to grow to as much as 70% by 2050.[16]

A variety of factors lie behind the global shifts influencing the digitization agenda. In his book *The World is Flat*,[17] Thomas Friedman argued that a collection of political and technological flattening forces has redrawn the global map for the Internet age. While some of his analysis has been openly criticized as being myopic and too narrowly defined,[18] [19] the value of his observations is that they place the globalization theme at the forefront of the debate and thus highlight the importance of a global perspective in planning future strategy. His basic message is an important call-to-action:

> The job of the politician [...] should be to help educate and explain to people what world they are living in and what they need to do if they want to thrive within it.

Friedman's work is just one of many examinations of the Internet's global impact and the changing nature of work.[20] It builds on a broader set of observations that takes a systems and service perspective on globalization. Almost 20 years ago, Richard Normann questioned the role of the Internet in terms of place, time, and distance.[21] He stressed that these three key concepts are redefined in a digital era where we think and act differently due to a revised understanding of where we are, who we are with, and how we view speed of action and decision-making. These observations were made in the context of us moving toward a service-based world, whose consequences can be seen in the popularity of social media channels and the rise of new business models such as outsourcing, crowdsourcing, and the gig economy.

Digitization

Technological advances over the past few years have led to wide deployment of high-speed broadband communications providing easy access to information at all times, and the extensive use of mobile devices. We have already passed the stage where the number of mobile devices exceeds the adult population of the world;[22] more than 260 million devices and over 80% penetration in the USA, with similar numbers across most European countries.[23] The speed with which this has occurred is both a driver and a direct consequence of digitization. All forms of information have now been turned into digital format for capture and processing by computers, making them suitable for electronic transmission over an increasingly interconnected infrastructure. Ubiquitous availability of mobile devices has led businesses and government agencies toward online and mobile delivery of information and services.

The move from physical to digital assets (from 'atoms to bits') is just a starting point. By taking a paper form and moving it online, for instance, we do more than just make an electronic version of the data previously captured through the act of writing on a piece of paper. One of the main consequences of ubiquitous communication infrastructure and the resulting flow of information is that we can also change the processes that surround the captured data. Access to the online form can be opened up to a wider audience, the data collected can be analyzed in near real time for common patterns, responses can be standardized to enable greater sharing, and feedback to users can be more immediate and efficient. The creation, management, and use of this digital format of information lends itself to new approaches. Not only can various manual activities (such as verification and error checking) be automated, but the very nature of the processes may also be redesigned to take advantage of the increased flow. Furthermore, as the processes themselves are expressed in digital form, the governance and control of the stream of activities can be digitally instrumented and managed. In this sense, the business processes are also digitized. The resulting "liquification" of business activities[24] removes much of the friction inherent in connecting, analyzing, and synchronizing a myriad of interactions.[25]

Dynamic Workforce

The 21st century has brought with it a number of fundamental challenges to business and society. Particularly in Western economies, the global financial crash that occurred at the start of the century was followed by a series of destabilizing political events with deep implications for business confidence, growth, and job creation. More recent concerns over the fate of European markets, currency fluctuations, and political change in several countries has dampened growth prospects.[26] Such uncertainty has been exacerbated by increasing business failure rates, churn in business start-ups, the rise in temporary fix-term and 'zero-hour contract' jobs, and many more factors impacting the nature of work and the workplace.

Large-scale job losses in the shrinking global economy between 2007 and 2010 have slowly begun to reverse and stabilize. Much of the job growth in the past few years has been due to increasing acceptance of Small-Medium Enterprises (SMEs) as a critical part of the economy. The acceleration of SME start-ups is often hailed as a success for the digital economy,[27] yet as many as 9 out of 10 new businesses fail.[28] The precarious nature of SMEs means that many workers are adjusting to a market where flexibility is essential to any continuity of employment. Hence, an increasingly large part of the workforce is choosing to manage their own portfolio career, with up to 43% of the US workforce (60 million people) expected to be freelance by 2020.[29]

This shift in perspective and expectations is important to how people plan their careers today; specifically, how they view the traditional prospect of a long-term career within a single company. This is particularly challenging for established companies that typically create their human resource mechanisms with the expectation that they will have a stable workforce through long-term employment of staff. Now, such mechanisms are under pressure from the drive for greater innovation within companies, the need to reskill quickly to respond to changes in the business environment, and entrepreneurially minded graduates increasingly attracted to start-ups. In what Accenture calls the "liquid workforce", the focus is on continual skills improvement, dynamically formed teams focused around projects, and more effective employee engagement to reward and retain high performers. The very nature and structure of organizations are being brought into question[30] as companies look to new forms that allow employees to maintain their individual identity and achieve personal goals while being part of a collective workforce.[31]

Consumerization

An organization's role and relationship with its stakeholders is constantly evolving. Many businesses are re-examining the nature of their products, who drives demand, and how they interact with the markets they serve. This has resulted in a great deal of experimentation in business models, particularly in sectors where new digital technologies have been deployed, as companies explore new ways to capture, share, and maintain value. For example, entertainment and social media businesses have begun to question whether the value they offer is not in selling products but in capturing knowledge of changing consumer tastes and behaviors. Such information is directly sold to partners or used to target customers with ads for third-party products. Similarly, retailers have reduced their focus on the profit margins of products sold in physical stores. Instead, they are using these locations to showcase products and create a high-street presence aimed at driving traffic to online purchases, and as pick-up points for these online orders. Likewise, the financial services sector has opened previously closed markets to create knowledge and integration platforms that enable a variety of value chains to be formed, for cross-selling products and combining services from many vendors through customer-centric alliances and joint ventures.

This reassessment of value can also be seen in the consumer's role, as individuals become more aware, informed, and demanding. With increased access and greater transparency of information, they expect more from the products and services that companies provide. As a result, the relationship between a company and its consumers are being driven by:

— **What I know about the company.** With information about its organization, products and services widely available, a company may find it difficult to manage its relationship with its customers. Its ability to control its dialogue with them is severely challenged as power shifts to consumers, industry specialists, and consumer advocate groups.

— **What the company knows about me.** Consumers expect the company to utilize its knowledge about them and their history with the company in all their interactions. Mass markets are essential to a company's growth, but consumers want personalized products and services that recognize their individual needs experiences, and circumstances.

— **What we share about the company's products and services.** Communities are constantly engaged in dialogue about products and services in near real time across many forums online; they become a primary voice in exploring a company's offerings. For example, many turn to online communities such as TripAdvisor, Mumsnet and PistonHeads to learn about new products and share opinions on their use. The nature of these communities is to amplify each individual consumer's experience (positive or negative) to those with whom they interact. Consequently, not only is a company now required to listen to such communities, it is also expected to be an active participant and to respond sensitively as part of an ongoing dialogue.

Issues and Implications

As businesses and communities come to terms with the increasing impact of digital technology, they need to reconsider core elements of their operating environment. All stakeholders need to be galvanized around common themes and priorities for without this, organizations could move in diverse directions; broad 'digital strategies' could devolve into uncoordinated lists of tasks with no common purpose.

Hence, organizations need to be explicit about the philosophy behind the direction taken, and to provide scope to the debate within and across business units. Encouraging an open approach not only recognizes the fundamental changes occurring in the business environment but is also essential for situating the discussions within the broader societal changes taking place. For many organizations, these conversations need to be grounded in what is driving change. They can be categorized into three areas of impact for digital transformation: Faster, Cheaper, Better.

Faster: The need for speed

Organizations spend a lot of time synchronizing different activities to establish a pace that meets stakeholders' and clients' expectations in complex and often unpredictable environments. Critical to their success is their ability to balance the stability and predictability they offer employees, clients, and investors with the operating agility necessary to remain competitive and relevant in the markets they serve. Much of the management theory and practical techniques produced by business schools and consultants explore this dynamic within different constraints.[32][33] However, digital transformation through the deployment of new digital technology has posed additional considerations.

Take for example, a typical structure in which the CEO, answerable to an appointed board of leaders from within and outside the company, is supported by central functions for marketing, human resources, and business operations. The CEO directs several business units that focus on product lines serving different customer groups. Their ability to sense and respond to changes in market demand for the company's offerings is typically an amalgam of historical data, opinions, predictions, and forecasts beset by incomplete and incompatible data sets, misinterpretations of market signals, and poor governance models. The hierarchical nature of the organizational structure, designed to maintain stability and control, struggles to adapt to disruptions in the business environment.

An increasingly digital world provides more rapid and sophisticated access to data generated from all parts of the business. Speed and efficiency in data analysis promises greater flexibility to help companies respond quickly to the signals received. Emerging companies designed to tap into this data are taking advantage of this new world with much tighter connections between information sources that highlight factors such as market directions, product use, supply chain dynamics, production efficiencies, individual and team productivity, and competitive positioning. Such companies build operational processes that are optimized to respond quickly to changes.

In contrast, existing organizations are often unable to react at the pace their markets demand. Consider for example, a retail company that receives data indicating that certain product lines are selling much better than predicted, which in turn leads to a shortage of stock in its stores and warehouses. Typically, the company would need to execute a series of management and operational decision-making procedures to change plans that may have taken many months to negotiate and put in place through careful multi-stakeholder interactions, and signed off by a complex network of stakeholders. Now the company will quickly need to review their contracts with suppliers, alter logistics for shipping to stores and directly to customers, hire new staff, negotiate new sales targets, and so on. Such changes are frequently seen to increase financial, reputational, and governance risk for the company, and thus require constant renegotiation with stakeholders. Often, no one feels empowered to take on this complicated set of changes.

Sensing and responding to market signals at an appropriate pace have become critical capabilities for all organizations looking to succeed in the digital economy. Data is being generated across all aspects of the business: from employee productivity, across the supply chain, within the solutions being delivered to consumers, and now increasingly, from the products and services reporting on the context in which they are being used. Organizations are now evaluated on their ability to generate and analyze these data streams to make better business decisions with immense operational, strategic, and investment implications.

In summary, a discussion about delivery speed highlights the need for a synchronized approach to decision-making in marketplaces evolving with new and more flexible entrants. Most established companies tend to be hindered by organizational inertia as they focus on stability and steady growth. Understanding the flow and pace within their organizations means they must recognize the need to prioritize changes in areas where they can overcome this inertia to reduce damage to the business.

Cheaper: Efficiency and control

As organizations seek to optimize tasks across all their business activities, digital transformation presents an opportunity to take new perspectives on the eternal challenges they face: to run their businesses more efficiently, to find out more about how their products and services are used, and to redesign processes to improve customer experience. Here, we highlight four key areas in efficiency and control presented by digital transformation.

Digital technologies help generate data for better efficiency. In the past, the management and operational information on which organizations relied was often incomplete, out-of-date, or incorrect. The use of digital technologies has changed this. For example, the availability of low-cost lightweight sensors coupled with standard identification schemes such as Quick Response (QR) codes have revolutionized asset management and tracking in many industries. In the retail sector for instance, the use of Radio Frequency Identification (RFID) tagging has improved the accuracy of inventory management and the flexibility of planning processes across multiple sales channels and outlets.[34] In fact, such data streams provide real-time feedback that is incorporated into many different product management processes. Leading companies such as Zara, IKEA, and Walmart attribute much of their success to their ability to reduce waste by using such RFID-generated data effectively throughout their organizations.[35] For instance, Zara is able to claim the following:[36]

- Design-to-store in 15 days (industry average: 6-9 months).
- Up to 12 inventory turns per year (industry average: 3-4 times per year).
- 85% of factory capacity reserved for in-season adjustments.
- Only 10% of unsold items (industry average: 17-20%).

Maximizing flow across digitally enabled enterprises. The adoption of lean manufacturing approaches across many industries in the 1980s and 1990s saw concepts such as minimizing waste, eliminating bottlenecks, and optimizing throughput incorporated into everyday management practice.[37] More recently, increased automation and deployment of digital technologies has given a significant boost to these lean concepts. New digital delivery approaches have made key business processes more accessible and transparent, while the use of more intelligent algorithms tuned by processing large amounts of operational data has enhanced predictive capabilities. In turn, communication has been strengthened through closer interaction between supply chain partners, customers, and employees.

Maximizing flow across digitally enabled enterprises is a critical underpinning of the Industry 4.0 movement. With its roots in the German manufacturing community, Industry 4.0 focuses on reducing friction in business processes through the end-to-end digitization of all physical assets and their integration into ecosystems with value chain partners. The flow of goods and services are improved by generating, analyzing and communicating data seamlessly and by leveraging a wide range of new technologies to create value.[38] Companies such as Bosch have adopted Industry 4.0 approaches across their manufacturing sites to increase shop floor transparency, improve process quality, find efficient ways of dealing with high levels of product variety, and adapt automation to support human workers and improve the working environment.[39] This last point is particularly important; advanced automation can relieve workers from monotonous or ergonomically challenging tasks and thus reduce accidents, improve accuracy, and speed up critical routine tasks.

Digitization of assets can lead to new supply chain models. By embedding sensors and other identification tags to their assets, businesses are seeking to learn more about the manufacture, distribution, and use of their products to streamline existing supply chains and increase intelligence in their operations. However, while the digitization of physical assets can improve access to available information, it can also overwhelm the organization's ability to analyze the data for better decision-making.[40] To help alleviate this, vendors of supply chain management systems such as SAP are investing significantly in new approaches to the storage, management, and analysis of operational data in areas fundamental to Enterprise Resource Planning (ERP).[41]

More importantly, greater real-time access to information on assets is changing the nature of supply chain management. New management and analytical models view supply chains as networks of suppliers operating within a cooperative ecosystem. Such an approach encourages and supports digital supply networks where information is more readily created, shared, and analyzed. The dynamics of such networked ecosystems support new ways for their participants to grow through the shared incentive approaches the platform provides.

Several business domains are already experiencing radical shifts in their supply chains. For example, companies such as Amazon, eBay, Alibaba, and Walmart act as major platform providers in the retail markets they support. They have created large communities of sellers (in 2015, Amazon claimed to have over 2 million sellers[42]) and are investing significantly in partnerships to streamline their logistics and delivery services across the world. For instance, eBay Australia has a substantial digitally focused partnership with SAP[43] while Walmart recently announced their use of an IBM-supplied blockchain solution to enhance digital traceability and transparency across their supply chain.[44] There are similar important changes in the automotive[45] and healthcare[46] industries.

Incomplete understanding of customers and their needs. Finally, it is essential to recognize that inefficient product and service delivery is not necessarily due to poor execution, but to an incomplete understanding of the customer and their needs.[47] Many organizations approach customer engagement using outdated strategies that are no longer effective in a digital world influenced by large, globally-connected communities of individuals who want more from the companies behind the products and services they consume. Edelmen's 2014 Brandshare study[48] found that nine out of 10 consumers want a more meaningful relationship with brands, but less than one in five believe brands are delivering on that wish. Two-thirds of respondents said that they have a one-sided relationship with brands, which request their information but do not share or engage in return. More than seven in 10 feel that companies have a self-serving goal to increase profits rather than a sincere commitment to understanding their customers better.

Many organizations are now focusing on doing so by increasingly paying more attention to how their products and services are designed and the role their customers play in the process. Companies like Apple, Valve, and IDEO are at the forefront of such a design-led view of product creation,[49] founded on the 'design thinking' approach pioneered at the Stanford d.school[50] and explored in detail by David and Tom Kelley at IDEO.[51][52] Their work focuses on a deeper understanding of who is the customer through the use of techniques from anthropology, psychology, and broader design disciplines such as architecture and the arts. By building empathy with the client's problem, greater insight is brought to "the job to be done"[53] and the resulting solution is a much simpler, optimized fit to the need being addressed. Constant testing of solutions in the client's environment ensures that misunderstandings are clarified before substantial intellectual and financial investment has been made, learning from early engagement is captured, and producers and consumers feel joint ownership of the outcomes. In this way, dead ends are quickly detected and backtracking is encouraged rather than avoided.

Companies adopting such a design-intensive view of product creation have seen improved customer experience. One example is the work carried out by IDEO at Bank of America to increase the use of savings accounts.[54] Closely observing the bank's customers, the IDEO team found that they emotionally identified more with the act of saving than with the amount saved. This inspired the 'round-up' concept, where customers save with every transaction by rounding up the amount to an agreed level (e.g., to the nearest $10). The concept was used by 2.5

million customers and resulted in 700,000 new savings accounts being created in the first year of its implementation.

Better: Knowing and doing

The real measure of all products and services is how well they meet users' expectations in addressing their needs. Organizations must understand how their products and services are used, and adapt their solutions in line with customer feedback. They must also optimize their processes to be as effective as possible in delivering these solutions. This requires them to leverage the skills of their teams in learning from current product use and adapting to change when reacting to these insights.

Customer service activities are organizations' most direct channel for understanding their customers' needs and responses to their offerings. Typically, a company invests significantly in a variety of online, phone, and face-to-face channels to support their customers in placing orders, requesting additional information, enquiring about process status, returning damaged goods, and making refund claims. These are important tasks for organizations to learn about their customers; the bedrock of better customer service.

The proliferation of online mechanisms for consumers to provide feedback means companies can now mine such data to understand usage patterns as well. This enables them to find areas for improvement, extract indications of value in the services being used, and identify opportunities for new features. Lowering computing costs mean these activities are boosted by sophisticated automation for processing natural language and powerful algorithms for machine learning. Consumer product and retail organizations now routinely examine customer emails and online communications not only to define the root causes of problems encountered with features and processes, but also to determine the sentiment and impact of each interaction. This data is used to optimize the way each interaction is handled and forms a critical input for ongoing strategy and planning exercises.[55]

Identifying and categorizing customer challenges is an important first step. The need for rapid response to changes in market conditions, competition, and customer feedback requires the organization to be able to reconfigure its processes at speed. For many companies such adaptation is difficult due to inflexible decision-making and production processes. Consequently, there has been a lot of interest in how to design products and organizations that inherently support restructuring to meet changing demands. From a product perspective, the componentization of solutions has long been a subject of study.[56] Techniques such as component-based design and service-oriented architectures have led to product line approaches, with solutions formed around product families that offer related sets of capabilities to meet a wide range of potential customer needs. Furthermore, they are extensible through common interfaces encouraging innovation from third parties and end users. This is most clearly seen in software-based products that now extensively use Application Programming Interfaces (APIs) as a general architectural principle to provide external users with easy access to product functionality.[57]

However, the challenge of reconfiguration and adaptability has been much more difficult from an organizational perspective. Structural and cultural inhibitors block many organizations' attempts to be more responsive to their dynamic environment. More radical management approaches have been proposed[58] [59] where hierarchies are flattened, and outcome-based prioritization is promoted. However, adoption of these organizational forms has been slow in most existing companies practicing traditional management styles. More successful are attempts to expand understanding of market dynamics, increase skills within teams, and break down the silos that exist across organizations. This push toward greater adaptability in organizations is what Peter Senge refers to as a "learning organization".[60] Senge emphasized the need to promote a broader systems-thinking approach to problem-solving where individuals and teams are encouraged to share their understanding to improve performance. His work has influenced a wide variety of approaches adopted by organizations looking to reshape how they grow their employees' skills, and build high-performing teams as well as a flexible organizational culture that adapts to changing market conditions.[61] These concepts celebrating team performance in very dynamic environments are at the heart of the agile software delivery approaches that dominate practices of software-intensive systems creation today.[62]

Summary

Driven by rapid technological change, organizations face new kinds of pressures to rethink their approach to business strategy in a world that is quickly moving toward digital products and services. For mature organizations the most critical task is to update existing infrastructure to take advantage of the efficiencies promised by new technology. Not only does this allow them to be 'Faster, Cheaper, Better', it also helps them reorganize to become more resilient in an evolving environment.

Within this context, digital modernization programs taking place across many organizations are accelerating the digitization of their core assets, rebalancing spending toward digital engagement channels, fixing flaws in their digital technology stacks, and replacing outdated technology infrastructure with cloud-hosted services. Such programs are essential for organizations to remain competitive and relevant in a world that increasingly rewards those that can adapt quickly to market changes, raise the pace of new product and service delivery, and maintain tight stakeholder relationships.

In many business domains, however, modernizing existing ways of working with digital technology is necessary but not sufficient. Beyond technology replacement activities, many organizations are rethinking their approach to all aspects of their business models: which customers they serve, what those customers value, which channels are most appropriate to reach them, how costs can be managed more effectively, where to compete and who to partner. Digital technology is driving a transformation in business, which we will examine in the next chapter.

References

1 Accenture (2018). *The Future of all Industry is Disruption – and That's a Good Thing.* Wired.co.uk. Available at: https://www.wired.co.uk/article/the-future-of-all-industry-is-disruption-and-thats-a-good-thing

2 Friedman, T.L. (2017). *Thank You for Being Late.* Penguin.

3 World Economic Forum (2016). *Digital Transformation of Industries: Demystifying Digital and Securing $100 Trillion for Society and Industry by 2025.* January. Available at: digital.weforum.org.

4 Tapscott, D. (2009). *Grown Up Digital.* McGraw Hill.

5 Schmidt, E. and Cohen, J. (2013). *The New Digital Age: Reshaping the Future of People, Nations and Business.* Vintage.

6 McQuivey, J. (2013). *Digital Disruption: Unleashing the Next Wave of Innovation.* Amazon Publishing.

7 Rogers, D. (2016). *The Digital Transformation Playbook: Rethinking Your Business for the Digital Age.* Columbia University Press.

8 McKinsey (2015). *Cracking the Digital Code. September.* Available at: http://www.mckinsey.com/ business-functions/digital-mckinsey/our-insights/cracking-the-digital-code

9 Gartner (2017). *Gartner Survey Shows 42 Percent of CEOs Have Begun Digital Business Transformation.* Press Release. April 24. Available at: http://www.gartner.com/newsroom/id/3689017

10 A good introduction to many aspects of this debate can be found at http://www.torch.ox.ac.uk/report-what-does-it-mean-be-human-digital-age

11 Maitland, A. and Thompson, P. (2014). *Future Work: Changing Organizational Culture for the New World of Work.* Palgrave Macmillan.

12 Carr, N. (2011). *The Big Switch: Rewiring the World from Edison to Google.* W.W. Norton & Co.

13 Brown, A.W., Fishenden, J., and Thompson, M. (2015). *Digitizing Government: Understanding and Implementing New Digital Business Models.* Palgrave McMillan.

14 Scott, L. (2015). *The Four-Dimensional Human: Ways of Being in the Digital World.* William Heineman.

15 Friedman, T.L. (2017). *Thank You for Being Late.* Penguin.

16 ITU (2018). *Measuring the Information Society, Vol 1.* ITU Publications. Statistical reports. Available at: https://www.itu.int/en/ITU-D/Statistics/Documents/publications/misr2018/MISR-2018-Vol-1-E.pdf

17 Friedman, T.L. (2005). *The World is Flat: A Brief History of the 21st Century.* Farrar, Straus and Giroux.

18 Aronica, R. and Ramdoo, A. (2006). *The World is Flat? A Critical Analysis of The New York Bestseller by Thomas Friedman.* Megan Kiffer Press.

19 See, for example, a summary of the arguments at https://hbr.org/2014/11/the-world-is-still-not-flat%E2%80%8B

20 For example, similar viewpoints are expressed in: Hamel, G.(2012). *What Matters Now?* John Wiley; Denning, S. (2010). *The Leader's Guide to Radical Management.* John Wiley; Gray, D. (2014). *The Connected Company,* O'Reilly; Carr, N. (2011). *The Shallows: What the Internet is Doing to Our Brains,* W.W. Norton.

21 Normann, R. (2001). *Reframing Business: When the Map Changes the Landscape.* John Wiley.

22 Evans, B. (2019). *The End of Mobile.* Available at: https://www.ben-evans.com/benedictevans/2019/5/28/the-end-of-mobile

23 Mobile phone penetration as share of the population in the United States from 2014 to 2020. Statista.com. Available at: https://www.statista.com/statistics/222307/forecast-of-mobile-phone-penetration-in-the-us/

24 Ng, I. and Wakenshaw, S.Y. (2017). The Internet-of-Things: Review and Research Directions, International *Journal of Research in Marketing*, 34, 3-21.

25 Ng, I. (2014). *Creating New Markets in the Digital Economy: Value and Worth.* Cambridge University Press.

26 Goodley, S. (2017). UK business confidence at lowest point for six years, say forecasters. 17 July. The Guardian. Available at: https://www.theguardian.com/politics/2017/jul/17/uk-business-confidence-britain-economic-growth-brexit-anxiety.

27 World Trade Organization (2019). *Technological Innovation, Supply Chain Trade, and Workers in a Globalized World.* Global Value Chain Development Report. Available at: https://www.wto.org/english/res_e/booksp_e/gvc_dev_report_2019_e.pdf

28 Tidd, J., and Bessant, J. (2018). *Managing Innovation: Integrating Technological, Market and Organizational Change.* John Wiley.

29 Accenture (2016). *Liquid Workforce: Building the Workforce for Today's Digital Demands.* Technology Vision Report. Available at: https://www.accenture.com/fr-fr/_acnmedia/PDF-2/Accenture-Liquid-Workforce-Technology-Vision-2016-france.pdf

30 See, for example, https://www2.deloitte.com/insights/us/en/focus/human-capital-trends/2017/organization-of-the-future.html

31 Birkinshaw, J. and Ridderstrale, J. (2017). *Fast/Forward: Make Your Company Fit for the Future.* Stanford Business Books.

32 Hamel, G. (2012). *What Matters Now? John* Wiley.

33 Drucker, P. (2007). *Management Challenges for the 21st Century* (Classic Drucker Collection). Routledge.

34 Visich, J.K., Powers, J.T., Roethlei, C.J. (2009). Empirical Applications of RFID in the Manufacturing Environment. *International Journal of Radio Frequency Identification Technology and Applications,* 2(3-4), 115–132.

35 Erply (2019). *In the Success Stories of H&M, Zara, Ikea and Walmart, Luck is not a Key Factor.* Available at: https://erply.com/in-the-success-stories-of-hm-zara-ikea-and-walmart-luck-is-not-a-key-factor

36 Petro, G. (2012). *The Future of Fashion Retailing: The Zara Approach (Part 2 of 3).* Forbes. Available at: https://www.forbes.com/sites/gregpetro/2012/10/25/the-future-of-fashion-retailing-the-zara-approach-part-2-of-3

37 Bicheno, J. and Holweg, M. (2016). *The Lean Toolbox, 5th Edition.* Picsie Books.

38 PwC (2016). Industry 4.0: *Building the Digital Enterprise.* 2016 Global Industry 4.0 Survey. Available at: https://www.pwc.com/gx/en/industries/industries-4.0/landing-page/industry-4.0-building-your-digital-enterprise-april-2016.pdf

39 http://i40.bosch-si.com/

40 EY (2016). *Digital Supply Chain: It's All About That Data.* Available at: http://www.ey.com/Publication/vwLUAssets/Digital_supply_chain_-_its_all_about_the_data/$FILE/EY-digital-supply-chain-its-all-about-that-data-final.pdf

41 https://www.sap.com/uk/products/digital-supply-chain.html

42 Perez, S. (2015). *Amazon's Third-Party Sellers Ship Record-Breaking 2 Billion Items In 2014, But Merchant Numbers Stay Flat.* Techcrunch.com. Available at: https://techcrunch.com/2015/01/05/amazon-third-party-sellers-2014/

43 Dingle, A. (2017). *How eBay Australia and SAP Ariba are Working Together.* Supply Management. 31 July. Available at: https://www.cips.org/supply-management/news/2017/july/how-ebay-australia-and-sap-ariba-are-working-together/

44 Kharif, O. (2018). *Walmart, Sam's Club Start Mandating Suppliers Use IBM Blockchain.* 24 September. Bloomberg.com. Available at: https://www.bloomberg.com/news/articles/2018-09-24/walmart-sam-s-club-start-mandating-suppliers-use-ibm-blockchain

45 EY (2016). *The Rise of the Digitally Driven Supply Chain Ecosystem.* Available at: https://advisory.ey.com/digital/rise-digitally-driven-supply-chain-ecosystem

46 Oleksy, C. (2013). *Surviving in the Medical Device Supply Chain's Evolving Ecosystem.* Medical Product Outsourcing. Available at: http://www.mpo-mag.com/issues/2013-03/view_features/surviving-in-the-medical-device-supply-chains-evolving-ecosystem/

47 Richards, K. and Jones, E. (2008). Customer Relationship Management: Finding Value Drivers, *Industrial Marketing Management,* 37(2):120-130 .

48 The study involved 15,000 consumers in 12 countries. See more at: https://www.edelman.com/insights/intellectual-property/brandshare-2014

49 See, for example, the "Human-centred" design toolkit provided by Ideo at https://www.ideo.com/ post/design-kit

50 https://dschool.stanford.edu

51 Kelley, T. (2016). *The Art of Innovation: Lessons in Creativity from IDEO.* Profile Books.

52 Kelley, T. (2016). *The 10 Faces of Innovation: Strategies for Heightening Creativity.* Profile Books.

53 https://hbr.org/ideacast/2016/12/the-jobs-to-be-done-theory-of-innovation.html

54 Knapp, J. (2016). *Sprint: How to Solve Big Problems and Test New Ideas in Just 5 Days*. Simon & Schuster.

55 Webb, N.J. (2016). *What Customers Crave: How to Create Relevant and Memorable Experiences at Every Touchpoint*. McGraw-Hill.

56 Brown, A.W. (2000). *Component-based Software Engineering*. Addison-Wesley.

57 O'Neil, M., Moyer, K. and Malinverno, P. *(2017). From APIs to Ecosystems: API Economy Best Practices for Building a Digital Platform*. Gartner Report, G00331662.

58 Birkinshaw, J. and Ridderstråle, J. (2015). *Adhocracy for an Agile Age*. McKinsey Quarterly. Available at: https://www.mckinsey.com/business-functions/organization/our-insights/adhocracy-for-an-agile-age

59 Denning, S. (2010). *The Leaders Guide to Radical Management*. Jossey-Bass.

60 Senge, P. (2006). *The Fifth Discipline: The Art and Practice of the Learning Organization, 2nd Edition*. Random House.

61 Heath, C. and Heath, D. (2011). *Switch: How to Change When Change is Hard*. Random House Books.

62 Schwaber, K. (2004). *Agile Project Management with Scrum*. Microsoft Press.

2 Fundamentals of Digital Transformation

Introduction

For several decades, there have been efforts to capture and share digital information. The early evolution of computers demonstrated the power and applicability of high-speed, reliable computation for many tasks across all business sectors. A key challenge was to manage the voracious appetite of computers to consume the data on which they operated. Much of computing history has been dedicated to finding new ways to encode, store, and transmit that data, from the early punch cards and magnetic tapes to today's solid-state devices, flash memory, and beyond. Naturally, much of the activity was on efforts to convert data in physical forms (e.g., books, photographs, and video tapes) for easy storage and manipulation. Digitization allows us to convert analogue information in any form such as text, images, and sound into a digital format so that it can be recorded, processed, analyzed, and communicated.

However, digitization takes on a broader implication when we also consider the new ways of generating data made possible by advances in electronics, telecommunications, and new material science. These enable us to generate new sources of data previously considered impossible or impractical, produce such data at high speeds and low costs, and use widely available communication technologies to distribute it to places where it can be recorded, examined, and used. Whether this is data about the human body from a wearable wristband, traffic patterns recorded by cameras across a busy city, or the minute variations in pressure detected by sensors inside an aircraft engine, the availability of such digitized data sources opens up once unimaginable opportunities for business and society.

Taking advantage of such availability of digital information, however, requires more than just a technology refreshment program. It also demands new approaches in using the data to optimize ongoing activities, and potentially a deeper review of the business models and organizational structures supporting them. As a result, the broader transformation that the organization must undergo will disturb the current status quo and significantly redirect how it plans, operates, and evolves.

For most organizations deploying digital technologies, their initial focus addresses four primary areas:

- **Product innovation.** Access to digital information, and the ability to process it quickly and accurately, has driven a host of new product opportunities across all business sectors. Consider image processing. The ability of smartphones to capture high-quality photographs and videos means that much of the world's population now carry with them a device capable of capturing, analyzing, and sharing images. This has opened up many new product possibilities in fields as diverse as healthcare, insurance, banking, and retail.
- **Brand awareness.** The rapid deployment of broadband and wireless Internet access has brought new opportunities for companies to market their products and services online to a global market. Moving advertising online has been a particularly strong trend over the past two decades. Marketing operations have also been completely redesigned to take advantage of digital technologies that enable a better understanding of user behaviors, activities, and attitudes.
- **Efficiency and performance.** Back-office operations are more efficient with digital technologies deployed to offer insight into business performance, monitor and manage day-to-day activities, and support planning and scheduling processes. Since the 1980s, ERP products have taken over business operational functions. More recently, cloud-based services have matured to the point that most back-office operations consist of rapidly evolving capabilities stitched together to provide an integrated system covering all aspects of business delivery.
- **Customer experience.** Product design and delivery has significantly improved with the use of digital solutions for concept design, prototyping, simulation, and construction. Products are easier to use, are designed to meet a wider variety of user scenarios, and are of higher quality than ever before. Beyond improvements to the user experience, greater understanding of consumer activities allows companies to gain deeper insights into their products and services in use. For example, new opportunities for improvement and customization arise with Internet-enabled products such as consumer goods, in-home monitoring technologies, and connected entertainment devices that report back to manufacturers in real time on their usage, performance, and status.

Here, we consider several critical dimensions of what's come to be known as 'digital transformation'. We first look at the importance of an ambidextrous strategy for organizations needing to improve current business practices while looking to the future. Then we make broader observations concerning the impacts of digital technology in moving organizations toward a new way of working in the digital economy. Finally, we provide a framework for understanding digital transformation, illustrated with several case studies.

Ambidexterity

Disruptive change affects all industries and organizations. Sometimes it may be unforeseen events that completely change the context in which the business operates. More often, however, such disruption is part of ongoing change whose impact is increasingly being felt. Whether the disruption arises from new technological advances or other changes in the business environment, organizations need to be able to continue operating while adapting appropriately. The challenge faced in such circumstances is how to manage and maintain the core business while simultaneously nurturing new opportunities. In facing this classic 'innovator's dilemma', ambidexterity is critical particularly given the uncertainty and ambiguity of today's digital era.[1]

Most organizations typically define and maintain their success through large-scale production and delivery mechanisms. These ensure stability in their current operations, but are generally ineffective in encouraging growth of new ventures. Such established structures are designed based on governance practices, key performance indicators, processes, and incentives suitable for mature business activities, but are much less appropriate for new ventures requiring greater flexibility and tolerance for ambiguity. Businesses optimize around currently deployed business models, often at the expense of exploring new business opportunities.

Digital disruption through the wide-scale accessibility of computer-based technologies is particularly challenging for mature organizations. They face a dual transformation:[2] their existing business operations must address the significant challenge of remaining relevant in a digital world, while new opportunities must be explored quickly. This requires a rethink of their fundamental value proposition in the context of potential threats from a reframing of the problem domain, the appearance of radical solution concepts, and the emergence of companies never previously considered to be competing in the same space.

To address these challenges, an organization needs to simultaneously pursue two distinct paths. The first concerns managing its existing business. To consolidate current activities, the company could employ digital technologies for efficiency and cost-cutting approaches to improve productivity, increase profit margins, and reinforce market dominance in critical areas. However, such defensive tactics are often insufficient on their own. The organization may need to look for more radical, structural actions internally (e.g., combining business units, consolidating product lines, withdrawing from particular markets) or pursue external actions aimed at more aggressive moves within and across adjacent industry sectors (e.g., acquiring smaller competitors, partnering with complementary offering providers, and exploring new channels to market). Such moves are direct reactions to the digital disruptions they face, and must align with the digital technologies and processes deployed as critical components of their execution. However, they do not attempt to change the organization's fundamental value proposition to the market.

In contrast, the second path is a journey toward a new way of working supporting a distinct set of customer challenges, or offering a radically new value proposition that changes customers' perceptions. In digitally disrupted markets, new opportunities arise from technological breakthroughs at a price point that enables new ways of solving existing problems, or now allows new challenges to be feasibly addressed. For example, the creative industries have been massively disrupted by the availability of affordable mass storage, acceleration of smartphone sales, and widespread deployment of reliable wireless and broadband connectivity. As a result, incumbent companies are investing heavily in new services and products outside their core businesses. Whether through organic growth or external acquisition, companies such as Sony, Warner Music, and Atlantic Records have been experimenting in such diverse areas as self-publishing of media, development of open-source media formats, and establishing music education academies.

Following both of these paths often requires ambidextrous organizations to create separate units outside their existing business, with distinct practices, structures, and cultures that enable the agility and flexibility inherent in early-stage start-up ventures. While both the old and new elements may logically be part of a single company, they differ substantially in their operating approaches and environments and therefore may also require different locations, management by different teams, and unique branding. For example, several existing insurance and financial services organizations have set up distinct Internet-based offerings aimed at markets underserved by traditional offerings (e.g., Aviva with QuoteMe-Happy.com, and RSA Group with MORE TH>N).

In terms of overall strategy, senior leadership teams deploy an ambidextrous organizational model to protect the two paths from each other: the larger existing business unit from stifling new business growth, and the new business unit from disturbing the ongoing operation of maintaining market equilibrium. This makes it possible for such organizations to manage an existing business while experimenting with new ideas that could potentially damage or destroy that business. Such an ambidextrous approach to management is particularly acute in a digital disruption context. The pace of introducing new technology, together with the volatility inherent in disrupted markets, brings enormous risks for mature organizations that need to maintain commitments to customers and suppliers, sustain large workforces in multiple locations, and manage significant investment in the assets that support them. The "creative destruction" first described almost a century ago by Schumpeter may be fine in theory,[3] but the reality for leaders in today's digital economy is often an organization at war with itself as it responds to the pressures of digital transformation faced simultaneously from many directions.

Toward the Second Machine Age

Technology-fueled disruption is not new. Many examples can be gleaned from the past to help us understand and scope the impacts of change brought by technical breakthroughs. Consider this: what the steam engine did to spark the Industrial Revolution in the late 18th century, computer technology achieved with the digital revolution toward the end of the 20th century[4][5]. Before the Industrial Revolution, the limitations of human power created a natural ceiling to the kinds of activities and approaches for addressing the problems faced in all aspects of life. The steam engine (among other things) broke through this ceiling by removing the barrier of human strength with much greater power provided by machines that began to augment, and subsequently replace, human effort. Similarly, the widespread availability of computer technology is now breaking through the barrier of limited human mental ability. Today, machines not only follow the steps programmed by humans to carry out calculations; they are also learning by analyzing, inferring, and adapting their capabilities over time to go beyond the bounds of human intelligence.

Capitalizing on highly-capable computer processors and the massive growth of new data sources, computing's focus has now moved from obtaining and manipulating data toward better ways of understanding and learning from the data to predict future behavior. Andrew McAfee and Eric Brynjolfsson call this the "Second Machine Age".[6] They argue that the changes underway in the digital world are as profound as those brought forth by the Industrial Revolution. The First Machine Age of the early 21st century was characterized by the deployment of digital technologies to optimize existing tasks through increased automation and open access to knowledge. In contrast, the Second Machine Age we have now entered has advanced to the stage that machines are capable of learning, connecting, and reconfiguring their ways of working in light of past experiences. Machines are now able to extract patterns from large amounts of data to adapt their behaviors and to look for new patterns, enabling them to predict future events.

However, as McAfee and Brynjolfsson emphasize, technological advances are only part of the equation. The Second Machine Age is driven by two further trends: the appearance of large, influential young companies disrupting incumbents across business domains, and the opportunity for organizations to tap into large communities providing knowledge, expertise, and drive. Organizations seeking to be successful in the Second Machine Age are beginning to recognize that adopting digital technologies is only part of their strategy. Also critical to their sustainability is a deeper analysis of the value they offer in a quickly evolving market, a broad examination of how they position their business activities in light of new entrants, and a careful review of management practices to adjust the pace of decision-making, establish appropriate levels of governance, and motivate a workforce driven by new expectations and concerns. Such activities are broadly considered to be a 'digital transformation'; a modernization of technology as well as a change in attitude and approach to spawn new business practices and structures.

Many recent surveys point toward the same conclusion: While business leaders recognize the importance and inevitability of digital transformation in their organization and throughout their industry, few believe they have sufficient grasp of the core elements that shape such a transformation. This dichotomy is repeatedly highlighted across areas such as marketing,[7] customer service delivery,[8] government IT,[9] and management strategy.[10] A broad framework is required to create a common set of concepts and vocabulary that helps to frame digital transformation activities, provides a way to outline its scope, and offers a basis for forming a narrative across the digital transformation landscape. We address this later in this chapter.

The Big Shift

Digital transformation is taking place in the context of formidable changes in business and society. The so-called 'big shift' toward greater use of digital technology (also described by Nicholas Carr as the "big switch"[11]) tracks the journey organizations take under intense competition from a global marketplace that forces them to enhance their capabilities for a digital world. In the UK this is exacerbated by decreasing productivity figures even as new digital infrastructures are being deployed.[12]

Understanding the relationship between worker productivity and digital transformation is not straightforward. There appears to be significant challenge in applying traditional methods for measuring productivity and value when considering the use and adaptation of digital technologies. One approach is to move away from holding value in knowledge assets, toward participating in knowledge flows.[13] In a world of volatile change, the measure of an organization's success may be more appropriately determined by its ability to sense and respond to the many different flows of knowledge around them rather than by its direct ownership of those knowledge assets. These flows occur internally across business units and supply chains, and externally with customers and in broader community interactions. The conversations taking place across these boundaries are important because they hold the key to behaviors and attitudes that inform the desirability of new and existing products and services, as well as strengthen confidence in decision-making on strategy and directions in times of massive uncertainty.

Understanding the importance of information flow has its implications, seen most strikingly in emerging platform technologies and their business models.[14] Platform models create value by connecting potential buyers and sellers through online marketplaces that encourage growth within and across these communities, to benefit all participants of this collaborative ecosystem. More buyers attract more sellers. More sellers attract more buyers. As a consequence, the platform provider financially benefits from the exchange of goods and services it facilitates and generates new business opportunities by mining the interactions within the ecosystem it has created. Platform companies are stimulating massive growth by encouraging large ecosystems of partners and consumers in the USA, China, and across the world. In practical terms, the Big Shift's impact can be seen in the stock market valuation of platform companies such as Airbnb (in mid-2017 valued more than all the major hotel chains combined despite owning no properties), Alphabet (parent company of Google), Amazon, Alibaba, and Baidu.

Major consulting firms are beginning to provide insight into how the Big Shift is evolving in industry and society. For example, the Deloitte Shift Index[15] tracks 25 metrics in the following three elements to measure what Deloitte terms "the waves of change" taking place in the digital world:

- **Foundation.** Tracks advances in the digital technology infrastructure and public policy that underlie business effectiveness, considered the core elements of digital transformation. Includes the current cost of storage and computing power, and the availability of high-speed Internet access to the communities being served.
- **Flow.** Considers the extent of interaction between knowledge, capital, and talent which amplify the flow. Typically requires acquiring more profound knowledge and understanding of the digital environment in use. Includes the use of wireless Internet, public and private transportation, and worker engagement in their jobs.
- **Impact.** Explores the effects of longer-term trends across industries. Requires a broader understanding of the industry sector and an organization's role in relation to its peers. Includes stock price volatility, return on assets, and brand loyalty.

Over the past few years the Deloitte Shift Index has highlighted strong growth in the foundational elements, driven by the continued fall in computing costs. Despite predictions to the contrary, this improvement seems set to continue. With flow elements, recent years have seen wide participation in social media and the use of collaborative tools to support group activities. Sharing of ideas and community activities is blossoming, but the main bottleneck is the lack of trained people in key areas such as Data Science and Artificial Intelligence. The impact elements are growing less quickly. A volatile economic environment has created a great deal of churn in business, with a high failure rate for start-ups and continued hesitancy in larger enterprises. Mature companies are grappling with new organizational models that reduce delays in decision-making and enable greater strategic flexibility.

Over the life of the Deloitte Shift Index there have been notable changes, namely several paradoxes highlighted in its most recent report:[16]

- between increased individual productivity and declining company-level return on assets.

- between the increasing power of individuals over their lives, and the declining autonomy at the workplace due to increased automation.
- between the increasing insight and transparency that digital technology provides, and the declining sense of being in control of critical elements of our business and home lives.

The Deloitte report offers useful insight into the digital transformation journey experienced by many organizations, concluding that "companies and individuals are increasingly willing to participate in knowledge flows but still learning how to understand and harness them".

Defining the Digital Economy

Intuitively, the digital economy encompasses all economic activity and impacts of digital businesses within a wide set of domains. However, this broad perspective means that the term 'digital economy' is often quite ill-defined. Almost all businesses make use of digitized assets in some form, even if this is limited to email and websites, and they increasingly rely on technology to manage and improve their performance, which involves installing and upgrading digital products and services. Defining the scope and extent of the digital economy is therefore challenging, with interpretations dependent on the definition source and how the resulting analysis is expected to be used. Here, we explore some of these discussions, and consider three particular viewpoints to understand the digital economy in terms of impact on government policy, statistical measurement of industry growth in key sectors, and the flow of online commerce.

Governments and politicians tend to use broad descriptions of the digital economy that highlight its importance in driving policy changes, particularly in times of political uncertainty and slow economic growth. Hence, the UK government's inclusive definition of the digital economy as "both the digital access of goods and services, and the use of digital technology to help businesses".[17] While the Organization for Economic Cooperation and Development (OECD) considers the term to encompass all economic impacts of digital transformation in business and society.[18]

Stricter measurement and analysis require a tighter scope. Statisticians and policymakers define the digital economy according to industry and output. Typically, this may cover Information and Communication Technologies (ICT) including manufacturing and services, and digital content involving everything from e-commerce to music to architecture.[19] Specific industries could be selected using Standard Industrial Classification codes to define the core activity of registered businesses. This means businesses categorized in certain industries (e.g., ICT) are considered part of the digital economy while those in other categories (e.g., pharmaceuticals) are not. Their economic activity, evidenced through employment profiles, reported income, taxes paid, can be used as a basis for assessing activity in the digital economy.

The narrowest definition of the digital economy is to consider it as the combination of two key mechanisms:[20] e-commerce transactions, i.e., the trading of goods or services over computer networks such as the Internet; and the deployment of enabling infrastructure such as hardware, software, and telecommunications networks to support e-commerce. This mechanistic view enables measurement by monitoring online commercial transactions together with the purchase, installation, and support of the technology facilitating the flow of goods and services. Both of these elements can be reasonably estimated. For example, in terms of online commercial transactions, figures from CapGemini indicate that UK online retail sales reached £133bn in 2016, an increase of £18bn, or 15.9%, year-on-year.[21]

The estimated size of the digital economy can also be determined using hybrid approaches, and the results can vary considerably depending on the scope selected. Accenture, for example, examines how digital aspects add value to the entire economy by tracing the use of digital skills, equipment, and intermediate goods and services in the production of all goods and services to offer a comprehensive view of what constitutes a digital economy. Their analysis shows that 22% of the world's economic output is linked to digital skills and capital.[22] Based on this definition, the US digital economy is the most developed, accounting for 33% of national GDP. Furthermore, 43% of the US workforce and 26% of its national capital is capable of supporting economic activities related to digital technologies. Elsewhere, digital economies range in value from more than 30% in the UK and Australia to 10% in China.

A lot has changed in the 20 years since Dan Tapscott introduced the term "digital economy" and began to explore its implications for business and society.[23] However, many organizations still see digital transformation as a technology issue to be figured out by the IT team, or partitioned as a problem to be sorted out by a separate 'chief digital officer'. More digitally mature organizations are beginning to view digital transformation as not just an internal technology infrastructure upgrade as they realize it is much more than an opportunity to shift to multi- or omni-channel service provision. The focus today is on a more fundamental review of business practices, a realignment of operations toward core values, and a stronger relationship between creators and consumers of services.

The excitement around ideas such as value co-creation, platform business models, and circular economy solutions is that digital transformation brings new ways to drive business success, ways that recognize changes in the value that consumers want and how they receive it. The explosion of interest in new digital technologies such as Artificial Intelligence and cognitive computing is a further indication of the changes that may render many existing business models unviable, to be replaced by new value propositions, organizational structures, and delivery approaches.

A Framework for Digital Transformation

Organizations undergo digital transformation when they adopt digital technologies to gain new insights and evolve their way of working. As a result, business activities are increasingly centered on digital assets, and their processes are evolving to take advantage of their particular characteristics. While sectors such as entertainment and online retail were among the first to embrace these changes, the effects of digital transformation are being felt across all industries and sectors.

It is useful to consider the primary target and emphasis of digital transformation in five key elements, as illustrated in Figure 2.1.

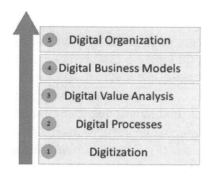

Fig. 2.1: The Five Elements of Digital Transformation

This framework defines five focus areas to understand the impact of digital technologies. In any digital transformation program, an organization may be engaged in activities that address one or more of these areas. Frequently, an organization's digital transformation strategy dictates that it proceeds in a linear fashion by applying increasing resources and energy from element 1 through to element 5. In reality, however, a much more complex profile of activities is usually being carried out across all five elements. Here, we outline the five elements and their relationships:[24]

Digitization. Converting data, transactions, and business artifacts into digital formats. In almost all cases, physical artifacts can be replaced or be represented by their digital equivalents to increase access, enhance quality, enable sharing, and improve processing capacity for those artifacts. Doing this raises new business challenges and opportunities in existing markets and creates new digitally focused solutions. For example, moving paper-based record keeping online does more than just reducing the cost of printing physical artifacts. The act of digitizing them presents new opportunities in how they are recorded, stored, curated, analyzed, connected, shared, transformed, and destroyed.

Digital Process Modeling. Deploying digital technologies and processes to support key business activities. Access to digital artifacts and deployment of digital tools and mechanisms has allowed organizations to redesign established control and operational management capabilities in areas such as human resource management, marketing, point of sales, help desks, and supply chain management. As a result, business operations are transformed to ensure they can be managed more efficiently, and optimized for the key tasks. Consequently, many projects largely involving upgrades to IT infrastructure and tools deliver key enablement capabilities to the organization that quickly result in changes to the core business processes across the organization.

Digital Value Analysis. Using digital technologies to generate new sources of value based on products and materials created, information captured and analyzed, and behaviors and actions monitored. Increasingly, digital technology is used to ensure greater intelligence is applied not only to creating products and services, but also to gain new insights into their production, distribution, and use. For example, embedding intelligence in consumer goods instruments production processes but also allows them to report back on their current performance, communicate with other devices, and adapt their behavior to their environment. Any physical device can now be wrapped with a digital capability that broadcasts information such as its location, environmental conditions, and operating status. Such a digital footprint provides insights into the product's value in use: information previously difficult or impossible to obtain. This information allows organizations to reassess the value offered by their products and services, and consequently to re-examine their go-to-market approach.

Digital Business Model Innovation. Restructuring and redefining existing markets and environments to encourage new digital business opportunities. Examples from many business sectors demonstrate that when digital products and services replace existing physical goods, or when the physical goods generate a real-time digital footprint, the nature of those markets is open to severe disruption by new providers with radically different business models. In the entertainment industry, for example, the move to digital forms of music and videos did more than just replace DVDs – it revolutionized the production and consumption of entertainment services. The ability to gain a deeper understanding of people's consumption of entertainment products in the home and on the move has changed pricing policies, altered their delivery formats and styles, encouraged new market entrants, and brought a diverse set of offerings to the market.

Digital Organizational Redesign. Reorganizing strategy to be better suited to digital technologies and business models, requiring changes to management structures to support the new strategy. Many companies competing in digitally disrupted markets are re-examining how they should organize their work, supplier networks, governance bodies, and other fundamental structures. Mature organizations such as GE[25] and IBM[26] are openly questioning what it means to be a successful company in a digitally disrupted economy. Meanwhile, newer companies such as Valve[27] and Zappos[28] operate with radically new forms of management behaviors and alternative decision-making processes across fundamental business areas such as procurement, hiring and staff development, product and project management, auditing, and compliance. For instance, a digitally disrupted business looks not just to hire people with different skillsets, but also to attract them through online channels or relevant online communities. It also manages its staff in smaller self-organizing teams, encourages them with impact-driven reward mechanisms, and places them in working environments designed to encourage creativity and innovation.

These shifts affect everyone: individuals, companies, markets, and industries. In some cases, they may prompt straightforward adjustments through updating existing approaches and practices. But primarily, digital transformation is raising fundamental questions in areas such as pricing strategy, supply chain dynamics, and labor management. Consider, for example, how a company digitizing its assets and workflows may need to update its auditing and compliance practices in areas such as privacy, security, data management, business continuity, and asset reporting. The implications of such changes will be felt across the business, from contracting and procurement through to staff training and project management.

Often, organizations do not welcome the disruption such changes bring to their core operating practices as they represent challenges to existing ways of working. However, they also bring new opportunities for companies to exploit, encouraging start-ups to take fresh approaches and existing companies to explore new business models more appropriate to the evolving environment in which they operate.

Case Studies

Two short vignettes provide useful insights into digital transformation using the conceptual framework described in Figure 2.1. While idealized to simplify their presentation, they capture key elements of real projects and their digital transformation experiences.

Case 1: FreshBrew Coffee shop

Far from the bland cafeterias of the past, today's coffee shops are community spaces where people meet, share ideas, connect to the Internet, get down to work, and consume a wide variety of beverages. Applying digital technology has been an important part of the changes taking place in these spaces, as digital approaches have been used to improve practices, deliver new services, and manage how the business is run.

Based near a university campus with a thriving community of students, the FreshBrew Coffee shop experiences periods of very high demand, often in short bursts, around timetabled lectures or special events. Let's consider the role of digital transformation in understanding and addressing these peaks and troughs of demand.

Digitization: At the first level, digitization enables the business to capture information such as which drinks are bought at what time, consumer preferences, flow of consumers through the café, average sale amount, and so on. Enhanced point-of-sale devices gather much of this data. However, data capture is also possible from different devices such as cameras in the café, tags attached to cups, smartphones carried by consumers, and through channels such as online ordering and downloadable apps. Analysis of such data significantly enhances insight into the current environment.

Digital Process Modeling: At the next level, the collected digital data is used to design processes that optimize efficiency in product ordering and across the supply chain of product suppliers, as well as in monitoring staffing levels and customer experience in the store. These digital information sources are more amenable to different forms of analysis than previously possible. The business can now obtain real-time information on the current status of operations and compare this with previous data to enhance forecasting to more accurately predict activity over the rest of the day. Processes can be further refined by connecting this data in real-time with other sources of information such as university timetables, weather forecasts, and public transport schedules.

Digital Value Analysis: Beyond current process optimization, the FreshBrew Coffee shop can be reframed in terms of its digital capabilities and activities. For instance, as a shared space used by individuals and communities, the coffee shop can be considered a digital workspace where user value is optimized around their broader needs and interactions. The different products and services offered can be examined in light of the outcomes received by their wide variety of clients.

Digital Business Model Innovation: Such reframing leads to a rethink of business models. Based on its underpinning digital infrastructure, the FreshBrew Coffee shop could now experiment with automated ordering based on predictive algorithms; the approach being tried includes new ordering processes based on predictive analysis and mobile phone data to ensure that a customer's drink request is waiting for them as they enter the shop. Pricing options for such services are also being reconsidered. Options such as subscription and surge-based pricing models for its beverages could be used to take advantage of peaks in demand. Additional business models are also being considered. For example, they are look at gaining income from less busy periods by using the café as a meeting space for businesses.

Digital Organizational Redesign: The FreshBrew Coffee shop is planning to re-design its organization to support these new business opportunities while exper-imenting with new product offerings in a rapid cycle. Any future organizational structure could incorporate more flexible staffing models and incentive schemes as well as models that allow teams to self-organize to address peaks in demand. New product streams may be handled in separate units running independently from the main organization.

Case 2: Zoetis PetDialog+

In animal health, digital technologies are enabling veterinarians to apply phar-maceutical products more effectively to fight disease and improve the lives of an-imals. With dog owners spending, on average, over $1,000 a year on their pet and at least a third of that on maintaining the animal's health,[29] digital disruption can bring particularly interesting opportunities to the market for companion an-imals. Such prospects have spurred Zoetis, the world's largest animal pharma-ceuticals company, to create a Center for Digital Innovation in 2014 with the goal of introducing new products that use digital technologies to enhance animals' lives.

Digitization: One such project involved attaching a small wearable device to a dog's collar to collect data about the animal's movement, activity, and behav-ioral patterns.[30] The first step was to consider what kinds of digitized data the device could generate, the fidelity and accuracy of the generated data, and how this digital information can be analyzed to understand potential health condi-tions. This information is assimilated into an online dashboard that pet owners can access through a mobile app to monitor their animal's nutritional intake, ex-ercise, and socialization patterns.

Digital Process Modeling: The use of this data allows pet owners, veterinarians and Zoetis-supplied pharmacists to review their activities as they look for effi-ciencies in maintaining an animal's health. For example, continuous availability of the animal's exercise and sleeping patterns could be used as primary input to diagnose illnesses, understand the efficacy of prescribed drugs, and reassure pet owners during treatments. This offers opportunities to change core processes for patient monitoring, drug prescription, and product evaluation.

Digital Value Analysis: The broad adoption of digital technologies highlights a new set of digital health concepts and principles to all stakeholders in the animal health value chain. Consider the role of the veterinarian in a digital world, for instance. Devices offering continual real-time monitoring of a dog's health allow the veterinary clinic to understand their patients' health, reduce uncertainties in diagnosis, evaluate the effectiveness of their diagnosis, and compare their practices to others based on outcomes received by their patients. This knowledge allows a deeper view of value creation across many aspects of the treatment of animals, and supports new business opportunities in digitally managed animal wellness.

Digital Business Model Innovation: A new set of principles makes significantly altered business model innovations possible. For example, the data generated from these wearable devices for dogs allow illness prevention and wellness-focused approaches to be considered. A variety of pricing strategies can then be examined based on a deeper understanding of an animal's continued health and treatment outcomes. For example, a core level of service can be defined at low cost with penalties introduced when animal owners or veterinary practices fall below performance norms. Practices willing to introduce such business models can significantly disrupt current approaches and differentiate themselves from the competition based on new evidence-based value models for their patients.

Digital Organizational Redesign: These digitally enabled ways of working signify a new relationship between drug supplier, veterinary practice, and pet owner that may require restructuring of the veterinary practice based on maintaining wellness of animals rather than focusing on fixing them when they are sick. For example, veterinary practices' activities may need to be more fundamentally re-organized around wellness. More broadly, however, the animal health industry may be affected across the whole supply chain. Consider, for example, the role of education establishments such as veterinary schools and the kinds of skills they need to impart to students. Veterinarians in a digital world may not only require basic training in digital technologies; they may also need to act as technology entrepreneurs in an increasingly sophisticated digital ecosystem. This could have enormous structural and organizational repercussions for all actors in the animal health supply chain.

Summary

Organizations face many challenges as they seek to reinvent themselves to compete in an increasingly digital world. The introduction of digital technologies across an organization opens up the opportunity to design new kinds of products and services, produce them with optimized processes, deliver them in new ways, gain fresh insights into their impact in use, and build more intimate relationships with consumers. Achieving this, however, often requires significant changes to the structures and practices already in place. Digital transformation is forcing organizations to not only undergo technology replacement, but to also consider a fundamental redesign of their processes and decision-making approaches.

To understand the different aspects involved in digital transformation we have provided a framework that highlights digitization, digital process modeling, digital value analysis, digital business model innovation, and digital organizational redesign. By addressing these five elements an organization can come to terms with the key challenges they face as they adjust to the digital world.

Organizations able to make these changes could potentially reap huge rewards. The Internet 'unicorns' that have successfully adopted new digital operating models have built substantial market positions, high valuations, and a clear momentum in the competition for consumers' attention. Many organizations failing to adapt have fallen by the wayside. A key focus for today's organizations is to build an effective toolbox that equips them for success in the digital economy.

References

1 Christensen, C. (2016). *The Innovator's Dilemma: When New Technologies Cause Great Firms to Fail*, Revised Edition. Harvard Business School Press.
2 Anthony, S., Gilbert, C., and Johnson, M. (2017). *Dual Transformation: How to Reposition Today's Business While Creating the Future*. Harvard Business School Press.
3 Schumpeter, J.A. (2010). *Capitalism, Socialism, and Democracy*. Routledge Classic Routledge.
4 Carr, N. (2011). *The Big Switch: Rewiring the World from Edison to Google*. W.W. Norton & Co.
5 Tapscott, D. (2014). *The Digital Economy (Anniversary Edition): Rethinking the Promise and Peril in the Age of Networked Intelligence*. McGraw Hill.

6 Brynjolfsson, E. and McAfee, A. (2016). *The Second Machine Age: Work, Progress, and Prosperity in a Time of Brilliant Technologies.* W.W. Norton and Company.

7 Edelman, D. and Heller, J. (2015). *How Digital Marketing Operations Can Transform Business.* McKinsey and Co. Available at: https://www.mckinsey.com/business-functions/marketing-and-sales/our-insights/how-digital-marketing-operations-can-transform-business

8 Moreno, H. (2017). *3 Steps to Digitally Transform Customer Engagement.* Forbes. Available at: https://www.forbes.com/sites/forbesinsights/2017/05/09/3-steps-to-digitally-transform-customer-engagement/#126fe3d37577

9 McKeown, N. (2017). *What does Digital Transformation mean to the Government?* The Digital Transformation People. Available at: http://www.thedigitaltransformationpeople.com/channels/the-case-for-digital-transformation/what-does-digital-transformation-mean-to-the-government

10 Boulton, C. (2017). *Proliferation of Digital Leaders Brings Confusion, Power Struggles.* CIO.com. Available at: https://www.cio.com/article/3184348/cio-role/proliferation-of-digital-leaders-brings-confusion-power-struggles.html

11 Carr, N. (2011). *The Big Switch: Rewiring the World from Edison to Google.* W.W. Norton & Co.

12 Hagel, J., Seely Brown, J. and Davison, L. (2009). *Measuring the Big Shift.* Harvard Business Review.

13 Friedman, T.L. (2017). *Thank You for Being Late.* Penguin.

14 Parker, G., Van Alstyne, M.W. and Choudary, S.P. (2018). *Platform Revolution: How Networked Markets are Transforming the Economy and How to Make Them Work for You.* W.W. Norton & Company.

15 Updated each year since 2009, Deloitte's Shift Index was constructed to define the key indicators for industries and countries that enable the Big Shift, and help executives understand and take advantage of them in defining strategy in an increasingly digital world.

16 Deloitte (2016). *2016 Shift Index. The Paradox of Flows: Can Hope Flow from Fear? Deloitte* University Press. Available at:https://www2.deloitte.com/content/dam/insights/us/articles/3407_2016-Shift-Index/DUP_2016-Shift-Index.pdf

17 House of Commons (2016). *The Digital Economy. Second Report of Session 2016-17.* Business, Innovation and Skills Committee. Available at: https://publications.parliament.uk/pa/cm201617/cmselect/cmbis/87/87.pdf

18 OECD (2014) *Measuring the Digital Economy: A New Perspective.* OECD Publishing. Available at: http://ec.europa.eu/eurostat/documents/341889/725159/OECD+Manual+Measuring+the+Digital+Economy

19 Portes, J. (2015). *The UK's Digital Economy.* National Institute of Economic and Social Research. Available at: https://www.niesr.ac.uk/publications/uks-digital-economy

20 Mesenbourg, T.L. (2001). *Measuring the Digital Economy.* US Census Bureau. 2001. Available at: https://www.census.gov/library/working-papers/2001/econ/mesenbourg-01.html

21 Econsultancy (2017). *UK Online Retail Sales Hit £133bn in 2016, up 16% Year-on-year: Stats. Available* at: https://econsultancy.com/blog/68709-uk-online-retail-sales-hit-133bn-in-2016-up-16-year-on-year-stats

22 https://www.accenture.com/us-en/insight-digital-disruption-growth-multiplier

23 Tapscott, D. (1997). *The Digital Economy: Promise and Peril in the Age of Networked Intelligence.* McGraw Hill.

24 https://www.accenture.com/us-en/insight-digital-density-index-guiding-digital-transformation

25 https://www.ge.com/digital/customers

26 Korsten, P.J,. Marshall, A. and Berman, S.J. (2016). *Digital Reinvention™ in Action: What to Do and How to Make it Happen.* IBM.com. Available at: https://www.ibm.com/thought-leadership/institute-business-value/report/draction

27 https://www.valvesoftware.com/el/publications

28 Vazquez Sampere, J.P. (2015). *Zappos and the Connection Between Structure and Strategy.* Harvard Business Review, June 3. Available at: https://hbr.org/2015/06/zappos-and-the-connection-between-structure-and-strategy

29 Money (2017). *We Did the Math: Here's How Much Your Dog Costs You Over its Lifetime.* Money. Available at: http://time.com/money/4884120/we-did-the-math-heres-how-much-your-dog-costs-you-over-its-lifetime/

30 https://vhive.buzz/cases/petdialog/

3 The Rise of the Machine

Introduction

Information management has always been at the heart of decision-making, whether it be government policy, corporate strategy or individual choice. In business, the tasks of collecting, administering, and querying complex data sources form the basis for their operating models and processes. Over the last half-century, corporate leaders and executives have striven to harness the power of such data by introducing powerful supporting systems for tasks like Customer Relationship Management (CRM), Supply Chain Management (SCM), Human Resource Management (HRM), and Enterprise Resource Planning (ERP). Recent migration of these systems to take advantage of maturing Internet-based technologies has led to these 'back-office' systems increasingly reaching out into 'front-office' activities so that end users in real time can monitor production processes, view current order delivery status, and engage in consumer collaboration. Today, consumers can depend on the power of these Internet-based systems to help make more meaningful decisions about every aspect of their lives, from savings and investment to physical wellbeing and medical care.

Despite massive technological advances in interconnectivity, computer processing, and information storage, the understanding and analysis required to improve the quality of business decision-making has yet to reach its full potential. For example, a recent study of over 5,000 employees in 22 global organizations concluded that "investments in analytics can be useless, even harmful, unless employees can incorporate that data into complex decision-making".[1] Despite massive amounts of data bringing unlimited insights and opportunities, most organizations remain far from being able to harness that potential into meaningful decision-making.

This chapter considers the missing link between a surfeit of information on every aspect of business and consumer activity and an effective means of harnessing the almost limitless supply of data. This missing link, often referred to as 'Machine Intelligence' or MI, combines technologies such as machine learning, natural language recognition, and artificial intelligence. At its heart, MI offers sophisticated software algorithms that can undertake non-routine, cognitive tasks to supplement and ultimately replace human intelligence.

In this respect MI is a central catalyst to deliver the full promise of Industry 4.0 – the coming together of intelligent systems, the Internet of Things, and cloud computing to enhance work activities across the entire manufacturing and services supply chain. Not only will this transform workflow efficiency, it is likely to change the industrial landscape itself as it increases the prospect of a seamless interlocking of innovative start-ups with the reach and power of traditional incumbents. Consumers should see equal benefits too, enhancing their daily experiences through the way products and services are packaged, priced, delivered, and consumed.

To enhance understanding of the opportunities, this chapter explores the context in which MI provides value, and brings insights into key areas of its use:
- Why MI can provide a solution to the management challenge raised by large quantities of data being collected as a consequence of hyper-connectivity and smart devices.
- How MI can help automate non-routine, cognitive tasks and thereby transform human experience, enterprises, and entire sectors.
- Where such transformations are generating new sources of value in the digital economy.
- What managers and decision-makers are doing to harness the power of new digital technologies such as MI.

Data, Data Everywhere...

With the advent of cloud-based services over the last decade, companies such as Apple, Amazon, Google, and Facebook have created vast, interconnected computer utilities across the globe. These are rapidly becoming the information hubs of the digital age[2]. Such centres are fed by exabytes (one billion gigabytes) of data generated by billions of consumers who have benefited from ubiquitous access to services and interaction via a plethora of mobile devices including tablets, smart phones, and wearables. For many people it is hard to imagine what life was like only a few years ago, without access to YouTube, Facebook, Google or WhatsApp from every Internet-connected device. Commentators such as Nicholas Carr view these leading digital economy companies as "rewiring the world" in a comparable manner to Edison at the beginning of the 20th century.[3]

This journey to hyper-interconnectivity appears to be only in its early stages.[4] Connected cars, homes and cities are likely to add further fuel to the fire in the coming years[5], as will the advent of powerful new mobile utilities such as fifth generation mobile infrastructure standards (5G) and software-defined networks that can support ever-increasing flows of data.[6] Cisco predicts that 5 billion people and 50 billion devices will be connected by 2020.[7]

Many challenges must be addressed to harness this explosion of hyper-connected computer power. The vast amounts of data currently generated by the interconnectivity of smart devices, computers and other entities is rapidly overwhelming individuals, communities, and businesses. Estimates of the amount and variety of data vary enormously, but Figure 3.1 provides a few illustrative statistics.

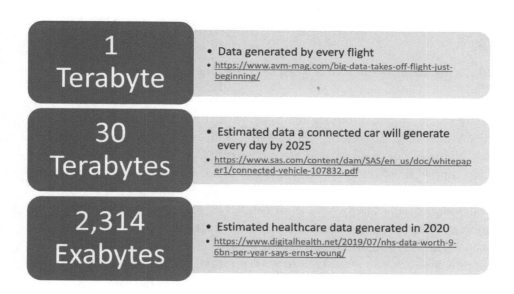

Fig. 3.1: Exponential Growth of Data

Such data takes many forms and is transmitted, processed, and stored in a variety of technologies. There is, however, little value associated with so much unstructured information without an ability to bring order and rigor to how it is managed, if it cannot be accurately examined to extract patterns of behavior, if lessons from its use are not captured to improve understanding of what happens in particular situations, and if it is not connected and aligned with decision-making processes.

Recent advances in computing and communication technologies have accelerated our ability to create and stream data in near real time from places that were previously inaccessible (e.g., inside the human body), and with increasing accuracy and frequency.[8] However, many business leaders believe we are in danger of creating so much success with 'big data' and 'open interoperability' that we are becoming overwhelmed and hence the value of data in improving business decision-making is diminished. As such, the current land rush to create and manage data will only be helpful if there is an associated improvement in techniques for understanding and analysing that data in the context of the tasks within which it is applied. It cannot be assumed that the availability of this data automatically leads to improvements in processes and outcomes. In fact, many studies and observations highlight that larger amounts of data increase the challenge to act effectively and efficiently in response to that data.[9] [10] [11]

Machine Intelligence in a Digital Economy

To extract economic and social value from the exabytes of information now being stored in global information hubs, we as individuals, communities, and businesses need to convert this powerful and ever-expanding resource into meaningful input that can help us with everyday decisions. The data must not only support organizations to be more profitable, it must also help address key societal questions, such as: Does greater insight into product and service consumption actually improve people's comfort, safety, and wellbeing? Will the connected car help us reduce congestion in cities and avoid accidents? Can banks' knowledge of financial markets be used effectively to advise us on our retirement needs and reduce poverty? Do wearable health monitors lead to earlier interventions and ensure a longer life and more active old age?

Smarter approaches to data-driven decision-making require significant investment in computer science and software engineering, particularly in solutions that enable organizations to bring together multiple data sources, filter out errors in the data, and extract meaningful insights from repeated patterns. MI is viewed as an integrative mechanism that transforms so much data into genuine sources of new value. In this respect it could readily be seen as the 'killer app' for the digital economy.

The computer industry has a long history of investigation into Artificial Intelligence (AI) approaches where computers attempt to mimic human behavior.[12]

While it can be argued that AI has long passed its fiftieth birthday, certainly since John McCarthy first coined the phrase in 1956, progress on intelligent data interpretation and machine learning has been quite slow and poorly applied to mainstream business challenges. More recently, however, several important developments, as illustrated in Figure 3.2, have made it possible for computers to begin emulating human cognitive capabilities. At the heart of AI and machine learning lies current generation algorithmic software that can simulate non-routine, cognitive tasks to help humans make meaningful decisions in all aspects of their business and social lives.

MI holds the promise of being able to make sense of large volumes of data by exploiting a combination of machine learning and AI to yield new sources of value. MI encompasses natural language processing, image recognition, interpretive algorithms, and other techniques to extract patterns, to learn from them by assessing what they mean, and to act upon them by connecting information together. MI is now possible as it builds upon core sets of relatively cheap hardware capabilities provided in massive centers that support large-scale data management (Data Lakes), with the move to virtualized storage and compute power accessible over the Internet (Cloud Technology, or 'Cloudification'), and managed distribution networks for architecting efficient systems that stitch together all the pieces of these complex systems (Interconnectivity).

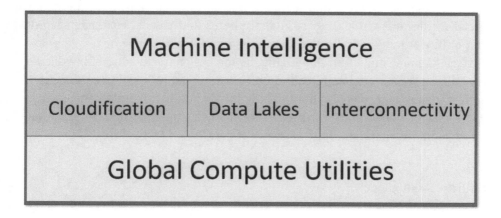

Fig. 3.2: The Foundations for Machine Intelligence

Discussions in this area are complicated since there is an abundance of terminology and no common vocabulary. Furthermore, the current set of terms continues to evolve; its common usage changes as new ideas emerge. Here, we offer a broad, illustrative overview of the key terms and concepts as a primer on their most frequent interpretation and use.

Machine learning

Machine learning is a form of data analysis that creates an evolving model of a problem from the data being analyzed. A set of algorithms is created to process the data with increasing accuracy as the data is classified and assessed. In this sense the computer system is able to learn from the data as well as gain new insights without being explicitly re-programmed. By gleaning insights from this data, often in real time, organizations are able to work more efficiently or gain an advantage over competitors in sectors such as financial services (e.g., fraud detection), government (e.g., cyber threat analysis), healthcare (e.g., medical diagnosis), and transportation (e.g., congestion avoidance).

Big data

Big data has become the general way in which we now refer to the challenge of a world where massive amounts of information are generated every day through a broad range of devices: information gathered through sensors in the home, social media interactions, stored digital photos and videos, customer records and online order details, and performance data from instrumented mechanical devices, to name but a few. IBM highlights the key characteristics of big data in four dimensions[13]: volume (creation and management of very large datasets); variety (heterogeneous collections of structured and unstructured items); velocity (speed of generation and processing of data streams); and veracity (assessing quality, timeliness, and accuracy of data).

Artificial Intelligence

Artificial Intelligence or AI refers to computer systems able to exhibit behaviors or perform tasks that normally require human intelligence. It is most frequently associated with cognitive tasks such as visual perception, speech recognition, decision-making, and translation between languages. However, industry commentators such as Accenture more broadly uses AI as a collective term for multiple technologies that enable information systems and applications to sense, comprehend, and act.[14] That is, computers are enabled to perceive the world and collect data; to analyze and understand the information collected; and to make informed decisions and provide guidance based on this analysis in an independent way.

Machine Intelligence

Machine Intelligence extends notions of AI and machine learning through computing techniques that allow systems to predict future actions and behaviors. As Numenta describes it,[15] rule-based models and data pattern analysis can be augmented with behavioral models that characterize normal and abnormal activities. This is essential in many situations that evolve quickly and involve many data sources such as weather prediction, modeling virus propagation, and social media analysis.

The Emergence of Machine Intelligence

MI is now regarded as the '*New* New Thing' by entrepreneurs and investors across the globe, with rapid growth seen in AI-related start-ups.[16] CBInsights reported almost 700 financial deals in AI companies in 2016,[17] with investment in such start-ups almost doubling between 2014 and 2016 to reach nearly $5 billion. As this focus expands, investment in MI could grow to $50 billion in the next five years, Deloitte recently predicted.[18]

More significant is the interest digital leaders such as Amazon, Google, and Facebook are showing in this fast-expanding area. Given the vast amount of data that each of these companies has collected, covering every aspect of our lifestyles, the race is now on to monetize this asset beyond pure advertising revenues. CBInsights estimated that between 2012 and 2016, the top five US tech companies invested in 420 private companies, led by Google (Alphabet) which backed 333 start-ups through its various venture arms[19]. Many of these investments are specifically aimed at expanding their AI-based technology base. For example, Apple has acquired Seattle-based machine learning start-up Turi for $200 million, while Google has bought UK-based DeepMind for $500 million. Intel recently took over Irish computer vision chipmaker Movidius. All these partnerships point to a deliberate focus on data mining and MI.

The maturing of this information technology (IT) sector reinforces the progress being made at the Research and Development (R&D) level. Huge strides in computer hardware and software provide fertile conditions for a commercial breakthrough, as witnessed by the increase in start-up activity particularly in global innovation hubs such as Silicon Valley, London, and Tel Aviv.

Big companies are also investing in their own projects. IBM Watson is perhaps the most visible with its longstanding Machine Learning program.[20] Since gaining initial public notoriety in 2011 by winning a popular US gameshow, *Jeopardy*, Watson has developed to the point that it is now able to store and interpret data in many different fields, from medicine and disease diagnostics to food recipes. In parallel, Google is creating an open-source library under its TensorFlow project that could ultimately connect the entire field of human knowledge.[21] What is especially significant here is the rapid flow of R&D discovery from academia into commercial environments, large and small.

Machine Intelligence and New Economic Models

Over the past few decades, global corporations have adopted integrated ERP systems that can monitor and control complex supply chains that link production and distribution networks across multiple business units and diverse regions. Despite efficiency improvements, these modern systems often prove to be far too rigid to adjust to the rapidly changing business and economic conditions being experienced recently. Data from recent surveys reveal that these organizations are attempting to dismantle their centralized systems, in favor of more adaptive cloud-based services that encourage agile decision-making appropriate for times of uncertainty.[22]

Within this context, the promise of MI and its associated self-learning algorithms could provide a radically new and improved way of assessing and responding to shifting supply and demand patterns at a faster rate. By combining the universal availability of data on every aspect of our lives with hyperconnectivity and AI, an opportunity is created to provide powerful new algorithmic systems that could form the basis for the digital economy of the future.

Much of current progress in the application of Machine Intelligence is concentrated on the limited automation of routine, repetitive tasks within administrative functions and supply chains via techniques such as Robotic Process Automation (RPA). In parallel, robots have been introduced into factories while software has aided routine decisions such as inventory management and production planning. Additional customer channels such as web and mobile access have been introduced to supplement physical outlets and improve the interface with customers. However, such technologies primarily reinforce the repetitive and relatively passive nature of today's supply-led economy and are aimed at efficiencies to drive current ways of working to be cheaper, faster and better.

With the advent of MI, organizations are seeking opportunities to transform such supply networks by introducing a new paradigm based on a 'sense-and-respond' approach. Through MI, commercial systems are becoming more adaptive to changes occurring externally, at speeds that humans would have difficulty emulating. Algorithms can use predictive analysis to anticipate customers' ever-changing needs by identifying patterns of change. In turn, supply networks are able to adapt in a continuous fashion. The pervasive nature of these capabilities raises the possibility that every industry will need to adopt intelligent software algorithms, driven by MI, to remain competitive and relevant.

The capabilities that MI can deliver may be summarized as:
- Converting routine, manual tasks performed by factory robots into non-routine tasks such as self-driving cars that exploit MI to learn through experience.
- Converting routine, cognitive tasks such as standard business process into non-routine tasks that require professional knowledge such as medical diagnostics and apply MI to automate complex workflows.

Such developments have enormous implications for all commercial and public organizations. A number of industry commentators envisage MI, big data, and interconnectivity creating transformational change in three areas:[23]
- **Rethinking humans.** In areas such as augmented reality, gestures, and emotional recognition, with consequences for enhanced experiences and increased productivity.
- **Rethinking enterprises.** In areas such as sales, security and authentication, HR and recruitment, marketing, and supply chain, by automating work flows.
- **Rethinking industries.** In areas such as medicine and healthcare, legal services, manufacturing, oil and gas, and automotive, by exploiting collective data and experiences.

This will have major implications for employment as many professional skills become targets for MI, in addition to the repetitive manual tasks already earmarked for automation. A study by Deloitte and Oxford University estimates that up to 10 million jobs are at risk in the UK alone.[24] The dystopian view of the future with MI is that by 2030, many professions will be 80-90% automated, with only a few creative tasks remaining in human hands.

Creating New Sources of Value in the Digital Economy

Rapid advances in digital technology have enabled existing ways of working to be optimized primarily by increasing access and reducing the friction of many business processes through enhanced automation and increased visibility. For many public and private organizations, the digital economy encourages a much broader reassessment of business practices, with a recognition that technology innovation frequently requires corresponding business model innovation which reconsiders value and guides their ongoing operation.

The relationship between technology innovation and business model innovation is much discussed across academia and industry. There is ongoing debate over whether business model innovation can be separated from technology innovation, the degree of influence each has on the other, where and how innovation in either impacts a firm's success, and how contextual aspects such as size and maturity of the firm and its markets affect the rate of innovation.[25][26]

Nowhere is this debate more heated than on the future of MI. The combination of MI, big data, and interconnectivity can help transform every aspect of our society, from the individual to entire sectors, in the following ways:

- **Connected self.** The plethora of connected devices and inputs around us can help predict and respond to our individual needs for high added-value services and enhanced experiences in areas such as physical wellbeing, lifelong learning and financial security.
- **Increased social context.** Identifying how individuals are influenced by social networking and the impact this has on our individual needs and aspirations can generate valuable insights for new products and services, as well as optimizing media spend.
- **Connected enterprise.** Interpreting the vast, real-time sources of data from all elements of business interaction amongst partners, platforms, and customers through the production cycle and across distribution networks can

yield massive efficiency improvements with both physical assets and human resources.

The combination of all three areas presents opportunities for radical transformation at the policy, economic, social, and technological levels of society and commerce. Organizations can collect vast amounts of data on our individual and collective behavior through omnipresent multi-channel engagements with the stakeholders they serve, powered by the rapid growth in smart devices. Equally, they can monitor the structures that support us such as our homes, cars, and cities. Companies such as Facebook, Google and Amazon are already capturing people's online interactions and are increasingly moving to introduce MI to interpret such interactions.[27] This could provide deeper insights into an individual's personal needs and aspirations that in turn will enable vendors to target such needs in an ever more intimate manner. Applying predictive analytics and MI to such information enables firms to discern distinctive patterns of behavior that can translate into new products and services; offerings that can both enhance customer experience and generate new sources of value.

Social media provides yet another lens on our individual and collective behavior, generating valuable intelligence in areas such as political and ethical issues, travel and entertainment, and media and advertising. This can provide a context for individual decision-making, as seen in examples such as TripAdvisor where individuals use other travelers' experiences to make hotel choices, and CityMapper which combines many sources of information to help commuters decide between transportation alternatives when travelling in London.

Enterprises Transformed

MI is predicted to have its deepest impacts inside enterprise organizations. Manufacturers and service companies have long been inhibited by lengthy and complex supply chains (physical and virtual) orchestrated by traditional HRM, CRM and ERP systems. Widely deployed, such systems are efficient at automating repetitive, routine tasks but do little to sense and respond to external changes. Deployments typically take years to be rolled out effectively and are complex to update as the organization's behaviors evolve.

Such challenges are exacerbated in large manufacturing organizations where supply chains can encompass many physical assets, such as machinery, as well as human-driven processes and workflows. They also involve multiple handoffs between different participants in the supply chain (several thousand in the automotive industry). Hence, such organizations are beginning to leverage MI to ensure cost-effective delivery of new processes and optimized operations. Manufacturing plants typically generate large volumes of data. The application of MI across enterprise operations enhances a stakeholder's ability to make decisions in real time, formulate strategy based on evolving trends, and ensure efficient support processes. The major impacts can be seen in four key areas:

- **Manufacturing.** Operational metrics to manage day-to-day operations and optimize maintenance of costly equipment.
- **Finance and IT.** Better management of IT infrastructure investments including prediction of cash flows and currency fluctuations for managing global finance operations.
- **Workforce Analytics.** Increased visibility of workforce productivity, skills development, and team-based decision-making across a diverse human capital base.
- **Sales and Marketing.** Insights into buying patterns, sales changes across different geographies, and social media feedback on new promotions.

A useful illustration is that of GE Digital, formed in 2015 to bring new thinking to complex, multi-party supply chains.[28] With its acquisition of Predix (an industrial cloud-based platform), GE was able to create a digital thread across the supply chain that links its components. By analyzing the productivity and resilience of all human and machine assets within the supply chain and optimizing workflows, GE improved efficiencies by 20-30%, thus reducing time-to-market and generating higher margins. Another industry with huge potential for MI adoption is oil and gas. Companies such as Tachyus offer similar machine learning capabilities to GE in oil and gas exploration that can increase the production capacity of oil sources by 20-30%, as well as find new sources of energy.

More generally, MI's ability to spot early signs of problems can be particularly useful for many companies. Call centers are applying chatbots to identify repetitive inquiries that represent process and product failures, helping managers track down their root causes and eliminate them. These chatbots can also start to displace human operators. Such developments illustrate the trend toward connected enterprises that can exchange information and use MI to adapt to prevailing conditions. The recent maturing of Software Oriented Architectures (SOA) and standard Application Programming Interfaces (APIs) toward microservices architectures also enables new industrial models to be implemented based on the principles of "plug and play".[29] This increases flexibility and agility in the construction, realignment, and reconfiguration of MI-based solutions.

Enabling New Business Models

MI is posing significant challenges to current thinking about where and how value is created in businesses across many industries. As we increase our ability to connect heterogeneous data sources, we can now gain insights into previously unseen activities, behaviors, and trends. This gives rise to emerging opportunities that enable businesses not only to respond to current, specific requests from customers, but to also anticipate their needs and evolve support for them.

The intelligent use of data to create new business models can be seen in the growth of the 'sharing economy' through companies such as Airbnb and Uber. Working on the basis that 'access is more valuable than ownership', these companies utilize advanced software algorithms to develop entirely new services based on asset sharing. The speed at which such new models have gained commercial acceptance has been remarkable, sending shock waves through many different sectors.[30]

In the taxi industry, for instance, Uber has long been associated with dynamic surge pricing; a mechanism that uses various sources of real-time information to adjust pricing schemes in an attempt to balance supply and demand across its ecosystem.[31] While this approach may be challenged on ethical grounds, there is no doubt that the closely guarded algorithms it utilizes to analyze data and predict future patterns of use have a huge impact on Uber's success.

In China, taxi aggregator Didi Chuxing takes the use of predictive analysis even further. Backed by Chinese internet giants Tencent and Alibaba (and a recent $1 billion investment from Apple), Didi currently operates in 400-plus cities and claims to control over 70% of the market in mainland China. It is heavily investing in MI to develop algorithms that can predict demand by taking into account multiple variables such as income earned by a driver during that day, distance of the ride, number of drivers in a locality, and past record of individual drivers. Didi Chuxing's use of MI is accelerated through an open competition managed by Udacity, with a $100,000 prize for the best algorithm submitted.[32]

One particular aspect of such businesses is their ability to use advanced software algorithms to respond rapidly to external changes such as traffic congestion or driver availability during periods of peak demand (in the case of Uber). By harnessing information across complex networks in real time, such organizations demonstrate the sort of adaptability lacking in traditional incumbents, but necessary for optimizing their business activities around current customer needs and adjusting internally to maximize service delivery efficiency.

New Architectures for Machine Intelligence

The arrival of cloud computing is by far the most conspicuous trend in computer architecture services delivery in recent times. It has already had widespread impact on software delivery, making inroads in both private and public sectors. Whether viewed as a natural extension of Internet-based computing or as a completely new phenomenon, cloud computing, with its high-bandwidth interconnectivity coupled with cheap processors and storage, serves organizations by creating large computing centers located at key points around the world. These centralized centers can be created by a single organization, shared between organizations, or provided by third parties as a resource to be consumed as and when necessary. This gives rise to digital technology infrastructures that can be coordinated more effectively via shared service centers, and supported more efficiently using flexible hardware and software services that can expand and contract as the consuming organization's needs evolve.

This move towards a centralized approach for greater flexibility and efficiency in service delivery is not new. From the earliest days of computing there have been efforts to centralize computer resources, share access to costly infrastructure, increase flexibility of access to common services, and improve responsiveness to peak demands for capabilities. What is new in the recent move towards cloud computing is the technology infrastructure that now makes that possible, the business environment forcing efficiencies across digital service delivery, the expanding global nature of many organizations and their supply chains, and a broader re-evaluation of the role of digital services supporting the organization's value to its stakeholders.

The main characteristic of a cloud computing approach is to deliver "convenient, on-demand network access to a shared pool of configurable computing resources (e.g., networks, servers, storage, applications, and services) that can be rapidly provisioned and released with minimal management effort or service provider interaction".[33] Such an approach offers a great deal of flexibility to users of those resources. In particular, capabilities can be rapidly and elastically scaled up when demand for them increases, and similarly scaled down when demand falls.

The flexibility possible with cloud computing is essential. Not only does it encourage dynamic relationships in the supply chain, it also provides much more explicit ways to look at infrastructure costs, to assign them to the role of each organization and team. And it encourages delivery approaches more suited to today's highly diverse and rapidly evolving organizations.

Taking advantage of these benefits, many traditional software-based solutions have been ported to a cloud platform. This is an important starting point for use of the cloud. However, it is only a fraction of the many important usage scenarios for cloud technology, where more sophisticated MI applications with large heterogeneous data sets are processed at high speed, using algorithms that evolve as the learning from the data increases.

Issues and Implications

The current convergence of MI, big data, and interconnectivity in a rapidly accelerating fashion signifies the need for all organizations to identify their priorities and start allocating their resources to achieving competitive advantage. Inevitably, there will be many challenges to overcome before the full potential of such technologies can be realized. Furthermore, different companies across a range of industries are at different phases of their journey to understand and adopt MI. Business leaders and managers exploiting current MI-based technology developments are executing three kinds of activities:

Research
- Familiarizing themselves with potential applications of MI-based digital technologies and considering where high pay-off areas might be within the organization.
- Mapping the MI landscape as it affects the organization's view of the industries in which it competes and examining new start-ups in their sectors as early signals of market change.

− Experimenting with new MI-based business models that could challenge the existing status quo or represent greenfield opportunities.

Experimentation

− Engaging in open, honest discussions with their teams about the extent of data-driven decision-making within the organization, and exploring new ways that data could be obtained, curated, and used.
− Conducting experiments or innovation sprints with appropriate partners to evaluate possibilities prior to scaling to identify minimum viable solutions.
− Engaging in small-scale pilot deployments of MI that focus on learning about the processes, skills, and impact on the organization.

Execution

− Ensuring that key roles and functional areas in the business are set up to act as appropriate entry points for MI-based innovations, by engaging with start-ups and technology leaders across the organization.
− Creating time in projects to capture and communicate stories around success and failures that inspire and motivate teams to gain a shared understanding and vocabulary about MI and its supporting technologies.
− Promoting internal successes within the organization to highlight behaviors and approaches to MI that the organization is seeking to encourage.

In the emerging digital economy with its many uncertainties, the path to success is often summarized as "fast start, fast fail".[34] Traditional R&D approaches must be infused with an "Experiment & Scale" mindset that encourages new approaches, and rewards attempts to try alternatives.[35] However, companies cannot assume unbounded risks, and must maintain stability across key elements of their business. MI is inevitably disruptive by nature. Hence, it is essential to recognize that MI and its associated digital business models may pose significant challenges, which are being addressed in several ways:

− **Changing the way data is collected and processed.** It is important to move away from localized databases associated with specific applications and form larger Data Lakes that can be exploited by new layers of intelligence such as MI and big data.
− **Ensuring there is a flexible, scalable technology infrastructure across the organization.** Business success requires integrating the many applications that constitute a complex set of workflows, by using SOA and API

techniques as well as connected platforms such as those provided by Google, Microsoft, IBM, and others.

- **Tackling the many cultural barriers that persist in every organization.** Success in the 20th century industrial era can work against 21st century changes as business leaders are inclined to cling to ageing business models and processes. New thinking will be required.

MI-based innovations will inevitably put stress on existing structures. Leadership is always a critical element of any major organizational change, and until the key business leaders are convinced of the need for radical change, little progress will be made. Companies across many different sectors are learning how fast progress can be achieved by increasing the capacity for change, and by opening the corporate culture to be receptive to new ideas.

Summary

As computer power continues to expand along with ability to interconnect using high-capacity mobile networks, we can expect to see MI embedded in more and more devices. The promise of MI is that it will enable organizations to absorb and interpret vast amounts of data quickly and easily to make meaningful decisions about all aspects of their business. However, to exploit these opportunities requires alignment across organizations and the confidence to create entirely new markets and radically alter existing products and services. In many cases this will require players from different groups and sectors to collaborate and share data. In many areas such as wellbeing, financial security and mobility, our human needs transcend today's sector boundaries. The integration of data from different sectors will provide new answers to our evolving needs. Imagine, for example, the opportunities to remove cost and improve the convenience of modern-day travel if it were possible to combine the data and intelligence of organizations such as Uber, Google Maps, Ford Automotive, EasyJet, and Shell.

Ultimately, we as humans face a dilemma. MI could help us achieve full self-actualization by informing and aiding us in every aspect of our lives. However, to do so, machines will need to acquire more and more personal information to the point that they could begin to take control of our lives. Many warnings have been issued in this regard. For example, in his book *Homo Deus: A Brief History of Tomorrow*, Yuval Noah Harari paints an alarming but plausible picture in which software algorithms have control over humanity. We as individuals become mere data elements within a ubiquitous processing system; a vision for the future that is as disturbing as it is empowering.

Equally, a machine's ability to take over non-routine and cognitive tasks in a manner that could replace human input has severe implications for today's workforce and will place a drastic strain on our political and social systems. In harnessing MI over the coming decade, organizations will be required to consider wide-ranging social, economic, political and ethical implications. However, far from it being the 'beginning of the end', we need to approach MI as a logical step that brings us to the 'end of the beginning' of our journey toward the application of computer-based intelligence to aid humanity. Much important work remains. Addressing these issues may well be the greatest challenge for Industry 4.0, and the essence of the future of business in the digital economy.

———

References

1 Shah, S., Horne, H. and Capellá, J. (2012). *Good Data Won't Guarantee Good Decisions*. Harvard Business Review, April.

2 Blum, A. (2013). *Tubes: Behind the Scenes at the Internet*. Penguin.

3 Carr, N. (2011). *The Big Switch: Rewiring the World from Edison to Google*. W.W. Norton & Co.

4 Ismail, N. (2016). *The Hyper-connectivity Revolution*. Information Age. Available at: https://www.information-age.com/hyper-connectivity-revolution-123463264/

5 Maddox, T. (2018). *Smart Cities: A Cheat Sheet*. TechRepublic. Available at: https://www.techrepublic.com/article/smart-cities-the-smart-persons-guide/

6 Fulton, S. (2019). *What is 5G? The Definitive Guide to Next-Generation Wireless Technology*. ZDNet. Available at: https://www.zdnet.com/article/what-is-5g-everything-you-need-to-know/

7 Evans, D. (2011). *The Internet of Things: How the Next Evolution of the Internet Is Changing Everything*. Cisco White Paper. Available at: http://www.cisco.com/c/dam/en_us/about/ac79/docs/innov/IoT_IBSG_0411FINAL.pdf

8 Marr, B. (2015). *Big Data: Using Smart Big Data, Analytics, and Metrics to Make Better Decisions and Improve Performance*. John Wiley & Son.

9 Evgeniou, T., Gaba, V. and Niessing, J. (2013). *Does Bigger Data Lead to Better Decisions?* Harvard Business Review. Oct 21. Available at: https://hbr.org/2013/10/does-bigger-data-lead-to-better-decisions

10 Marr, B. (2016). *Data-Driven Decision Making: 10 Simple Steps For Any Business*. Forbes. Available at: https://www.forbes.com/sites/bernardmarr/2016/06/14/data-driven-decision-making-10-simple-steps-for-any-business/#7bddcfe85e1e

11 Lloyd, C. (2011). *Data-Driven Business Decisions*. Wiley.

12 Boden, M.A. (2018). *Artificial Intelligence: A Very Short Introduction*. Oxford University Press.

13 https://www.ibm.com/it-infrastructure/solutions/big-data

14 https://www.accenture.com/us-en/insights/artificial-intelligence/what-ai-exactly

15 https://numenta.com/

16 Knight, W. (2018). *Nine Charts That Really Bring Home Just How Fast AI is Growing*. MIT Technology Review. Available at: https://www.technologyreview.com/s/612582/data-that-illuminates-the-ai-boom/

17 https://www.cbinsights.com/research/report/artificial-intelligence-trends/

18 https://www.deloitte.com/insights/us/en/focus/tech-trends.html

19 CBInsights (2017). *Big 5 Private Market Bets: Google Leads Top US Tech Companies in Investments*. Available at: https://www.cbinsights.com/research/google-amazon-microsoft-facebook-ibm-startup-funding/

20 https://www.ibm.com/watson

21 https://ai.google/

22 Surrey CoDE (2016). *Escaping Legacy: Removing a Major Roadblock to a Digital Future*. University of Surrey White Paper. Available at: https://www.surrey.ac.uk/sites/default/files/2018-11 /escaping-legacy-report.pdf

23 Teich, D. A. (2018). *Machine Learning and Artificial Intelligence in Business: Year in Review*. Forbes. Available at: https://www.forbes.com/sites/davidteich/2018/12/26/machine-learning-and-artificial-intelligence-in-business-year-in-review-2018/#6d4ac762041c

24 Frey, C. and Osbourne, M.A. (2013). *The Future of Employment: How Susceptible Are Jobs To Computerization?* White Paper. Available at: http://www.oxfordmartin.ox.ac.uk/downloads/ academic/The_Future_of_Employment.pdf.

25 Baden-Fuller, C. and Haefliger, S. (2013). Business Models and Technological Innovation. *Long Range Planning*, 46, 1–8.

26 Doganova, L. and Eyquem-Renault, M. (2009). What do Business Models Do? Innovation Devices in Technology Entrepreneurship. *Research Policy*, 38(10), 1559–1570.

27 See, for example, the discussion of Google's RankBrain activities at https:// www.bloomberg. com/news/articles/2015-10-26/google-turning-its-lucrative-web-search-over-to-ai-machines

28 https://www.ge.com/digital/iiot-platform

29 Newman, S. (2015). *Building Microservices*. O'Reilly.

30 Wosskov, D. (2014). *The Sharing Economy: An Independent Review*. UK Government Report BIS/14/1227, November.

31 Prasad, L. (2016). *How a Chinese Cab Service Uses AI to Purge the Surge*. The Indian Express. Available at: http://indianexpress.com/article/technology/tech-news-technology/chinese-company -didi-chuxing-uses-artificial-intelligence-peak-hour-surge-pricing-ola-uber-2779421/

32 Shen, C. (2016). *Didi and Udacity Team Up for $100K Grand Prize Machine Learning Competition!* Udacity. Available at: http://blog.udacity.com/2016/05/didi-and-udacity-team-up-for-100k-grand-prize-machine-learning-competition.html

33 The US National Institute of Standards and Technology (NIST) definition of cloud computing: http://csrc.nist.gov/groups/SNS/cloud-computing/cloud-def-v15.doc

34 Blank, B. (2013). *Why the Lean Startup Changes Everything*. Harvard Business Review.

35 Schrage, M. (2018). *R&D, Meet E&S*. MIT Sloan Management Review. Available at: http:// sloanreview.mit.edu/article/rd-meet-es-experiment-scale/

4 The Human Dimension

Introduction

Ask any organization what their most important asset is, and the most common answer will be "our people". All companies seek to develop motivated individuals and organize them into teams with inspiring leaders who set directions to achieve the aims of the business. Despite this, however, employees often feel that their needs and aspirations are poorly understood and inadequately addressed.

According to Hay Group's *What's My Motivation?* report from 2015,[1] just 15% of UK workers consider themselves "highly motivated", with almost 24% admitting to "coasting" and a further 8% being "completely demotivated". More worrying is that poor staff motivation is reducing productivity by close to 50%, with just 21% of British workers considering themselves "very effective" in their current job role. These figures are similar to those from the USA, where a 2017 Gallup report on the state of the American workplace found that over 51% of the US workforce is not engaged with their work, and only 22% believing that their company has leadership with a clear direction.[2]

Given this data, it is more important than ever that we consider the human dimensions of the digital transformation taking place in organizations. This is particularly so because digital technologies are frequently viewed as dehumanizing the workplace through automation of tasks, replacement of face-to-face activities with online alternatives, and eradication of human judgement in favor of data-driven decision-making. Although intended to support human creativity and value, the pressures from these changes, if left unchecked, may further diminish employee engagement and job satisfaction.

To highlight some of these concerns, this chapter considers three particularly important human aspects in a digital world. First, we provide a perspective on workforce motivation in the digital era, and the rising expectations of the 'born digital' generation. Second, we examine the impact of digital transformation on businesses today. This is to offer a perspective on how such challenges are perceived by organizations building a successful workforce while undergoing digital transformation, and the approaches taken to address them. Finally, we consider how automation and further developments in digital technologies will increase opportunities, as well as concerns, for humans in our fast-paced world.

What Motivates People in a Digital Era

In his book *Grown up Digital,* Don Tapscott discussed a \$4M research study that took place between 2006 and 2008 to better understand how the Net Generation[3] uses digital technologies.[4] His observations are part of a broader examination of what drives individuals and shapes their communities in our digital world. Interviewing over 6,000 people, Tapscott was particularly interested in the way the Internet has changed the social context for individuals and families. He concluded that those generations 'born digital' have a radically different approach to absorbing knowledge, interacting with their peers, and perceiving the world around them. It is not that they have a better understanding of digital technologies than those introduced to them later in life; rather, the way they act is more fundamentally aligned with digital concepts. Alan Kay summarized this aptly when he said that technology is "technology only for people who are born before it was invented". For everyone else it is simply part of the fabric of their lives, invisible and intrinsic to how things happen.[5]

The consequences of a 'born digital' approach are broad and profound, with important implications for any organization involved in digital transformation. These are nicely distilled in Tapscott's eight new norms for the Net Generation or Net-Geners:

Freedom. Internet connectivity brings diverse sources of information from around the world, wide-scale access to all kinds of goods and services, and real-time interaction with peer groups. The Net Generation's use of their digital skills opens up freedom of choice in many areas, changing their attitudes towards brand loyalty, career development, friendship, travel and mobility. For example, when deciding where to work, a Net-Gener is likely to prioritize aspects such as flexibility of workplace location and working practices, direct interaction with clients, and variety of engagement in cross-functional teams.

Customization. The flexibility of digital products such as smartphones, tablets, and media streams has encouraged many forms of customization to suit every user's needs. Over time these products have been adapted to the usage scenarios in which they are employed. Net-Geners now eschew standardized products and services aimed at large audiences, expecting products and services to be specialized according to particular individual tastes, activities, and actions. For example, in education there is a growing rejection of a 'one size fits all' approach and a move toward personalized learning curriculums delivered through blended channels utilizing video, audio, and textual media.

Scrutiny. Digital information is notoriously easy to manipulate. From Photoshopped images to email phishing scams and 'fake news' tweets, we see people trying to gain advantage through various devious behaviors. The Net Generation has grown up dealing with such issues. Having instant access to information, communities, and individuals means that Net-Geners are aware of the importance of very quickly verifying what they see. Net-Geners respect honesty and authenticity, and actively seek out and reveal instances where they consider such values not being upheld. This intense scrutiny means that businesses must be more transparent with their actions as they will be judged on their ability to speak with an authentic voice.

Integrity. Exposing and connecting large pools of information has an additional consequence for the Net Generation. The purpose and impact of actions are now more readily analyzed and discussed. A broad sense of what is acceptable behavior is brought to bear on activities that can quickly be exposed, highlighted, and propagated. Errors and inappropriate actions are expected to be corrected. Organizations found to lack integrity suffer immediate backlash and risk being rejected by Net-Geners, who move on to other sources of products and services.

Collaboration. The Net Generation interacts frequently and without barriers. The wide adoption of social media tools and sharing platforms through mobile devices has revolutionized how individuals connect with each other to share all aspects of their lives. The broader consequence is an increased reliance on interactive tasks and collaborative problem-solving. In the business world a Net-Gener would want a similar experience in which they communicate frequently with co-workers and colleagues, participate in decision-making, and view their role as both a willing producer and consumer of new ideas.

Entertainment. Getting your message heard has become increasingly difficult in the digital world. Greater access to online channels has increased competition for the Net-Gener's attention. It has become essential for companies to bring novelty and entertainment to their connectivity with the Net Generation. A focus on engagement and experience is important. The blurring of lines between work and play is also an essential aspect of the Net Generation, who frequently have no clear separation of work and private lives. Instead they multi-task, expecting to move seamlessly between work tasks and personal needs.

Speed. Access to high-speed broadband and ubiquitous wireless Internet, along with the rapid drop in computer technology prices have brought powerful digital capabilities to many people and communities across the world. Along with this comes growing impatience with products and services that are slow, lack intelligence, and are poorly interconnected. The Net Generation demands quick responses and expect businesses to bring together the necessary information to facilitate smooth interactions.

Innovation. In a fast-evolving digital world, the Net Generation is accustomed to change. Traditionally, businesses have been optimized toward stability, and change management in most organizations is designed to reduce the risk of errors in offering new capabilities and services. However, Net-Geners value product innovation and have become used to receiving a constant stream of new features in the products and services they use. They also prioritize speedy access to such features over their robustness, and respect an organization when it tries out new ideas, even if they subsequently fail.

Figure 4.1 usefully illustrates how different generations exhibit distinct behavioral characteristics that can have significant impact on their work interactions, motivations, and activities. If we consider learning style for example, traditionalist staff members will look for organized learning opportunities through classes and events, while their Net-Gener colleagues will be more spontaneous and interactive, turning to co-workers, online learning platforms, and their broader social networks for immediate and continuous support and advice. Hence, organizations must consider a breadth of approaches to encourage and support the ongoing learning of their workforce.

Beyond the individual, building effective teams is critical to success when creating organizational units capable of moving quickly and responding to uncertainty.[6] An essential first step is to encourage and support the growing diversity in digitally driven teams. The fast pace of technological change and the increasing global footprint of many organizations have encouraged their workforce to be:
— globally distributed across multiple time zones.
— drawn from many countries and cultures.
— designed to operate both onsite and offsite, with frequent remote working.

- constructed from a wide range of experiences, backgrounds, and ages so that, for instance, new entrants to the workforce join experienced employees who now continue to work for longer.
- representative of the diversity of the communities and customer base being served.

	Traditionalist	Boomer	Net Generation	
			Gen X	Gen Y
Training	Scheduled, regular	As needed	Required for success	Continuous and expected
Learning style	Classroom	Facilitated	Independent	Collaborative, interactive
Communication style	Top down	Community-based	Hub and spoke	Collaborative
Problem-solving	Hierarchical	Horizontal	Independent	Collaborative
Decision-making	Seeks approval	Team informed	Team included	Team decides
Leadership style	Command and control	Authorize and review	Coach and inspire	Partner and support
Feedback	At end of project	Once per year	Weekly / daily	On demand
Technology use	Uncomfortable	Unsure	Unable to work without it	Unfathomable if not provided
Job changing	Avoided	By necessity	To broaden skills	Part of my daily routine

Fig. 4.1: Behavioral Characteristics of Different Generations[7]

Consequently, teams in today's workplaces represent a variety of backgrounds, perspectives, aspirations, work approaches, collaborative skills, and learning styles. Such diversity brings strength and opportunity to the organization.

Drive – Mastery, Autonomy, and Purpose

Beneath the surface of learning styles, collaborative behaviors, and modes of interaction lies a deeper concern regarding an individual's motivation. Motivation has been studied for decades, and leaders in the workplace have used a variety of assessment tools such as Myers-Briggs[8] to ascertain personality types and gain a deeper understanding of the variation in individual and team performance, or as input for structured exercises to form high-functioning teams.[9]

A multitude of business books offer advice on how to increase motivation and help individuals gain more from their working life, balance it with their home life more effectively, and contribute more to their employer organizations. Such approaches, frequently part of broader organizational initiatives, can help inspire both short-term and long-term performance. However, underlying such efforts must be an understanding of what drives people in today's digital era.

Dan Pink has raised some of the most interesting insights into motivation from his research exploring how incentives influence workers.[10] Pink examined the role of money in motivating workers to work harder and improve their performance in cognitive tasks. He found that motivation is not driven by rewards or punishment. Rather, once workers are paid enough to live comfortably, they look for other kinds of outcomes. Pink observed three factors that motivated workers to go beyond basic tasks and increase performance and satisfaction:

- **Autonomy.** Our desire to be self-directed. Individuals value the opportunity to manage their time and effort, and to be active participants in planning future steps. In this way workers feel supported in increasing engagement rather than overwhelmed by the need to comply.
- **Mastery.** As individuals we seek to improve our capabilities, learn new skills, and hone them through application to complex tasks. Workers look to new challenges as a chance to augment their skills and to share them with colleagues.
- **Purpose.** Increasingly, workers want to be inspired. As humans we have a need to do something that we believe has meaning and contributes toward a defined outcome. Businesses that only focus on financial motives without valuing the broader business and social impact often find they face poor customer service and dissatisfied employees.

Experiments carried out by Pink and his team demonstrated various elements of these motivational factors. In one particular scenario, when monetary rewards were offered to workers carrying out a task, the time they took to complete the task increased. Pink concluded that the reward only succeeded in narrowing the focus of the task, which may be healthy for manual work, but counterproductive for knowledge workers needing to solve problems more imaginatively or where customer needs are less well-defined.

These observations are especially relevant to digital transformation contexts where an organization's flexibility in the face of significant uncertainty is critical to success. In such circumstances it is essential to focus on the broader motivational needs of workers beyond monetary incentives and to provide a context in which today's digitally inspired individuals can flourish.

Dealing with Digital

The introduction and application of digital technologies brings many additional challenges for organizations looking to nurture their talented individuals and build high-performance teams. In 2016, MIT's Sloan School of Management and Deloitte carried out a comprehensive survey of 3,500 managers and executives on their digital business attitudes and activities.[11] The survey's analysis highlighted the specific challenges organizations face in building a successful workforce while undergoing digital transformation, and made observations at three macro levels: individual, team, and organizational.

Individual

Organizations face significant challenges in attracting and retaining talent in a world where individuals are much more inclined to pursue a portfolio of jobs throughout their working life,[12] rather than have career longevity with a single company.[13] The rise of the current "Tech Start-up Culture"[14] based on smaller, more flexible companies offers today's workers a dynamic environment in which they can quickly build skills, take on extensive responsibilities, and see ideas implemented as actions in short order. For the individual, the breadth of opportunities such environments offer and the speed at which they gain their experiences help to offset the downsides of an unpredictable portfolio career that can be financially unstable.

Hence, larger, more mature organizations frequently find it problematic to convince digitally savvy employees that they offer a challenging, fast-paced working environment tuned to their workers' expectations. In most markets there is a massive shortage of staff highly skilled in data science, digital marketing, and customer-centric product delivery. These individuals are usually attracted to companies and locations where they can find like-minded colleagues, stimulating workplaces, and living conditions that they value. For this reason, organizations operating in traditional industrial sites have been investing to equip their older buildings for more modern working practices. They are also seeking to open satellite offices with business accelerators on university campuses and within emerging digital hubs.[15]

As they review the skills of their existing workforce, these mature organizations face an additional challenge; what the CIO of a large UK-based aerospace and defense company described bluntly as "a 50/50 issue".[16] He observed that in key areas of his business, more than 50% of his staff were over 50 years old. While they brought a tremendous amount of stability, experience, and domain knowledge, their level of expertise in new digital technologies and business practices was understandably quite low. They were also less likely to introduce many new ideas or challenge orthodox approaches, which tended to inhibit risk-taking and experimentation. All this makes the organization less attractive to potential newcomers looking for a young, vibrant work environment.

Upgrading the skills of an existing workforce, however, is far from straightforward. Many such companies have traditional learning and development approaches involving occasional training classes and centrally-driven training agendas controlled through a bureaucratic budgeting process. But today's young workforce demands a more personalized approach to learning that recognizes individual learning styles, driven by the individual's agenda. They also expect a combination of online and offline approaches that can be more dynamically scheduled as part of their regular working life, including optimized "learning moments" during dead time such as while travelling.[17]

Today, many also look for immersive experiences through online communities, where skilled individuals participate in problem-solving in contexts that reinforce learning and build confidence. This approach has resulted in the rapid rise of online learning portals such as Coursera, Udemy, and edX, and wide participation in community projects as exemplified by the Apache open-source software products[18] and the Bloodhound project.[19] Dynamic, digitally aware individuals identify themselves with the communities to which they contribute, and they use these communities not just to advance their skills but also to showcase their talents for prospective employers, find like-minded workmates who share common goals, and establish strong team relationships that often extend beyond their loyalty to a single organization.

A related problem many organizations face today is retaining digital talent. Keeping good people has always been high priority for any company, but the pressure to do so has been heightened by a very dynamic marketplace, the shortage of digitally experienced people, and changing attitudes toward long-term career progression. One of the most outstanding responses in the MIT Sloan study was that employees and executives wanted their organizations to encourage and support them to advance their digital skills and give them opportunities to apply these skills to drive new business activities. Without this, senior executives were 15 times more likely to want to leave the organization within a year. Most compellingly, this response was consistent across the Information and Communications (ICT) sectors as well as others including healthcare, public services, and construction. Even in those non-ICT areas, the use of digital technologies to enhance capabilities and optimize service delivery was seen as critical to an individual's choice of where they wanted to work.

Team

Organizations are increasingly focusing on the impact of high-performing teams.[20] In a rapidly-changing environment, the ability of teams to work together to respond to change and deliver customer-facing value is now seen as critical. Such teams provide something of a 'shock absorber' when a business needs to pivot quickly, or when broader management strategies shift due to unforeseen macro-level trends – driven by new technologies, innovative business models, and emerging platform companies – that could potentially have a huge impact on the company. The best-performing teams work at incredibly high velocities, delivering solutions quickly with interaction patterns that reinforce the group's cohesion. Various studies have demonstrated this in practice,[21] showing that the best-performing teams build internal cohesion through frequent inter-team interactions and open their activities to external communities to broaden their experiences. The conclusion is that organizations can learn how to identify and encourage appropriate communication styles to shape and guide teams so that they develop team skills necessary to sustain their growth.

For many organizations, a starting point for rethinking the role and importance of team structure is the move toward platform-based architectural models as the basis for products and services. With the rapid growth of a wide variety of Software-as-a-Service (SaaS) capabilities, many companies have re-architected their enterprise solution to build on the commoditized service offerings that SaaS provides. They then organize their teams around the capabilities created to extend these platforms with customer-specific features that add value and differentiate the company's offerings in the market. Such an architectural approach based around common service platforms encourages tightly integrated team interactions to deliver new features and cultivates a certain level of independence and competition between teams.

Ericsson offers a good example of this practice.[22] Based on its traditional approach of software project delivery, Ericsson's initial organizational structure comprised component teams and a sequential, waterfall-type, process. As such, each component team included between 10 and 20 people across multiple sites using teleconferences to communicate on a weekly basis. However, the agility and speed necessary for new product innovation required smaller, tightly integrated teams to be created to support delivery of a flow of finer-grained features. The lessons from Ericsson's subsequent move to agile cross-functional feature teams, in line with other studies of agile practices,[23] emphasize the importance of stable teams formed around a common agile delivery framework.

Rather than working privately and without context, these service delivery teams become an integral part of broader ecosystems formed around these service platforms. The multi-sided marketplace dynamics of such platforms foster a form of alignment across the ecosystem through a cooperative shared set of platform incentives.[24] For example, consider the many, varied product offerings built by small, integrated teams around platforms such as Salesforce[25] and SAP.[26] Such an approach is now used more broadly as a design and organizational model in many enterprise solutions.[27]

An additional benefit of this approach is that the move to platform thinking and ecosystem support also encourages teams to be more transparent within and outside company boundaries. Local and dispersed teams can work collectively through widely used, shared environments such as GitHub.[28] These environments not only bring teams together to enhance productivity while working on common capabilities, they also promote teams across their wider peer communities, act as showcases for team best practices, and aid recruitment to teams as they compete for the most talented individuals within and beyond the company.

Wide adoption of agile approaches in many organizations, particularly in those sectors where software plays an important role, has been at the root of many team dynamics activities. Agile practices are becoming increasingly important for companies offering digital products and services, and an essential part of every organization's digital operating environment. Driven by demands for more software more quickly, organizations have studied the practices of high-performing teams to see how they could be replicated,[29] including how those teams tried to shake off the overly constraining processes they believed were hampering innovation and creativity. From this emerged a series of principles for agile development, most famously captured in the "Agile Manifesto"[30] and a series of development practices that encapsulate those principles – notably the Scrum method.[31]

Many of the ideas and approaches toward team agility are obvious to the individuals in these high-performing teams, who may argue that they represent no more than years of 'common sense' techniques that experienced teams accumulate over time. However, less clear to the organization is how it can scale and manage such teams as part of a concerted effort of improvement across their integrated delivery units, and more broadly throughout the organization. Initiatives such as Disciplined Agile Delivery (DAD)[32] and the Scaled Agile Framework (SAFe)[33] have been formed largely to encourage and support scalability for collections of agile teams.

Consequently, Agile thinking has galvanized several important ideas relevant to contemporary team dynamics. Critical to success in this mindset is placing emphasis on the following key elements:

- **Collaboration.** Agile approaches focus less on paperwork and more on conversations across the team and with actively involved stakeholders.
- **Quality.** Agile practices encourage inclusion of test activities as early as possible in projects and continuous execution of tests to maintain quality.
- **Evolution.** Agile projects create loosely coupled, highly cohesive architectures, and frequently refactor to keep them that way.
- **Working solutions.** Agile projects monitor progress based on what they can show works more than on designs and descriptions of what should or could be produced.
- **Individual and team flexibility.** Agile team members are 'generalizing specialists' who are experts in some areas but may perform many tasks on a project and work for the good of the team.

The move toward greater use of digital technologies has also encouraged the emergence of new roles essential to the success of teams creating, capturing, and delivering value across the company. Grounded in traditional management capabilities, these coordinating roles combine skills from disciplines typically found in disparate silos in the organization. Several of these hybrid roles, such as Product Managers and User Experience Designers, aim to reduce the friction between consumers and providers of products and services that can slow down decision-making. Particularly important is a focus on translating the requirements of increasingly connected users into online interactions and experiences that match their needs. Service delivery via online channels has heightened expectations for responsive, personalized services as well as raised the bar for the design, accessibility, and usability of these offerings.

Much of the evolution in team performance is driven by easy access to online data analysis tools such as Google Analytics and a variety of marketing automation software tools, as well as to ever-growing volumes of data. Consequently, companies now expect all team members to be capable of using data effectively in decision-making, and that they will build increasing insight into the methods used for designing, delivering, and managing the products and services they create. Three data-driven hybrid team roles are particularly critical in today's digital economy:

Marketing Automation Specialists who combine traditional marketing skills with emerging information technology capabilities to design technology-enabled marketing programs and rapidly respond to ongoing feedback with digitally delivered marketing campaigns. Many marketing tasks are increasingly driven by data extracted from product delivery and usage contexts. Also, as companies digitize more aspects of their products and operations, they are increasingly using quantitative approaches to target customers and manage marketing campaigns. Hence, Marketing Automation Specialists require deep mathematical and technical skills more commonly found in statistical or IT roles. They need to know how to combine these with traditional marketing skills to interpret data-driven signals in the context of the company's current market strategies.

Product Managers who draw on capabilities from engineering management through to business planning and strategy and are increasingly expected to have basic computer programming skills to generate accurate status and reporting data from their teams. Product Managers coordinate team activities to deliver products, often taking responsibility for setting the product strategy, maintaining the cooperation of external teams across engineering and marketing, and preparing the product for a variety of sales channels. Product Managers also rely heavily on their ability to communicate and present data using effective data visualization strategies to a plethora of stakeholders with varying understanding of the company's products and their uses.

User Experience Designers who not only bring together skills from graphics, design, and computer programming, but are also increasingly required to understand consumers in depth by employing techniques from psychology and anthropology. In contrast to user interface design, User Experience Designers go far beyond a product's 'look-and-feel' to explore the usage context, define user needs, and specify the optimal approach to meet stakeholder expectations. This requires a combination of research and communication skills bridging technical, market, and business domains.

Organizational

Some organizations have found ways to become more flexible in their ability to absorb growth, and to react to changes in market conditions by moving quickly into new areas, adapting to different delivery channels, and forming new alliances as necessary for more efficient delivery. In examining the objectives of these "elastic enterprises", Vitalari and Shaughnessy[34] highlight five key elements:

- A **clear business strategy** where business rules and relationships are well-aligned to address customer needs and support supply chain opportunities.
- The development of a **healthy business ecosystem** where participants are motivated to deliver major functional capabilities and services to support the organization's business goals.
- Explicit **creation of universal connectors** to services offered by the organization through interfaces that encourage and leverage business partners.
- **Use of cloud infrastructure** for rapid deployment and low overheads in the internal management of critical core services and external delivery of capabilities to clients and partners.
- A **leadership approach that recognizes the transformational impact of digital business** and is unafraid to drive the organization in new directions toward reshaping its role, purpose, and operating model.

Management in such 'elastic' organizations must adapt to a different approach toward leadership, strategy, and decision-making, as traditional top-down hierarchies are unlikely to work effectively. The bureaucratic approach developed during the industrial age emphasized the importance of productivity and efficiency through standardization and rigor. Hierarchical management models organized large teams into manageable units aimed at achieving a common purpose through adherence to shared processes. In the information-driven age that followed, successful companies leveraged their insights and access to new knowledge to build organizations based on meritocracy.[35] Rational analysis and expertise were celebrated as they guided future directions. Strategic decision-making was based on evidence drawn from data.

However, such organizational models are sub-optimal in many digital transformation situations characterized by massive uncertainty and a fast-changing environment. Here, the focus must be on speed of reaction to the weak signals received, with strategic intuition and opportunistic risk-taking playing a more significant role. This opportunistically focused adhocracy approach[36] is based on a fast-paced experimental learning cycle that encourages a form of 'planned serendipity'.[37]

Many companies' strategic approach to problem-solving is a critical determinant of their dominant culture; the way they handle problems is particularly illustrative in understanding the differences[38] across the range of organizational models. For example, when bureaucratic organizations solve complex problems, they would typically rely on their hierarchical management structure to understand roles and responsibilities, delegating and escalating decision-making as necessary. In contrast, problems faced in a meritocratic organization are solved through collecting data and using rational data-based arguments to justify a particular course of action. In an adhocracy, the default problem-solving approach is to experiment to learn more, using feedback to refine direction, and continue operating through swift act-learn-refine cycles. The focus in an adhocracy is to maximize learning in the shortest possible time. The key differences between these three management approaches are summarized in Figure 4.2.

In digital transformation, adhocracy is particularly appropriate as it brings structure to highly uncertain situations. Three key features of adhocracy make this management approach attractive to companies embarking on digital transformation journeys:

- **Coordinating activities around opportunities.** Flexibility in the formation and disbanding of teams focuses on achieving outcomes rather than maximizing outputs. Each team has a clear mission and declares success once this is accomplished before disbanding to move on to new challenges.
- **Making decisions through experimentation.** Incremental learning helps to refine understanding in unprecedented situations. Early release of minimal viable products to customers brings realistic feedback that helps to coordinate effort around the highest priority activities. Intuitive insight into

challenges is encouraged, with speed of action prized above depth of analysis.

— **Motivating people through achievement and recognition.** Motivation arises from challenging individuals and teams to excel, and through offering extraordinary levels of support that enable teams to perform at the highest possible levels.

	Bureaucracy	Meritocracy	Adhocracy
Focus	Stable, well-known environments	Technically-advanced products and services	Unknown and exploratory ventures
Approach	Work package and rule-based	Flexible aimed at maximizing learning	Problem-oriented and dynamic
Decision Making	Hierarchical, top-down	Technical skills and experience	Trial and error
Motivations	Pay and career advancement	Personal mastery and peer recognition	Solution and outcome based

Fig. 4.2: A Comparison of Three Organizational Models

Thus, the objective for digital transformation is to create an organization with a more dynamic, agile approach to change and with the flexibility to adjust to unforeseen circumstances, helping them maintain their relevance to customers in the digital economy. Digital transformation is therefore about rethinking business strategies and adjusting organizations to be more flexible and responsive to change, enabled by deploying new technology.

The Future of Work

As we look toward the future, we see a number of key megatrends that will shape the work environment in a digital age.[39] Most prominent of these are:

- The continued impact of technological breakthroughs automating manual tasks and reforming markets.
- The demographic shifts that will bring older populations and workforces to some geographical regions and large younger populations to others.
- Rapid urbanization growing our largest cities way beyond their current boundaries.
- Shifts in global economic power toward emerging countries with growing working populations and low labor rates.
- Resource scarcity driving demand for new energy sources in new places.

At a macro-level, such megatrends set a foundation for the opportunities and challenges businesses face in our digital world, and how such major themes will play out in practice remains to be seen.

Without a clear framework it is difficult to make sense of these megatrends to drive business strategy. To assist with this, an analysis by a consulting company considers future scenarios in which four primary categories of working environment emerge.[40] Centered on the human elements essential in any organizational view, PwC examined two dimensions in its analysis: the collective versus individual approach to organizational structures, and the forces for integration versus fragmentation that dominate businesses. The result is a distinction between four "future worlds of work" that they label red, blue, green and yellow.

In the **Red World,** where individualism is strong and there is a great deal of market fragmentation, businesses innovate to create personalized solutions that serve emerging niche markets. The workforce must be highly innovative, supported by digital platforms and technologies which enable workers with the most in-demand skills to be successful. More mature organizations will be chasing talented individuals and partnering with smaller, more agile companies to deliver the skills they need while maintaining flexibility.

Blue World organizations value individualism but in a larger corporate setting integrating a wide set of services for consumers. These companies can leverage their size and market position to dominate the markets in which they operate. They will need to identify their key-performing individuals and support them with teams that amplify their impact. Non-essential activities will be automated to focus efforts on where they can differentiate value for their customers. Digital technologies are particularly useful in managing and optimizing internal processes, and in guiding managers to identify important signals in the mass of data they receive.

In the **Green World** there is a collective approach to meeting market needs in an integrated organizational structure. There is strong motivation to build a trusted environment that prizes social responsibility with a deep understanding of ongoing demographic changes driven by a responsible social agenda. Digital technology is important as it can reduce the need for travel, improve innovation in communications technology, and support promotion of a social agenda that is integral to the business. Employees value flexibility in the workplace and collaborate in creating a learning culture across the organization.

Yellow World organizations work together to address the needs of a highly-fragmented business environment. Innovation in business models and practices is essential, centred on a strong ethical framework. Workers participate in the funding and support of new ideas via crowdfunding schemes and shared personal commitments of their free time to projects with which they feel strongly connected. They are incentivized and rewarded through cooperative ownership models and social impact. Adoption of digital technologies is encouraged, but only when workers have considered their potential negative impacts on individuals and society, and are satisfied that these are being transparently monitored. Employee skills development is particularly critical for the longer-term interests of individuals and communities.

While many organizations have invested significantly in digital technology, there has been much less focus on the future workforce and their needs. The PwC report may have highlighted the different worlds that are emerging, but the challenge now is to ensure that digital transformation sufficiently addresses the design of future workforces. Digital technology can play an important role, but companies are realizing that the differentiator is not the technology *per se*; it is a talented workforce enabled with such technologies that remove friction, augment human creativity, and extend reach and impact.

While many factors may be considered important in creating a digitally enabled workforce, three initiatives are particularly notable:[41]
- Widely-deployed digital technology **offers new insights** into customers, marketplaces, production processes, operations, and much more. Such information is vital not only for efficient business operations, but also in understanding, supporting, and predicting the organization's workforce needs.[42] Such predictive analytics can offer a foundation for improved decision-making across talent management functions and differentiated workforce strategies.

- Digital technology is **expanding the footprint of today's workforce**, redefining who can be classified as a worker, what is shared across a partner ecosystem, and how tasks are carried out by teams of workers from both within and outside a company's traditional employment boundaries. Far beyond remote working, tasks can now be outsourced to partner organizations, shared across geographically distributed teams, issued as challenges to broad communities, and crowdsourced.[43] The ability to source talent in new ways is becoming a key competitive area for many companies.
- Traditional notions of learning and development in the workforce are being **swept away by digitally enabled learning management systems** with on-demand access to materials that combine classroom activities, multimedia content, games and simulations.[44] These capabilities not only support improvement of existing skills, they are also being used to prepare workers for the digital future by encouraging continuous re-skilling that helps to sustain the organization's workforce through unpredictable changes.

As organizations look to the workforce of the future, they are increasingly using digital technology as a critical enabler. The most successful companies in the digital economy are not only hiring the best digitally aware talent, they are using digital technologies to augment their impact and sustain their value to the organization. Such activities are increasingly seen as a competitive advantage in a talent-scarce environment.

Summary

Success in a digital economy demands a talented workforce that uses digital technology effectively and feels supported in a working environment where change and uncertainty may be the norm. The challenge, then, is to create a future workforce that can adapt itself to the world as it evolves, and where digital transformation recognizes the critical role of the human dimension as companies and markets form and reform in a world of constant change.

————

References

1 Korn Ferry Institute (2016). *The Battle for Motivation*. Briefings Magazine. Available at: https://www.kornferry.com/institute/the-battle-for-motivation
2 http://news.gallup.com/reports/199961/7.aspx

3 The Net Generation is defined by Tapscott as those born between 1977 and 1997. They are intimately familiar with the Internet and digital technologies, embedding them in every aspect of their daily lives.

4 Tapscott, D. (2009). *Grown Up Digital.* McGraw Hill.

5 Widely referenced, e.g., https://en.wikiquote.org/wiki/Alan_Kay

6 Pentland, A. (2012). *The New Science of Building Great Teams.* Harvard Business Review, April.

7 Adapted from: Lancaster, L.C. and Stillman, D. (2003). *When Generations Collide: Who They Are. Why They Clash. How to Solve the Generational Puzzle at Work.* Wheaton, IL. Harper Business.

8 https://www.myersbriggs.org

9 Forsgren, N., Humble, J. and Kim, G. (2018). *Accelerate: Building and Scaling High Performing Technology Organizations.* IT Revolution Press.

10 Pink, D. (2011). *Drive: The Surprising Truth about What Motivates Us.* Canongate Books.

11 Kane, G.C., Palmer, D., Nguyen Phillips, A., Kiron, D. and Buckley, N. (2016). *Aligning the Organization for its Digital Future,* MIT Sloan Management Review, July 26. Available at: https://sloanreview.mit.edu/projects/aligning-for-digital-future/

12 Petriglieri, G., Ashford, S.J. and Wrzesniewski, A. (2018). *Thriving in the Gig Economy.* Harvard Business Review, March-April. Available at: https://hbr.org/2018/03/thriving-in-the-gig-economy

13 Korkki, P. (2011). *The Shifting Definition of Worker Loyalty.* The New York Times, 23rd April. Available at: https://www.nytimes.com/2011/04/24/jobs/24search.html

14 McAveeney, C. (2013). *How Do You Define Startup Culture?* WIRED. Available at: https://www.wired.com/insights/2013/09/how-do-you-define-startup-culture/

15 Viki, T., Toma, D., and Gons, E. (2019). *The Corporate Startup: How Established Companies Can Develop Successful Innovation Ecosystems.* Management Impact Publishing.

16 From a personal interview with an Aerospace executive, April 2018.

17 Banerjee, P.M. and Belson, G. (2015). *Digital Education 2.0: From Content to Connections.* Deloitte Review Issue 16. Deloitte Insights. Available at: https://www2.deloitte.com/insights/us/en/ deloitte-review/issue-16/future-digital-education-technology.html

18 https://www.apache.org/

19 http://www.bloodhoundlsr.com/

20 Keller, S. and Meaney, M. (2017). *High-performing Teams: A Timeless Leadership Topic.* McKinsey Quarterly. Available at: https://www.mckinsey.com/business-functions/organization/our-insights/high-performing-teams-a-timeless-leadership-topic

21 Pentland, A. (2012). *The New Science of Building Great Teams.* Harvard Business Review, April.

22 Paasivaara, M., Behm, B., Lassenius, C. and Hallikainen, M. (2018). Large-scale Agile Transformation at Ericsson: A Case Study. *Empirical Software Engineering,* 23(5): 2550-2596. Available at: https://doi.org/10.1007/s10664-017-9555-8

23 Dorairaj, S., Noble, J. and Malik, P. (2012). *Understanding Team Dynamics in Distributed Agile Software Development.* In: C. Wohlin, ed., *Agile Processes in Software Engineering and Extreme Programming.* XP 2012. Lecture Notes in Business Information Processing, Vol 111. Springer.

24 Cussamano, M., Gawer, A. and Yoffie, D.B. (2019). *The Business of Platforms: Strategy in the Age of Digital Competition, Innovation, and Power.* Harper Business.

25 https://www.salesforce.com/products/platform/products/force

26 Hinchcliffe, D. (2019). *How SAP's Partner Ecosystem is Built for Long-Term Growth.* ZDNet. Available at: https://www.zdnet.com/article/how-saps-partner-ecosystem-is-built-for-long-term-growth/

27 Riggins, J. (2015). *Agile Management: How to Manage Microservices With Your Team.* The New Stack. Available at: https://thenewstack.io/agile-management-how-to-manage-microservices-with-your-team/

28 https://github.com/

29 Dyer, J. and Nobeoka, K. (2000). *Creating* and Managing a High-Performance Knowledge-Sharing Network: The Toyota Case. *Strategic Management Journal* (Special Issue), 21(3): 345-367.

30 https://agilemanifesto.org/

31 https://www.scrum.org/

32 Ambler, S. and Lines, M. (2012). *Disciplined Agile Delivery: A Practitioner's Guide to Agile Software Delivery in the Enterprise.* IBM Press.

33 https://www.scaledagileframework.com/

34 Vitalari, N. and Shaughnessy, H.(2013). *The Elastic Enterprise: The New Manifesto for Business Revolution.* Telemachus Press.

35 Whitehurst, J. (2014). Meritocracy: *The Workplace Culture That Breeds Success.* WIRED. Available at: https://www.wired.com/insights/2014/10/meritocracy/

36 Birkinshaw, J. and Ridderstrale, J. (2017). *Fast/Forward: Make Your Company Fit for the Future.* Stanford Business Books.

37 Muller, T. and Becker, L. (2012). *Get Lucky: How to Put Planned Serendipity to Work for You and Your Business.* Jossey Bass.

38 Birkinshaw, J. and Ridderstrale, J. (2017). *Fast/Forward: Make Your Company Fit for the Future.* Stanford Business Books.

39 Jones, T. and Dewing, C. (2016). *Future Agenda: Six Challenges for the Next Decade.* Third Millennium Publishing.

40 PwC (2017). *Workforce of the Future: The Competing Forces Shaping 2030.* PwC. Available at: https://www.pwc.com/gx/en/services/people-organisation/publications/workforce-of-the-future.html

41 Lyons, M., Biltz, M. and Whittall, N. (2017). *Shaping the Agile Workforce.* Accenture Strategy Report. Available at: https://www.accenture.com/_acnmedia/PDF-60/Accenture-Strategy-Shaping-Agile-Workforce-POV.pdf

42 Harris, J.G., Craig, E., and Light, D.A. (2011). Talent and Analytics: New Approaches, Higher ROI. *Journal of Business Strategy*, 32(6): 4-13.

43 Lacity, M. and Willcocks, L.P. (2009). *The Practice of Outsourcing: From Information Systems to BPO and Offshoring.* Palgrave Macmillan.

44 https://www.learninglight.com/best-elearning-white-papers/

Part 2: **shaping the path**

5 Agile

Introduction

Today's companies are able to design, test, and deliver new products and services more quickly than ever before. This is due to new technologies that support rapid user-centered design, constant field testing, and instant deployment on a very broad scale. More fundamentally, however, there has been a tremendous change in mindset. Today, digitally aware organizations' engagement and delivery is very much based on short delivery cycles using lean start-up techniques, where Minimum Viable Products (MVPs) trialed with consumers drive feedback that can help the organization find the winning business model through multiple "pivots" in market strategy, capabilities, and positioning.[1][2]

Meanwhile, organizations have made huge investments in technology to automate and optimize their maturing business processes. In contrast to more recent agile practices, IT approaches need to create stability, predictability, and consistent quality in software-based services. The resulting enterprise software solutions (in areas such as Database Management, Customer Relationship Management, and Sales Management) were architected and deployed for long-term shared use. While they bring significant benefits, they also have many limitations in respect to speed of change. This has made them brittle and unyielding when faced with demands for flexibility inherent in the rapid business model innovation prevalent in the digital economy.

Consequently, we have learned much in the past decade about how agile change is defined, delivered, and managed. Much as agility has benefitted an organization's productivity, quality, and effectiveness, it has not been without significant challenges and missteps. Such experiences have forced organizations to rethink many aspects of how they perform their functions. Attention needs to be given to three fundamental observations in the context of digital transformation:

- The short, medium, and long-term value a business derives from digital technology deployment is frequently not understood in relation to the technology investment itself.
- Business processes undergo constant change, and their ability to evolve is poorly addressed in principle, and expensive to support in practice.
- Most of the costs and value of digital transformation initiatives occur beyond the technology's initial purchase and introduction, yet much attention

and investment is focused on the initial technology selection, testing and deployment.

For over two decades there have been efforts to increase flexibility by applying agile practices within enterprise software delivery. The intent is to shorten the time-to-delivery through optimized rapid iterative delivery, early visibility into problems and blockages, reduced late rework through continuous feedback, and greater cooperation at all stages across distributed teams.

Increasing agility in enterprise software delivery introduced ideas and approaches that seemed like obvious solutions to those involved in the projects; it builds on common practices for small, well-integrated teams to work closely together in rapid cycles. However, what's less clear to the organization is how it can scale and manage agile practices as part of a concerted effort of improvement across an integrated supply chain within a broader digital transformation effort. For without due care and attention, these agile approaches not only have limited success, they can also be harmful:[3] existing ways of working can become unstable, control and governance of projects unpredictable, and employee productivity and satisfaction may begin to fall.

Experience also shows that any digital transformation will be partial and ineffective if it does not address the clash of cultures and practices across an organization's development, delivery, and management.[4] Hence, in this chapter we review the context for agile practices and address what it means to increase agility within an organization and across an ecosystem of partner organizations. We first consider the adoption and adaptation of agile practices in software delivery to offer a broader view of agility, before we look at the key elements in moving from agile software development toward an agile organization. Then we focus on the ways in which this agility can be scaled and adopted as part of a broader digital transformation.

The Agile Software Delivery Context

The earliest uses of computers were for scientific tasks, mathematical calculations, and statistical analysis. However, as businesses began to appreciate the value of rapid, accurate computation, the job of programming computers moved from the scientist to a new role: the computer programmer, supported by business analysts who translate business needs into processes amenable to computer-based solutions. The deployment of the resulting software into mission-critical business environments demanded that these programs be adequately tested, could be maintained once in production, and evolved appropriately according to new requirements. Software tasks were structured as complex construction and maintenance processes modelled and managed along similar lines to manufacturing and construction projects.

Despite their many successes, software delivery organizations had a poor reputation throughout the second half of the 20th century, as projects creating or deploying large software systems were frequently late and ended up costing far more than originally anticipated.[5] Large-scale software development projects were implemented through compliance-driven processes that managed the long-term delivery activities. They were executed by extensive teams of people through a series of phased tasks whose progress was measured in terms of incremental steps toward output-based delivery targets. Such a linear approach to successive phases aimed to ensure that completeness and accountability could be verified throughout the project's lifetime. Success relied on extensive planning, well-defined processes, and reuse of predictable architectural solution patterns and components to ensure stability and predictability in operation.

These bureaucratic approaches were very successful for many styles of project development. They brought strong governance and rigorous consistency to demanding multi-dimensional programs that delivered the critical functionality organizations were increasingly relying on for their operations. However, they also had their disadvantages, particularly when the priority was to deliver solutions quickly in volatile or poorly-understood contexts. Often, the rigid and bureaucratic overhead significantly reduced the effectiveness of the processes, and the software produced was costly, over-engineered, and inappropriate for the situation.[6] Those involved in such projects increasingly began to see themselves less as creative solution designers, and more as mechanics in a software factory process.[7]

In response, more flexible team-based methods were created under the general banner of "agile methods".[8] Unlike previous approaches, these methods recognized that the variability and unpredictability of the problems being addressed required greater human creativity in the design process, shorter discovery-focused iterations that combined design and delivery activities, and strong collaboration across integrated teams and with external stakeholders. Instead of armies of people organized hierarchically to mirror manufacturing production processes, agile methods sought to:
- Highlight individuals with insight and skill.
- Bring together small cross-functional teams.
- Interact closely with product and service consumers.

– Organize work based on near-time, line-of-sight priorities rather than ex-
trapolated longer-term projections.

The key characteristics of emerging agile methods were summarized and pro-
moted through an "agile manifesto" created by a group of prominent software
delivery experts.[9] They comprised a set of values considered fundamental to
these agile ways of working that encouraged a focus on:
– Individuals and interactions over processes and tools.
– Working software over comprehensive documentation.
– Customer collaboration over contract negotiations.
– Responding to change over following a plan.

This set of priorities led to an emphasis change in software delivery; a move
away from heavyweight processes towards more flexible, experiment-based
methods such as Scrum,[10] Dynamic Systems Development Methodology
(DSDM),[11] Extreme Programming (XP),[12] Crystal,[13] and many others.

While widely debated,[14] several aspects of agile delivery methods are now dominant across many software development contexts.[15] The use of agile methods
and techniques are viewed as being particularly suited to projects characterized
by volatile requirements, diverse capabilities of those consuming the products
and services, and rapid evolution of the technology utilized. More broadly,
however, the principles that underlie agile methods are seen to be applicable in
other contexts that require a more emergent understanding of problems, or
when there is uncertainty surrounding critical aspects of the solution to be delivered.[16] As such, agile methods are now considered a key part of any digital
transformation program. This crossover of agile software delivery into other
areas is a particularly important aspect of current business strategies.

Toward a Broader View of Agility

Today's organizations are increasingly under pressure to respond ever more
quickly to the needs of their customers and broader stakeholders. Not only is
the drive for increased flexibility resulting in more new products being brought
to market faster, it is also accelerating the evolution of existing solutions and
services. Handling such change is critical for business success, driven by external factors such as market fluctuations, new technologies, competitive offerings, and new laws.

The instability driving business change has become a dominant issue for many organizations. The disruption that digital transformation triggers within a market context of fast-paced evolution has analogies in military combat.[17] In recent years, much military strategy has focused on techniques appropriate for extremely fluid situations with unprecedented, confusing scenarios. These situations are referred to with the acronym VUCA, which represents four key dimensions of unpredictability. In terms of digital transformation, VUCA defines the challenges obstructing success:

- **Volatility.** An increasing range of type, speed, volume, and scale of change in the business environment that places strain on planning processes for stable contexts across agreed planning horizons.
- **Uncertainty.** Lack of predictability of future market conditions and consumer expectations that leads to high levels of risk and inaccurate forecasting.
- **Complexity.** Emerging forms of networked interactions and dependencies across business environments that cause widespread confusion and increase the challenge of establishing clear cause-and-effect traceability when diagnosing problems.
- **Ambiguity.** Unprecedented problems, lack of precision, and wide contradictory interpretations of current status that paralyze decision-making and raise doubts about future steps.

More traditional problem-solving approaches would seek to optimize the stable aspects of strategy to control variations and anomalies. VUCA situations are, however, characterized by their lack of uniformity and therefore require approaches that recognize and thrive in conditions of inherent instability. But change cannot mean chaos. Every organization's activities, in particular its changes to ongoing ways of working, must be governed by a plethora of formal and informal procedures, practices, processes, and regulations.[18] These governance mechanisms are essential to the organization's success in managing and controlling how products and services are delivered into production, maintained, evolved, and brought to end-of-life.

Much has been learned over the past two decades to offer a clear direction in agile delivery. The rapid evolution of digital technology and resulting digital transformation activities have forced organizations to invest in techniques that remove friction and increase flexibility in their delivery approaches, without abandoning all forms of control. They face pressure in balancing their delivery capabilities across four key dimensions:

- **Productivity of individuals and teams.** Traditional productivity approaches are based on the quantity of units of capability (i.e., new features, lines of code, or function points) delivered over time.[19] Producing more in a shorter amount of time may, however, not be the most effective metric for productivity in highly-volatile environments. Other metrics have begun to emerge, such as those based on rapid learning through adoption of experimental techniques.

- **Time-to-market for projects to complete and deliver a meaningful result to the business.** Long planning cycles and multiple levels of sign-off may be appropriate in well-understood environments. However, their value diminishes where speed of delivery and early feedback with customers is necessary. In such cases, rather than focus on overall project completion, it is more effective to optimize the delivery of usable capabilities in short bursts into the hands of product and service users.

- **Process maturity in the consistency, uniformity and standardization of practices.** External auditing and internal corporate mandates often require procedures to conform to rigorous scrutiny. Often it is not just the quality of the outputs that are assessed, but also the way in which those outputs are produced and maintained. Various industry frameworks can help, but usually bring with them a heavy overhead in documentation, sign-off, and management.[20]

- **Quality in delivered product and services, errors handled, and turnaround of requests.** A focus on high-quality products and services is essential. However, for the viability of many solutions the risk of product error (and the impact of that error) must be aligned with the resources needed to achieve specific levels of quality. Traditional measures of success are typically combinations of defect density rates and errors fixed per unit time. These must be balanced with a broader view of quality, one that focuses on how efficiently products and services better able to achieve the outcomes that matter to consumers are put into their hands.

Finding an appropriate balance across these success factors when delivering digital transformation is a constant struggle. One of the most challenging aspects is achieving the change in perspective necessary to balance speed of delivery with governance and predictability of the delivery process.[21] Traditionally, methods and processes for any transformation placed the highest priority on ensuring that everything was rigorously specified before they were executed, and that comprehensive assessment plans were followed to satisfy external auditors that the changes conformed to the specification as closely as practically possible. But such approaches assume that significant elements of the future desired state are both knowable and known when embarking on the transformation. In a digital context this may not be the case.

Also, many organizations in today's digital economy view the relationship between 'operational risk' and 'delivery risk' to be very different than it was a few years ago. There are many occasions where the risk of delivering late or with capabilities that do not meet evolving market needs outweighs the risk of failing to analyze every possible usage model, run every possible test case, or follow every step in the defined delivery process. This is particularly true in situations where changes to existing products and services must be quickly understood, analyzed, and brought into the hands of consumers. This kind of flexibility, or agility, in delivery has become an essential element of the digital economy.[22] Providing this flexibility is an essential aspect of an organization's strategy and approach to product and service delivery.

Focus Areas for the Agile Organization

To have the flexibility required for success in a digital economy, organizations must invest in the collaborative process, from idea generation to solution delivery. They also need to enhance innovation practices to be flexible and repeatable, and train leaders willing to lead innovation-focused teams. The organizational transformation they undergo is aimed at developing the structures, strategies and operating environment capable of differentiating how they deploy digital technologies and processes.

This ideal is often referred to as the 'agile organization'. It is a new way of operating based on a set of principles, practices and tools emerging across a range of disciplines in engineering, information technology, and systems delivery. This focus on agility is the driving force for the new digital economy, and those organizations unable to progress toward this practice and increase their capacity to innovate at internet speed may struggle to survive.

While there are many elements to consider on this journey, our experiences across a range of digital transformation initiatives enable us to focus on several key areas for agility, grouped into the following three major themes:

Technology
- Create and maintain flexible system architectures.
- Rethink the role of agile software delivery.
- Create a new agile discipline for the role of Product Manager.

Process
- Place agile delivery in the context of lean practices.
- View agile software delivery as a series of experiments.
- Encourage and support process maturity in scaling agile practices.

People
- Move to more flexible leadership through empowering people and teams.
- Encourage and reward agile thinking to reinforce agile behaviors.

We now consider these three themes in further detail and explore the importance of an accelerated innovation approach in creating an agile organization.

Technology

Agile methods have been applied in developing and delivering software for more than 20 years now, so it is possible to highlight some important aspects of agile maturity distinguishing those organizations that have succeeded in bringing flexibility to the way they work. Particularly important is their ability to transform their overall approach to product management from a *development* focus to a *delivery* focus, to improve their operating speed and flexibility. This subtle distinction in wording represents a dramatic change in the adoption of the principles driving the agile management philosophy and its governance models.

Software Development Perspective	Software Delivery Perspective
Distinct development phases	Continuously evolving systems
Distinct handoff from development team to maintenance team	Common process, platform, and team for development and maintenance
Distinct and sequential activities requirements to design to code to test	Sequence of usable capabilities with ever-increasing value
Role-specific processes and tools	Collaborative platform of integrated, web-based tools and practices
Co-located teams	Distributed, web-based collaboration
Governance via measurement of artifact production and activity completion	Governance via measurement of incremental outcomes and progress/quality trends
Engineering discipline: track progress against static plans	Economic discipline: reduce uncertainty, manage variance, measure trends, adapt and steer

Fig. 5.1: Software Development and Delivery Perspectives

As summarized in Figure 5.1, the shift in perspective from a *development* to a *delivery approach* affects several dimensions. This is because a delivery perspective[23] focuses on:

– **Continuously evolving systems.** Products and services undergo a continual process of change. Traditionally, the goal is to optimize the steps toward the initial release of these offerings, but in agile organizations the emphasis is on speed of delivery with frequent releases of new capabilities. Investment should be made in supporting and encouraging this evolution.

– **Blurring of boundaries between development and maintenance.** A clear distinction is normally made between development and maintenance, often involving organizational, process, and cultural implications for a 'handover' of the products and services to maintenance. With an evolutionary view of delivery, the distinction between these two is blurred to the point that development and maintenance are just two aspects of the same need to create and deliver value to users of deployed products and services.

– **Sequence of released capabilities with ever increased value.** A development view operates from the understanding that after a deep analysis, the requirements for products and services are agreed (often with a formal 'sign-off') and development activities begin with the goal to meet those requirements and place the products and services in production. But the reality is that further requirements emerge and evolve as more is discovered about the needs of customers and as understanding of the delivery context grows. A more realistic approach views delivery not as a sequence of major discrete releases, but as a continuous series of incremental enhancements providing increasing value to the customer.

- **Common platform of integrated processes and tools.** Organizational approaches for software development usually consist of role-based teams offering resource pools of capabilities to support several projects. This siloed organizational approach is supported by processes and tools optimized for each silo. This occurs because most organizations define processes and acquire tools individually per role, function by function, with little thought for the end-to-end flow of information and artifacts. In contrast, a delivery view recognizes that these processes and tools tend to interoperate to optimize toward speed of delivery and increase cohesion within teams.

- **Distributed collaboration.** A development approach focuses on teaming and teamwork within functional areas, but a delivery view defines the team more broadly, recognizing that stakeholders in delivery tasks may vary widely in function, geography, and organizational approach. Technology support to include all stakeholders in team activities is essential. While a variety of collaborative, web-based technologies have emerged in recent years, many organizations have deployed them in an ad hoc way, with insufficient investment in adopting them across their enterprise organization.

- **Economic governance tailored to risk/reward profiles.** To manage software development, most organizations use a collection of processes, measures, and governance practices that focus on development artifacts such as the software code, requirements documents, and test scripts. A delivery view shifts this governance focus to the business value of what is being delivered, aiming to optimize the features delivered and time-to-value of delivered capabilities, increase burn down of new request backlogs, reduce process volatility, and sustain velocity of delivery teams.

- **Business value and outcome-led approach.** Many organizations pride themselves on their technical skills and the depth of their knowledge in technology infrastructure for creating and operating delivered products and services. They see these as vital to their success. However, this emphasis on technical prowess can create the perception in the organization that technological novelty is prioritized with little regard to where and how such technology investments help the business achieve its goals. A delivery focus emphasizes the business outcomes as the ultimate determinant of success and gives greater emphasis to the business value of technology investments to create a more balanced view.

Consequently, a delivery perspective can radically alter how an organization approaches its business. It encourages a move away from early lockdown of decisions to reduce variance in processes and tasks toward controlled discovery, experimentation, and innovation.

Process

Established organizations devote significant attention to managing their ongoing business activities, which typically takes up to 80% of all costs.[24] Hence, an agile organization must recognize that agility cannot be confined to new projects, and agile practices must be adapted to the business's existing culture and practices. For many organizations, the entry point is to apply agile practices through lean process improvement programs for more efficient delivery.[25]

Based on lessons learned from the manufacturing sector in the 1980s and 90s, lean techniques consider resource expenditure for any goal other than creating customer value to be wasteful, and thus needs to be eliminated. Value is defined as any action or process for which a customer would be willing to pay. Hence lean thinking is centered on preserving value with less work. The essence of a lean manufacturing style is to optimize flow, increase efficiency, decrease waste, and use empirical methods to decide what matters, rather than uncritically accepting pre-existing ideas.

Software delivery organizations[26] [27] have adapted the original lean practices used by Toyota in its car assembly plants, but they have ensured that the key elements of lean thinking remain true to the original lean vision.[28] Interpreted in the context of increasing organizational agility, the key steps include:

- **Define value.** Specify value from the customer perspective and focus on outcomes that are important to the customer in their current context.
- **Map the value stream.** Identify the value stream for each product or service and challenge all non-value adding steps (waste) to determine if they are necessary. Add nothing other than value to processes.
- **Create flow.** Ensure the product or service creation and delivery processes maximize the flow of activities across all steps that add value.

- **Establish pull.** Rather than create bottlenecks where delays occur, introduce pull between all process steps so that continuous flow is possible.
- **Pursue perfection.** Manage toward perfection to minimize the number of steps and the amount of time and information needed to create and deliver the product or service.

Increasingly, agility in software delivery is driving important advances in lean thinking as it applies to organizational transformation.[29] In the move toward an agile organization we see a focus on lean practices that aim to ensure fast cycles to improve feedback and learning across the value chain. The result is an agile approach viewed as a series of experiments governed by well-defined hypotheses, a focus on the speed of testing those hypotheses, and recognition that a clear approach to measurement and management is essential to ensure any experimental approach converges toward meaningful decision-making. Some key principles are emerging, well-summarized by Eric Ries[30] as:

- **Agility is management.** Too many people associate an agile organization with a chaotic, 'anything goes' attitude to governance and planning. Nothing could be further from the truth. In any agile organization there must be a very strong management dimension to ensure progress is coordinated and aligned. Large numbers of small incremental changes must be made based on feedback and analytical data. That cannot occur without discipline and rigor.
- **Validated learning.** Agile decision-making requires constant feedback and is consolidated through frequent reflection. An agile organization must learn from the experiments it undertakes and validate that learning with real-world inputs. This leads to constant reprioritizing and refactoring to ensure activities are well-targeted.
- **Innovation accounting.** Measuring progress in conventional ways (e.g., source lines of code delivered, function points coded) offers limited value to an agile organization, as it is optimized for rapid decision-making, flexibility in adopting new capabilities, and ease of adapting to evolving customer feedback. Consequently, a new planning approach based on innovation accounting is required, one that focuses on establishing benchmarks for these areas and accelerating the pace of delivery based on managing those measures.
- **Build-measure-learn cycle.** The most critical life cycle process in an agile organization is the 'build-measure-learn' cycle. A great deal of attention is directed toward its definition, execution, and enablement. The speed and consistency of executing this cycle are important for understanding the

success of an agile organization because they indicate how well ideas can be realized and delivered.

Ries further observed that what distinguishes organizations successful in adopting an agile approach is that they welcome and embrace change, making many adjustments as they learn what works and what doesn't, including changes in value proposition, customer segment, business model, and partner network. Their key attribute is their ability to *pivot* when they gain feedback that is contrary to their expectations: they change directions but stay grounded in what they have learned. They also focus on validated learning and employ a rigorous method for demonstrating progress through positive improvements in core metrics and key performance indicators (KPIs) critical to the software-intensive business.

People

Many recent studies into high-performing organizations highlight the dominant role people and team dynamics play in product delivery success.[31] Peter Gilles[32] states that "while the agile company is configured in a particular way, it is the agility of its workforce which determines the success or not of this potential". Despite this, many businesses fail to take adequate account of the human elements of an improvement program, and instead, focus much of their attention on technology and processes.

In many regards, the agile manifesto issued two decades ago[33] focused on the impact of people in software-intensive businesses. Several agile software development methods provide clear guidance on how to motivate teams to encourage greater innovation,[34] with Jim Highsmith[35] offering the most straightforward advice on creating and motivating self-directed agile teams, namely:
— Get the right people.
— Clearly articulate the project vision, boundaries, and roles.
— Encourage interaction.
— Facilitate participatory decisions.
— Insist on accountability.
— Steer, don't control.

But such broad descriptions take inadequate account of the challenges most organizations face in aligning and evolving their workforce. Supporting talented individuals has always been a priority for sustainable success and finding and retaining such individuals has become more intense in the digital economy, as discussed in Chapter 4. Three particular aspects of talent management are seen as essential for creating an agile organization:

- **Using digital technologies to learn more about the workforce.** A better understanding of individuals' skills and capabilities helps to optimize talent where it can be most effective, while targeted educational opportunities can be more directly and effectively provided where skills are seen to be insufficient.
- **Adopting a broader concept of an agile workforce.** An agile organization needs to move beyond traditional notions of workers as it is essential to have a diverse workforce drawn from different backgrounds.[36] To attract the best talent, employment boundaries must be stretched to include new forms of partnerships, outsourcing, occasional employees and crowdsourced workers.
- **Existing employees must be upskilled for a digital economy.** Employees need to be supported in picking up new skills appropriate for the digital world in which they operate. Learning to use new digital technologies is essential. However, upskilling must also emphasize new working approaches based on collaboration, self-organizing teams, and outcome-based risk management; skills essential for success in a digital economy.

Addressing individual- and team-level concerns is an obvious starting point for agile organizations to improve their organizational capabilities. However, succeeding in digitally transforming a workforce is much more challenging in practice. Much more radical management principles can and should be adopted.[37] Also, individuals and teams operate within a broader organizational culture and context. According to Steve Denning, the drive for greater organizational agility inevitably challenges traditional management practices, and requires quite different approaches to:

- How an organization sets its goals.
- The role of managers in achieving them.
- How coordination occurs across the supply chain.
- How incentives are set for individuals and teams.
- What the communication paradigms are within the organization and across the extended ecosystem in which it operates.

At the organizational level, agile organizations must constantly adapt to meet the demands of continuously changing business environments. Although it is tempting to believe that this can be driven through high-level corporate initiatives, the most common approach in agile delivery involves building the visibility and credibility of leaders throughout the organization and encouraging communities to be led by those they themselves elect (so-called 'meritocracies'). In this way an agile organization builds an environment that encourages action from bottom up and naturally develops employees who embrace and share new ways of thinking and working.

A 2012 CIO-level study[38] revealed six key findings for promoting an effective organizational context to encourage agile thinking in individuals and teams, emphasizing close attention to individual, team, and organizational interactions:

- Organizations require significant time to absorb changes and react to new norms. Typically, it takes more than two years for major shifts to be accepted. Attempting more rapid change in organizational structures can overwhelm the improvements introduced.
- Where businesses experience fast-paced changes, their employees' ability to adapt is more significant to success than their productivity and performance. Not only do they enhance their own impact on the organization, they also learn from others, seek feedback, and support their peers.
- Agile organizations must improve communication, increase transparency, and focus on sharing information that helps employees be self-directed, autonomous, and develop their own solutions to problems.
- The highest-performing individuals and teams in an agile organization create strong networks and use them as a primary source of communication, problem-solving, and social interaction.
- The enablement role assumed in most software-driven businesses must be revisited for agile organizations. They must prioritize coaching, connect employees to the right networks and communities, and emphasize honest retrospection and feedback.
- The focus on agility is a cross-functional effort. It affects all aspects of the organization including its approach to hiring and training employees, performance management models, external communications and public relations, strategic planning, and technology investment.

How Not to be Agile

While agile approaches are now widely used not just in mainstream software development but also in other sectors,[39] their application in mature organizations remains fraught with difficulties. 'Agile health checks' conducted at large-scale organizations reveal a common pattern: early enthusiasm and grassroots success for agile practices soon face barriers to broader acceptance when they come up against concerns about their scaling, governance, and institutionalization. Too often, an organization rushes into a 'corporate agile improvement program' but end up smothering the growing enthusiasm with a blanket of management oversight, and within a short time the efforts are mired in disappointment, skepticism, and a lack of quantifiable results. This gives 'going agile' a negative connotation, regarded as a byword for lack of planning, poor management, and chaotic delivery schedules.

Organizations also find themselves increasingly polarized. On one side are those advocating rapid delivery cycles and close collaboration across the team, colocation of people, and speedy feature release, while on the other side are those focused on delivery governance and control, schedule predictability, and accountability for resource use. The solution is to recognize that a range of approaches may be required for the different cultures, contexts, and experiences that make up an organization. The fundamental questions to ask in such situations are:
— Which aspects of the organization require more agility?
— What outcome is to be achieved with this change?
— How would the current status, and the impact of this change, be measured?

Strangely, this simple set of questions is rarely asked, and if it is, the answers are frequently not clear. Usually, a debate ensues within the organization as different people seek to clarify and prioritize what they expect, and how they will ensure they succeed. The diversity and depth of this debate clearly indicates the extent to which agile adoption is understood and planned. From these experiences, we identify four 'anti-patterns' for agile success; characteristics that underlie the failure of agile adoption.

Using agile as an excuse to avoid good management practices

Organizations typically spend many years adopting and refining management practices to suit the context in which they are used. Representing years of corporate history, deeply integrated with common practices and tools and embodying key aspects of the organization's culture, these practices cannot and should not be put to one side. Many complaints about agile adoption are around the idea that well-understood, functioning processes are abandoned without sufficient thought to their replacement, or to the impact on skills, projects, and management practices.

A classic illustration is that of ongoing software process improvement programs such as the Capability Maturity Model (CMM).[40] CMM is a simple five-level structuring framework used to assess the repeatability and predictability of software delivery practices. As with many structured change programs, it is easy to argue that most CMM implementations end up being overly bureaucratic, inflexible, and expensive. However, they give a framework and a phased approach to software process improvement and measurement that is widely understood and supported in many sectors, where CMM has become part of the organizations' culture, language, and operations. Hence, agile adoption in such organizations cannot be successful without addressing basic questions about the relationship of newly adopted practices with established CMM efforts, and the concomitant shift in mindset that must be undertaken.

Adopting agile for new development, not as an end-to-end delivery approach

Most agile adoption efforts begin with small teams of software developers introducing agile practices within software development tasks with limited scope and impact. In many cases these practices are not part of any formal enablement activity; they are simply local efforts by individuals and teams doing what they believe is most effective in writing and delivering good software. With broader adoption of agile practices, other software development teams quickly see the benefits and pick up these ideas as their own.

Such grassroots adoption, while valued and celebrated, inevitably introduces challenges across the organization. The dispersed and diverse nature of product and service delivery means that those involved in the core software production have much less insight and understanding of what has taken place with the agile teams. Often, they are only aware of the additional challenges that agile approaches bring to their traditional delivery mindset and techniques: no clear upfront commitments to a fixed budget, lack of medium- to long-term planning, and progress measures that do not align with company baselines. They may see agile as bringing more problems, not as a source of benefits.

In the worst cases this results in stalling agile adoption as it is stifled by project managers, business analysts, contract negotiators, and auditors who do not feel empowered by agile approaches; instead, they feel out of control. In the better cases this can lead to a clear two-tier approach to agile adoption, sometimes referred to as an "ambidextrous organization"[41] as discussed in Chapter 2. Here, some of the teams adopt agile methods such as Scrum, while the rest of the organization remains committed to more traditional phased-based methods. While some progress is possible this way, it can be challenging to keep these two worlds interconnected and aligned.

Believing agile to be the new silver bullet

As with any new technological advance, early successes are often overhyped and underanalyzed, resulting in unrealistic expectations. Agile adoption has seen its successes, with organizations such as Google, Microsoft, eBay, and Facebook all claiming that agile approaches allow them to deliver more of what customers need more quickly. Hence, expectations are naturally very high.

The reality, however, is that every organization is different in its structure, history, culture, and market position. Lessons from other organizations' experiences are very helpful as guides, but by no means do they guarantee that approaches successful in one company will work in another. These lessons need to be analyzed, understood, and adapted. Knowing how, where, and when to apply agile practices is just as important as knowing what it is, and who else has used it successfully. Unfortunately, many organizations try to introduce agile practices much too quickly, with overblown expectations of what results will be achieved. This is counterproductive as it diminishes executive management interest in smaller-scale impacts and demotivates all other staff trying to change behaviors well established over many years.

Focusing on agile as technological change

There has been much interest in agile practices as a new way to design and deliver software, resulting in agile methods such as Scrum, XP, DSDM and Crystal that capture these ideas for use by software-intensive businesses. Each method has its supporters and detractors and is eagerly supported with training and consulting. These in turn are encapsulated in a myriad of open-source and commercial tools that help the application of these methods. As a result, adopting agile practices is seen in many organizations as an IT issue, and reduced to questions of which software-specific method and tools to acquire, which training classes are needed, and how do software development teams accelerate creation and delivery of more software into production.

Unfortunately, such a narrow perspective obscures the bigger questions to be addressed: how do I get my organization to think and operate from a more agile viewpoint given my technical, commercial, and economic context? Invariably, one of the main challenges to agile adoption lie in the lack of skills and education that inhibits progress when organizations overemphasize the software delivery methods and tools.

Our experiences with several large agile organizations suggest that agile approaches can be successfully applied in almost every kind of development team, and in almost all organizations. While each situation has its own specific needs and variations, the core agile principles can provide significant results when applied with care, and with realistic expectations.

Lessons and Observations

Here, we make several observations of critical success factors for agile adoption based on our experiences with agile organizations. Understanding and addressing these concerns provide a solid basis for embarking on the journey toward becoming an agile organization.

Lesson 1: The roles most challenged in an agile transformation are executive managers, product managers, and project managers

To a large degree, agile approaches focus on development roles and pay little attention to those in management. Agile methods such as Scrum and XP are frequently described in terms of reducing unnecessary controls on developers and testers and introducing new development roles such as Scrum master and product owner.

Hence, their introduction can cause executive managers, product and project managers to feel rather lost. It is not unusual to find tensions arising when developers perceive agility as an excuse to avoid burdensome management practices and ignore long-term planning in favor of shorter cycles and continual replanning. Management however can perceive this as being dangerous and chaotic, reducing both their insight and impact on the projects. A typical anecdote

is that of senior managers asking product owners for plans and progress updates of agile development teams but obtaining no clear view of the project
beyond its current iteration or sprint – often only a few weeks away – and being
brushed off with the comment that "we don't do long-term planning because
we are agile".

As a result, great care needs to be taken to help each manager understand how
adopting agile approaches will affect them, how their role will evolve, and how
planning and management activities support and adjust to an agile approach.
Often, education in new management techniques is required to improve their
understanding of these approaches. For example, project managers and product owners working in agile projects may need support in writing requirements
as epics and stories, improved approaches to itemize backlog analysis and prioritization, and more accurate estimation techniques for systems that will undergo significant evolution. Members of senior management will need to understand that introducing techniques such as self-managed teams are not simply a
way to abdicate responsibility, but a necessary adjustment to increase flow and
reduce friction.

Rather than reinforcing the divisions between the management and delivery
roles, agile teams can be a catalyst for including them in new ways. For example, in one large electronics company, the scaling of agile practices using Scrum
methods was struggling to gain management support. The way forward was to
work more closely with product managers to leverage their skills within the
software delivery teams. The product owners had a significant role in defining
and managing new versions of consumer products for the market and hence,
they had well-developed skills in feature prioritization, value analysis, and
market assessment. Rather than being considered 'outside' of the main software
delivery team, these product owners were found to be critical players in backlog
analysis, sprint planning, and complex priority analysis. Including them in the
software delivery teams had the dual benefit of improving the delivery cycle
while also gaining important advocates with the company's management.

Lesson 2: Plan at multiple levels, and adopt a 'measure-and-steer' approach to agile planning

In adopting agile approaches, different techniques need to be used for planning
product and service delivery. Specifically, planning must take into account
multiple levels of needs, based on an understanding that the plan is a current

snapshot of tasks and deliverables that will evolve as the teams deliver more capabilities to satisfy customer needs.

Several agile methods discuss planning approaches in terms of development teams and projects (sometimes referred to as 'two-level planning') but say little about how those ideas roll up to high-level planning needs. Our experience suggests four levels of planning that must be addressed:

Enterprise level. The traditional planning approaches provide a global strategic view of the organization's business objectives, KPIs, and resource usage. Such planning is highly dependent on historical data amenable to different forms of analytics as well as being compared against benchmark data, analyst studies, and industry norms. It must be clear to the company's executive management and strategists what impact, if any, agile practices will have at their level. For example, with one global System Integrator (SI) we observed major concerns around cost management and outsourcing that were driving many strategic decisions on resources. Broader scaling of agile approaches was effectively blocked by these managers, until a detailed study was carried out to understand the impact of the SI-specific agile delivery model on the offshore delivery approaches they were using as the basis for key business decisions.

Portfolio level. Most organizations engage in a wide variety of projects, often considered in terms of one or more portfolios of activities and managed as a whole in terms of resource use, return on investment, business value, technical investment, and prioritization. Agile approaches have been found to bring risk and uncertainty to portfolio-level planning. For example, in one large retail organization we found that portfolio planning pushed toward pooled resources, matrixed approaches to using people on projects, and flexibility for moving people between projects. However, their pilot agile initiative strongly advocated dedicating resources to projects. This clash of cultures resulted in several practical implications for matrix management, incentives alignment, and end-of-year promotions. Before meaningful progress could be made, both parties needed to discuss their philosophical differences and gain a clearer understanding of the way forward.

Project level. In the most straightforward cases, projects are easily identifiable by the teams contributing to the projects' success. However, the reality for many organizations is that projects vary greatly in size, complexity, and organizational structure. Project management plays a critical role in controlling and managing delivery of systems across these structures. But we often see project management facing many challenges where teams have little shared experiences or techniques. Take for example, large enterprise back-office systems on mainframes that have been in place for many years and supported for most of that time by the same team with well-established methods of work and a long history of delivery success. This team would often react defensively when a new team appears, professing support for agile approaches to build new capabilities that must integrate or have an impact on that back-office system. Special attention must be given to planning and delivering those mixed-mode projects, often with additional support for working with both teams to gain a common view of plans and progress.

Team and individual level. A lot of work has taken place around agile planning for individuals and teams.[42] This has helped organizations understand how to gain greater insight into project status and progress when planning based on epics and stories, estimating time using story points and 'ideal days', and measuring using metrics such as velocity, burndown, and technical debt. While retraining using such approaches has been effective, a larger problem remains. Many team managers are using such measures inappropriately to compare and contrast individual and team performance and making false abstract summaries from the lower-level data. For example, one large software product company insisted on transparency of all individual and team work item lists and backlogs, together with detailed accounts of time taken on each activity. This is very much in line with the agile principles of honest interaction and aids whole-team thinking and planning. However, it soon became clear that project managers and executives had been using this data to rate and rank individuals and teams based on their daily performance, using criteria that had never been discussed with them. This resulted in a period of confusion and hostility during which the individual- and team-level planning approach collapsed. Some level of normality returned only after discussion and education on how to use agile planning and measurement.

Our experience is that traditional planning approaches do not easily fit with agile projects. The basis of most organizations' project planning is a detailed list of (more or less fixed) requirements, against which a work breakdown structure divides the tasks estimated and managed using a set of Gantt charts. This approach is widely understood and well supported by project planning tools and best practices, and is used as the basis for status reporting and governance procedures.

Unfortunately, it offers very limited flexibility when confronted with evolutionary delivery styles typical of more agile approaches. Many organizations find conflict between the need for stability and control with traditional planning techniques, and the push for increased flexibility, continual re-planning, and late decision-making in agile methods. Perhaps the simple analogy is that traditional planning is based on an 'aim-and-shoot' philosophy while agile planning is more about 'measure-and-steer'.

Addressing this difference in viewpoint requires a clear, explicit set of choices to be made about how agile projects will be planned, managed, and reported. Additional awareness training and education will be essential to help the organization understand the broader impacts of agile planning.

Lesson 3: Don't use agile methods for everything. Match practices to project characteristics.

It is tempting to think that an agile approach is right for every project and organization. Certainly, its broad principles have a lot to offer many business sectors, and they provide valuable insights and techniques when interpreted intelligently and in context. However, experience suggests that in practice it is essential to limit the scaling of agile approaches to projects with properties well matched to the characteristics of agility, at least when establishing new practices in a complex organization undergoing significant change.

In Figure 5.2, project properties are summarized through a number of dimensions, according to how well those properties align with the agile ideals. This is simplified to three basic categories of projects: maintenance, process improvement, and business innovation. For each we list the properties that pertain to the projects in that category. Agile approaches are clearly matched with business innovation projects which possess an evolutionary approach to requirements, flexibility and frequent re-planning, and a drive toward incremental delivery of new capabilities.

Maintenance and business improvement projects are less aligned with agile approaches, making the mapping of agile methods much more complex. This does not mean that agile approaches cannot be used. Rather, such a mapping requires greater care, increased training, and additional piloting may usually be necessary. Many organizations tend to scale agile approaches in stages, with the initial phases targeted at projects with a greater affinity to agile concepts.

	Maintenance	Process Improvement	Business Innovation
Project Type	Repeated, predictable	Understood, variable scope	New, Exploratory
Requirements	Fixed, clear	Variable, clear	Emergent
Management Metrics	Cost	Time	Quality
Management Effort	Low	Medium	High
Primary Sourcing	Offshore, or outsourced	Offshore-Onshore	Onshore
Contract Type	Fixed price	Time and materials	Results, value
Development Method	Waterfall	Iterative	Agile
Collaboration	Low, fixed handoffs	Medium, fixed handoffs	High, variable handoffs
Project length	Long (>3 months)	Medium (1-3 months)	Short cycles (<1 month)

Fig. 5.2: A Simplified Analysis of Project Properties

Lesson 4: Adapt and 'harden' the agile processes as the project gets closer to delivery

An important lesson from agile adoption is that the agile process does not remain consistent throughout a project's lifetime. Usually, the governance and control elements must increase as the project moves toward formal delivery milestones. In practice, specific discrete points may be needed where a project moves into a more constrained period during which many important 'hardening' activities take place, e.g., finalizing tests, obtaining conformance sign-offs, completing documentation.

Figure 5.3 illustrates this evolution of an agile approach. Here we see a high-level representation of the agile delivery process used in the enterprise software delivery team within a large financial services company. Three distinct project phases are utilized to categorize the sprints, or iterations, into different clusters.

In the early phase of the project lifecycle, the initial sprint is defined as a 'warm-up' phase where the project objectives are clarified, the initial architectural principles and assets agreed, and common communication channels established. Then a series of ongoing sprints implement the system's key capabilities, following practices typical of agile methods. In the final phase, time is allocated to activities such as asset handover, system users training, and documentation completion.

It is also worth highlighting that there are explicit sign-offs at the end of each sprint. These involve demonstrating capabilities to stakeholders and agreeing on progress made, reinforcing the iterative nature of the process. These formal reviews play an important role in subsequent project auditing and compliance exercises.

As the project evolves, there are also increasing restrictions on development. Initially this takes place through increased scrutiny in sign-offs, greater attention to performance metrics, and explicit inclusion of mandatory non-functional requirements in the later sprints. However, additional restrictions are also introduced as the project proceeds. For example, as delivery deadlines approach, the teams may restrict who is allowed to initiate a new work stream, kick off builds, or reprioritize work item backlogs.

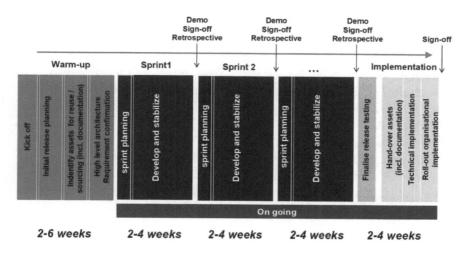

Fig. 5.3: An Example of a Modified Agile Delivery Process

In understanding the process described in Figure 5.3 it is important to remember the context in which it is applied: significantly risk-averse organizations. Hence, the additional governance and control steps in the process bring a level of coordination viewed as essential for broader acceptance of agile techniques within such a setting. Other approaches to agile process hardening may be more appropriate for other organizations with different pressures.

Three Agile Organization Vignettes

An organization's journey to agility can vary considerably. Here are three vignettes from the banking sector illustrating such journeys and their outcomes.

Danske Bank

Over the past few years Danske Bank has been undergoing a significant redesign of its IT operations. Key to that transformation is the adoption of agile software delivery techniques aimed at speeding up responses to user demands, and accelerating time to value from project initiation through to completion. In its initial phases, Danske Bank's agile practices pushed software project delivery times from an average of 14 months to under nine months, with associated improvements in quality and efficiency of the delivery cycle.

More importantly for Danske Bank, however, is the shift in mindset accompanying the move to more agile approaches.[43] Volatility in the banking industry demands new approaches to IT delivery that recognize the importance of closer stakeholder involvement in IT projects, a more integrated team approach to problem resolution, and greater transparency of project progress and outcomes. The results, according to Peter Rasmussen, Senior Vice President, IT Development Processes & Tools of Danske Bank is that "the business units experience closer cooperation with the IT department and a direct prioritization of the tasks – and thus a higher degree of certainty that the right developments are taking place." Risk management is improved through agile software delivery practices that change the rhythm of project delivery to more closely match the needs of business in the digital economy.

Lloyds Banking Group

Speed of change has long been a focus of software development organizations as they adopt more agile delivery practices throughout their teams. However, scaling agile approaches successfully in complex organizations requires a problem-solving stance that moves well beyond technology; one that embraces experimentation and supports fast-learning cycles driven by a management that needs to achieve clear outcomes.[44] But agility cannot mean chaos. The energy and fast delivery cycles must be coordinated and managed.

Tony Grout, Head of Digital and Non-Digital Agile Transformation at Lloyds Banking Group describes this as "moving the needle".[45] Even in adopting agile approaches, his focus for managing risk is to establish agreed outcomes for each project, with project members aiming at clear metrics and achievable increments against established baselines. Grout sees the situation as follows: "The problem is that an agile organization needs to think and act differently, and agile methods are only part of the story. Each organization is different and any change on this scale is going to have to adapt to emerging conditions." He believes his role is defined by the need to adopt an "agile culture" across more than 23,000 people that deliver IT and business services across Lloyds Banking Group.

BBVA

Francisco González, the chairman and CEO of BBVA, has adopted a striking stance – for an incumbent – toward the impact of digital on financial services. He has declared that "banks need to take on Amazon and Google or die",[46] and that "BBVA will be a software company in the future".[47]

BBVA embarked on its "digital journey" nine years ago, with its model for "conscious coupling" between operation and innovation maturing over time.[48] At first, management of digital initiatives was centralized within IT. The model then decentralized as a number of digital centers of excellence emerged to address strategic priorities, such as big data and mobile banking. The pendulum swung back toward centralization, with responsibility consolidated into a digital banking unit reporting to the CEO with a mandate to lead the digital agenda across the organization. Most recently, there has been a transition toward a catalyst model, with digital dispersed back into the business. For example, a new unit leads global development of end-to-end customer experience, with an innovation lab conducting live customer trials.

By now, many senior executives have considerable digital experience, having risen through the ranks internally or been recruited from external digital-native companies. This has been instrumental for the major change in BBVA's organizational DNA in relation to its digital transformation journey.

Summary and Conclusions

Agile thinking has galvanized several important ideas to drive innovation and encourage flexibility across an organization. In this chapter, two aspects have been highlighted: an innovation acceleration practice focused on rapid introduction, experimentation, and evaluation of new ideas; and adaptation of an agile software delivery perspective to how products and services are designed, created, and placed into production.

In making the journey toward agility, organizations can learn much from the experiences of software-intensive businesses adopting agile software delivery approaches. These experiences highlight several critical themes for broader adoption of agile approaches to accelerate new ways of working as well as to adapt to fundamental practices. In particular, a view of agile delivery beyond the agile software development context is necessary.

Despite early successes, many organizations have seen their ambitions thwarted when their agile software development teams become swamped by overbearing, slow-moving engineering and management practices. Hence, from an agile software delivery context, it is critical that substantial effort is invested in essential activities such as hiring staff, obtaining and setting up test equipment, interacting with project and program management coordinators, and training sales teams on new capabilities. Without that focus, the gains from agile software development become insignificant in the daily cut-and-thrust of a project, or else they are choked by broader organizational inertia and inefficiencies. Any organization with ambitions to be more agile must understand and support those leading the way.

Perhaps the biggest challenge of transforming into an agile organization is to achieve a shift in thinking, from which agile actions must flow. For many organizations this change is simple in theory, but very difficult to execute in practice due to a variety of scaling issues. As a result, moving to an agile organization mindset requires focus on practical areas where demonstrable, measured progress can be made: technology, process and people. Here, we have discussed the change in thinking required in becoming an agile organization and highlighted the essential areas of focus for succeeding with agility in a digital economy.

References

1 Blank, S. (2013). *Why the Lean Startup Changes Everything*. Harvard Business Review, March.

2 Ries, E. (2011). *The Lean Startup: How Constant Innovation Creates Radically Successful Businesses*. Penguin.

3 Brown, A.W., Ambler, S. and Royce, W. (2013). Agile at Scale: Economic Governance, Measured Improvement, and Disciplined Delivery. *Proceedings of the 35th International Conference on Software Engineering, IEEE*, May.

4 Rowels, D. and Brown, T. (2017). *Building Digital Culture: A Practical Guide to Successful Digital Transformation*. Kogan Page.

5 Jones, C. (2008). *Applied Software Measurement*. McGraw Hill.

6 Kruchten, P., Nord, R. and Ozkaya, I. (2019). *Managing Technical Debt: Reducing Friction in Software Development*. Addison Wesley.

7 Grier, D.A. (2019). *Software Factories*. IEEE Computer Society. Available at: https:// www. computer.org/publications/tech-news/closer-than-you-might-think/software-factories

8 Abrahamsson, P., Salo, O., Ronkainen, J. & Warsta, J. (2002). Agile Software Development Methods: Review and Analysis. *Proceedings of Espoo 2002, Finland: VTT Publication*, 478: 3-107.

9 http://www.agilemanifesto.org

10 http://www.scrum.org

11 http://www.agilebusiness.org/

12 http://www.extremeprogramming.org/

13 http://explainagile.com/agile/crystal/

14 Abrahamsson, P., Salo, O., Ronkainen, J. & Warsta, J. (2002). Agile Software Development Methods: Review and Analysis. *Proceedings of Espoo 2002, Finland: VTT Publication* 478: 3-107.

15 See the "State of Agile" reports at: https://www.stateofagile.com/

16 Rigby, D., Sutherland, J., and Takeuchi, H. (2016). Embracing Agile. *Harvard Business Review*, May.

17 Denning, S. (2018). *The Age of Agile*. AMACOM.

18 Royce, W. (1998). *Software Project Management: A Unified Approach*. Addison-Wesley.

19 Jones, C. (2008). *Applied Software Measurement*. McGraw Hill.

20 CMMi for development, version 1.3, CMU/SEI-2010-TR-033, November 2010.

21 Brown, A.W. (2012). *Global Software Delivery: Bringing Efficiency and Agility to the Enterprise*. Addison-Wesley.

22 Ambler, S. and Lines, M. (2012). *Disciplined Agile Delivery: A Practitioner's Guide to Agile Solution Delivery in the Enterprise*. IBM Press.

23 Royce, W., Bittner, K., and Perrow, M. (2009). *The Economics of Software Development*. Addison-Wesley.

24 Jones, C. (2010). *Software Engineering Best Practices*. McGraw Hill.

25 Liker, J. (2004). *The Toyota Way: 14 Management Principles from the World's Greatest Manufacturer*. McGraw-Hill.

26 Poppendieck, M. and Poppendieck, T. (2009). *Leading Lean Software Development: Results are Not the Point*. Addison Wesley.

27 Poppendieck, M. and Poppendieck, T. (1997). *Lean Software Development: An Agile Toolkit*. Addison Wesley.

28 Womack, J.P. and Jones, D.T. (2003). *Lean Thinking: Banish Waste and Create Wealth in Your Corporation*. Free Press.

29 Coplien, J. and Bjornvig, G. (2011). *Lean Architecture for Software Development*. John Wiley.

30 Ries, E. (2011). *The Lean Startup: How Constant Innovation Creates Radically Successful Businesses*. Penguin.

31 Curtis, B., Hefley, W., and Miller, S. (2009). *The People Capability Maturity Model: A Framework for Human Capital Management, 2nd Edition*. Addison Wesley.

32 Gilles, P. (2018). *Cultural Agility: The New Basics of Organizational Development*. Createspace Publishing.

33 http://agilemanifesto.org/

34 Cohn, M. (2006). *Succeeding with Agile*. Addison Wesley.

35 Highsmith, A. (2009). *Agile Project Management: Creating Innovative Products*. Addison-Wesley.

36 McCuiston, V.E., Wooldridge, B.R. and Pierce, C.P. (2001). Leading the Diverse Workforce: Profit, Prospects and Progress. *Leadership & Organization Development Journal*, 25(1): 73–92.

37 Denning, S. (2010). *The Leaders Guide to Radical Management*. Jossey-Bass.

38 https://www.gartner.com/smarterwithgartner/category/marketing/

39 Rigby, D., Sutherland, J., and Takeuchi, H. (2016). Embracing Agile. *Harvard Business Review*, May.

40 CMMI Product Team (2010). CCMMi for Development, Version 1.3, CMU/SEI-2010-TR-033. Software Engineering Institute Technical Report, November. Available at: https://resources.sei.cmu.edu/asset_files/TechnicalReport/2010_005_001_15287.pdf

41 O'Reilly III, C. and Tushman, L. (2004). *The Ambidextrous Organization*. Harvard Business Review, April.

42 Highsmith, A. (2009). *Agile Project Management: Creating Innovative Products*. Addison-Wesley.

43 Brown, A.W. (2012). *Enterprise Software Delivery: Bringing Agility and Efficiency to the Global Software Supply Chain*, Addison Wesley.

44 Brown, A.W., Ambler, S. and Royce, W. (2013). Agile at Scale: Economic Governance, Measured Improvement, and Disciplined Delivery. *Proceedings of the 35th International Conference on Software Engineering, IEEE*, May.

45 Telephone interview with Tony Grout, September 16, 2016.

46 González, F. (2013). Banks need to Take on Amazon and Google or Die. *Financial Times*, December 2.

47 González, F. (2015). *In the Future, BBVA Will Be a Software Company*. Finextra, March 5.

48 Kaufman, E., Bailey, A., Berz, K. et al. (2015).*The Power of People in Digital Banking Transformation: The Digital Financial Institution*. BCG Perspectives, November 5.

6 Innovation

Introduction

Innovation is now considered a business priority essential for success. For businesses to have meaningful growth, the collaborative process from idea generation to solution delivery must be optimized. Innovation practices must be flexible and repeatable, and leaders must be willing and able to lead teams in an innovation-focused interactive environment. In the past innovation was slow and risky, and largely left to the experts in the R&D department. Today, tremendous importance is placed on "democratizing innovation" by establishing practices that increase innovation speed while decreasing risk.[1]

Yet in the fast-moving digital economy, the fundamentals of innovation practice come up against a number of barriers. A PwC survey from 2015 highlighted one of the most critical issues faced: too frequently, digital technology investments are not meeting the business's expectations for growth.[2] Technological advances alone are viewed as interesting sideshows poorly exploited within the day-to-day context. So how should organizations focus their innovation efforts to ensure their digital transformation is successful?

Technology refreshment across all organizations is a constant challenge. Rapid advances in the performance, availability, and cost-effectiveness of digital technology have optimized existing ways of working, primarily through increasing access and reducing friction in many processes with enhanced automation and increased visibility. For many public and private organizations, digital technology advances can encourage a much broader reassessment of their business practices, with a recognition that innovation in technology frequently requires innovation in business models to reconsider their value and guide their ongoing operations.[3]

To address these needs, many organizations have moved their focus on innovation toward two key areas: agility and openness. Consumers require businesses to maintain constant open dialogue on product improvements and prototypes, and at the same time engage in new forms of producer-consumer partnerships such as co-creation, evolutionary design, and micro-customization. This is necessary to ensure that the business produces its goods and services at the speed required to maintain market advantage. Through a combination of agility and openness, companies of all sizes must pursue a market-driven conversation with consumers on the benefits of flexibility to take on the challenges of a turbulent economic environment.[4] The goal is to deliver a stream of consumer-tested ideas that can position the organization as a leader in the knowledge-driven marketplace.

However, the generation of new ideas is only the starting point. Success requires overcoming obstacles to bringing those innovations into routine practice. It has been estimated that up to 80% of corporate innovations fail and only 10% of SMEs can sustain the innovation necessary to generate significant employment.[5] In particular, speed is of the essence in introducing innovation: Intel Corporation, for instance, claims that 90% of the revenues the firm derives on the last day of the year are attributable to products that did not even exist on the first day of that same year.[6]

In this chapter we reflect on the background, practices, and implications of innovation in driving digital transformation. We look at the particular characteristics of innovation important to digital transformation. We then consider the relationship between technology and business model innovation, followed by a series of practical insights into innovation based on digital transformation experiences across a range of organizations.

Understanding Innovation

As a key concept that has received increasing attention in recent years,[7] innovation is often narrowly defined in terms of technological invention or creation of new features in existing systems. A much broader perspective would be helpful, so it is particularly useful to view innovation in practice as the alignment of three critical components (see Figure 6.1):

- **Desirability.** Successful innovation solves a problem that matters to a customer. Whether these are internal or external customers, any innovation must address a problem that someone cares about, and provide a solution that the customer can readily consume.
- **Viability.** Innovation must address a product or service need in a way that meets any constraints of the operating environment and market conditions in which it will be deployed. A myriad of issues must be considered including production cost, strategic fit, impact on market and ecosystem, sustainability and maintainability.

– **Feasibility.** A new idea must be able to be realized and maintained given current market and engineering constraints. Not only must it be practically possible to create, it must also generate value for potential customers and profit for those involved in its creation, management, and maintenance.

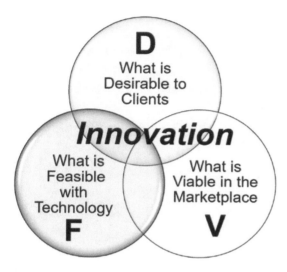

Fig.6.1: Innovation: Desirability – Feasibility – Viability

Many have provided insights into the innovation process and explored the elements critical to success. For instance, Peter Drucker emphasized that innovation is not an isolated activity, but part of a broader value creation process.[8] He defined innovation as:

> The effort to create **purposeful, focused change** in an enterprise's economic or social potential...**the means** by which the entrepreneur either creates new wealth-producing resources or endows existing resources with enhanced potential for creating wealth.

Several aspects of Drucker's definition are worth highlighting:
– First, the goal of innovation is purposeful change with an economic or societal impact. It is the outcome of innovation that guides and dictates the parameters essential to its success.
– Second, it is not just the resulting product or service that is important to innovation, but the approach taken. Innovation is as much about process as it is about ideas.

- Third, the actor in innovation, an entrepreneur, aims to make a financial or societal difference through their actions. Hence, the characteristics, experiences, and personality of the entrepreneur play a key role in innovation.
- Finally, and most significantly, Drucker sees the process of innovation as a set of activities that organizations can take as a systematic approach to becoming successful.

Building on this definition, Drucker identified seven sources of opportunity that will ultimately drive innovation:
- The organization's own unexpected successes and failures, and also those of the competition.
- Incongruities, especially those in a process such as production or distribution, as well as those in customer behaviour.
- Process needs.
- Changes in industry and market structures.
- Changes in demographics.
- Changes in meaning and perception.
- New knowledge and discoveries.

The mindset and culture of innovation can also play a significant role. Such a broader perspective of innovation has been recognized by many organizations, industry bodies, and government agencies. For instance, the US National Innovation Initiative (NII) defines innovation in terms of impact on society:

> Innovation is a societal, not a technological, phenomenon, one that arises from the intersection of invention and insight, leading to the creation of social and economic value.

Hence, innovation is perceived not just as an isolated event focused on a 'lightbulb moment' from a lone scientist. It involves the whole process across opportunity identification, idea creation, solution realization, prototyping, production, and marketing and sales. In a digital economy, there is also pressure on ensuring that innovation includes the capacity to quickly adapt to changing conditions as well as to the complexity of an incumbent organization. The impact of innovative activities is seen as a much wider issue, with implications for society as a whole.

The dimensions of innovation

The earliest seminal writings on innovation from Schumpeter,[9] Drucker,[10] and Christensen[11] have examined the role and impact of innovation in driving business success. Subsequently, much has been written on how innovation creates value in an organization. Broadly, four dimensions of innovation have emerged as critical to establishing and sustaining value:[12]

– **Products and services**. The search for new technologies and solutions is the starting point for many businesses. Product and service innovation is typically delivered in many forms, through the use of new digital technologies and application of emerging knowledge.
– **Process.** The way products and services are created, distributed, and maintained is a clear target of innovation. With time to market such a dominant factor in many sectors, organizations must be able to operate more efficiently to survive and grow.
– **Business model.** For many companies, new ways of operating are essential to augment or replace traditional business models based on high-volume sales, discounting, and standard transactional behaviors. Many new business model approaches are emerging, often based on exploiting broadband connectivity, direct customer interaction offered by Internet-based technologies, and ease of interaction provided by smart devices.[13]
– **Societal.** Our society has undergone rapid evolution due to increasing technological sophistication, educational standards, economic wealth, and changing demographics. Dramatic changes are taking place with consumers' needs, expectations, and the contexts in which they interact with digital products and services.

Consequently, the drive for innovation is particularly dominant in any business, and a constant factor in decision-making at all organizational levels. It is not overstating the case to say that the resulting organizational, managerial, and legal structures of most businesses can be directly traced to their decisions on how they address innovation across these four dimensions.

The changing nature of innovation

In fact, the nature of innovation itself has evolved quite dramatically over the years. Organizations no longer seek innovation by looking inwardly toward their own R&D teams that are tightly tied to five-year business plans. Rather, to reduce the risk of long-term programs unable to evolve in contexts of rapid change, they take a more expansive view of innovation through an active role in emerging ecosystems comprising diverse organizations with various viewpoints. This shifts the balance of effort and cost away from in-house R&D to externalized experimentation and scaling on stable technology platforms.[14]

Hence, for many organizations the nature of innovation is increasingly:[15]
- **Open** to outside ideas, and actively seeks input from consumers, partners, academics, and the wider community.
- **Collaborative** across teams and individuals to allow ideas to be shared, co-developed, and jointly sourced.
- **Multi-disciplinary** to derive the best thinking from many domains, aligned toward common goals and themes.
- **Globally managed** to take advantage of the best skills wherever they reside, and **locally informed** to ensure that they are well matched to consumers' specific contexts.

Recognizing innovation as being at the forefront of many organizations today, some, mainly software-intensive businesses, have renamed the traditional CIO or Chief *Information* Officer title to Chief *Innovation* Officer.[16]

The Innovation Challenge in a Digital Economy

To become successful, organizations must overcome significant challenges. These include the need for agility and openness in today's digital economy, as discussed in the introduction of this chapter.

To improve their innovation practices, large organizations and SMEs need to pioneer a way of rapidly introducing ideas from concept through to deployment. By tapping into new methods of rapid pre-market testing, idea development, and intellectual property management, they can de-risk the introduction of new products and services. However, this reinvention of innovation for a digital economy must come to terms with several major trends that today's organizations face:
- **Removal of barriers to collaboration** across geographical boundaries, industry silos, and supply chain networks, due to easy availability of technologies for remote working.

- **Increased information transparency.** Competitors, consumers, and employees now have access to data of all forms, leading to more informed customers, greater scrutiny over operational practices, and narrower windows of opportunity to exploit market insights.
- **Shortening cycle from idea creation to market saturation.** In areas such as app development, the lifetime of new products and services can be measured in hours or days.
- **Huge penalties for getting to market late or missing deadlines.** Market and consumer expectations are such that failure to deliver new capabilities may quickly lead to mass migration of customers to new providers.
- **A more holistic view of product and service delivery.** Aligning the three elements of desirability, viability, and feasibility requires wider collaboration across disciplines and specialties within and across organizations.
- **Recognition that external expertise may be needed to solve problems and improve diversity in thinking.** The closed nature of many organizations can stifle new ideas. Increasing the range of ideas and encouraging new ways to approach problems often requires a more expansive view.
- **Leveraging ownership of ideas becoming more complex.** The concept of intellectual property is being re-examined in light of new media forms, open access to data, and shifting societal norms for sharing artifacts. Laws and regulations are not catching up with technological advances. This gap poses a challenge (and opportunity) in many sectors.

Consequently, many organizations are experimenting with different approaches to innovation. At the most fundamental level, they recognize its importance and are encouraging workers to seek out new ways of working that change the status quo by offering incentives tied to yearly objectives, enhancing public recognition of new ideas translated into practice, and introducing internal competitions for new thinking. An interesting example is Adobe Kickbox,[17] a broad internal program that encourages workers to investigate new ideas by offering them a small amount of money plus the time to investigate new ideas and their potential impact.

To innovate better, some organizations are also acting as Venture Capital (VC) groups investing in external ideas. This may be through setting up an innovation fund like Centrica's $100m investment fund which finds, supports and accelerates new technical innovations that can subsequently be embedded across the company.[18] Extending this concept, some organizations have created incubation programs to support and grow new ideas through funding, guidance, and access to expertise. Telefonica's Wayra incubator is a particularly interesting example;[19] it is a program comprising a set of locations, educational activities, and mentors where entrepreneurs with new business ideas can be nurtured and supported through access to Telefonica's extensive network of partners and customers.

Each of these approaches can help create new practices and insights that encourage innovation across the organization, increase the pace at which new ideas are explored and rejected, and drive experimental learning in a digital environment characterized by tremendous instability and uncertainty. We emphasize, therefore, that innovation practices have evolved significantly in the past decade. As summarized in Figure 6.2, the stepwise activities that guided homegrown technology-based inventions from initial idea to product have been replaced with a more open, collaborative solution delivery that explores new approaches to solve client-facing problems. Building capabilities for delivering such changes is a differentiator for organizations adapting to do business in a digital economy.

From	To
Invention	Innovation
Linear innovation model	Dynamic innovation mode
Build to forecasted demand	Sense and respond to demand
Independent	Interdependent
Single discipline	Multiple discipline
Product functions	Value to customer
Local R&D teams	Globalized open knowledge networks

Fig. 6.2: The Shifting Sands of Innovation

Business Model Innovation

As we have noted throughout this book, rapid advances in digital technology performance, availability, and cost-effectiveness have optimized existing ways of working. Enhanced automation and increasing operational transparency have increased access to information and reduced the friction inherent in many business processes.

Often, an organization may understand how to create and deliver a technological enhancement long before it has grasped where it is useful or how it can best be used to improve business practices. As a result, digital technology advances are encouraging many public and private organizations to broadly reassess their business operations, and to recognize that innovation in technology frequently requires innovation in their business models. This enables them to reconsider the value the firm creates and captures, and to use that knowledge to guide its ongoing operation.[20]

Echoing experiences from earlier revolutions in IT,[21] the dynamics of this "technology push vs business model pull" has seen a renaissance in studies into business models and their utility during fast-paced technological change.[22] Two specific strands of that investigation are highly relevant to digital transformation: the evolving view of a business model's role in understanding a firm's strategies and behaviors, and the relationship dynamics between technology and business model innovation.

Reassessing the Business Model's Role

A business model is "a blueprint for how a company does business".[23] It encapsulates what the company does and how it does it, connecting "the workings inside the firm to outside elements including the customer side and how that value is captured or monetized".[24] This concept has been much studied and discussed for well over a decade, and has seen a particular surge of interest in recent years due to the emergence of e-business initiatives and the current wave of digital technology transformations.[25]

This in turn has resulted in a much more complex analysis of the motivations, goals, and uses of business models, providing deeper insights into their characteristics. Essentially, business models play a variety of roles[26] including their use as:

– Market devices that help in understanding uncertainty, and act as prescriptions for change.[27]
– Models to follow, providing exemplars and illustrations of best practice.[28]
– Recipes or patterns that can be instantiated in particular contexts.[29]
– Expressions of strategic intent, enabling exploration of a firm's unique value and competitive advantage.[30]
– Stories that provide a narrative to capture and communicate a firm's reason for being.[31]

Classifying this range of roles is useful for academics and practitioners alike as it guides our views on how and when a business model needs to evolve. This enables us to review the relevance of the business in today's digital economy, and to use it to act as a set of guiderails to shape the digital transformation taking place. In this regard, a useful distinction explored by several academics[32] is to consider an "inside-out" versus an "outside-in" perspective on a firm's business model. With the former, a business model is seen as a cognitive configuration that can be manipulated in the minds of managers and academics, while the latter considers it as a practical tool for driving an operational plan.

Fundamental to this is a perspective that considers a business model as "a useful representation of how the organization creates value".[33] This view allows us to focus on the impact of the business model (and consequently any business model changes) on various stakeholders, and establishes an "outside-in" emphasis on business model analysis to complement the "inside-out" view more typically considered.[34] More broadly, academics[35] have addressed business models by considering their attributes in direct relationship to the value chain they define, including value capture, value proposition, value creation, value delivery, value experience, and value communication.

At the root of much discussion on business models is the explicit consideration of the value of products and services.[36] From a value-in-exchange perspective, every product or service has a market value determined by what the consumer is willing to pay (or exchange) for it. This value is ascertained by current market conditions, and hence affected by the time and place of the exchange. In contrast, value-in-use is contextual and qualitative based on the consumer's 'satisfaction'. Digital technologies can play a significant role not only in creating new channels to market for products and services, but also in reshaping how value is determined by enabling new insights into product and service use.[37]

This broad set of perspectives offers many useful insights. However, while they conclude that establishing clear understanding of actual and perceived value is fundamental to any firm, achieving this in practice is far from easy. Not only is the concept of value not consistent between creators and receivers of that value, as Irene Ng discusses[38], it is also highly related to the context in which that value is received. Furthermore, as Ng highlights, with the rapid adoption of digital technologies there is an increasingly important and complex relationship between how the value is created and the stakeholders' value experience. Every offering needs to consider the contexts which it serves, and the value experience delivered through different types of value exchange within those contexts.

Several practical conclusions can be drawn from these analyses:
- Academic studies highlight a business model's contribution in coordinating people and activities toward a common view. In fact, the business model is in many ways the central artifact holding together disparate views and motivations across an organization.
- The business model's dual role of conceptual model and operational blueprint, with its fundamentally distinct usage scenarios, presents a particular challenge to the way it is described, communicated, shared, and evolved.
- As the capabilities and impact of new digital technologies are better understood, experimentation in business model variations will be critical. Flexibility and adaptability to business model changes will be a key skill for organizations in a rapidly moving digital economy.

Technology and Business Model Innovation

Undertaking digital transformation requires a combination of technology and business model innovation, and a major change in the organization's operating model. To relieve growing pressures to change, business units need to focus on rethinking, redesigning and optimizing their services, and placing the user (consumers, residents, businesses, and partners) at the center of their operations, rather than the needs of internal stakeholders and service providers. To succeed, they need to move rapidly and effectively away from outdated business models, management cultures, technology, and processes inherited from earlier eras.[39]

Consequently, the relationship between technology and business model innovation has been much discussed among academics, commentators, and practitioners. Debates range from whether business model innovation can be separated from technology innovation and the degree of influence each has on the other, to how innovation in either or both impacts a firm's success, and how contextual aspects such as size and maturity of both the firm and its market sector influence the rate of innovation. Our understanding of this relationship is evolving and needs considerable further research,[40] particularly as the new opportunities created by digital technologies have increased the challenges for those looking to make sense of these issues.

From a practical perspective, digital transformation requires an intense focus on business model impact and use. Illustrative of this is Weill and Woerner's digital business model framework which has three components:[41]

– **Content.** Reconsiders what the customer consumes, which may be digital products such as software or electronic documents, or other forms of information such as product details, service descriptions, and comparison data.
– **Customer experience.** Explores the best way to package the content to meet a customer need. The results may include a community experience, a personalized product experience, or an open information access experience.
– **Platform.** Offers a way to deliver that experience, perhaps via well-defined data management practices, an open interface, or through a mobile device's operating system.

This simple framework makes it possible to explore the characteristics of any digital business model. For example, we can view publishing companies as doing much more than putting documents online. Through this lens we see how proprietary, tightly integrated packages of content, i.e., articles, photos, and news items, have been unpacked to offer wide collections of community-provided or syndicated materials accessible through many different channels. The experience offered to consumers is highly personalized to different tastes and profiles, and delivered on demand through the use of intelligent algorithms, or at the user's specified time frame to various devices that the user owns. The infrastructure supports the curation, coordination, and management of all these data sources, made accessible through a flexible software platform supporting many possible delivery models.

Charles Baden-Fuller's work offers perhaps the most succinct summary of the current business model evolution in the context of digital transformation,[42] emphasizing that:

- Choice of business model influences how technology is monetized and the profitability of a firm using that technology.
- The business model frames the thinking of managers, entrepreneurs, and developers, and strongly influences technology choices.
- There is a two-way, complex relationship between business model and technology innovation that is still widely misunderstood and under-researched.

It should be emphasized, however, that this complex relationship should not be viewed as just a theoretical debate amongst academics. Nor should it be seen as confined to less technologically advanced areas of the business world. This lack of clarity has important, practical implications. Indeed, the misunderstanding of the relationship between innovating through the introduction of digital technology, and the business model innovation associated with implementing a digital strategy, is pervasive and common in both the public and private sectors. Forrester's State of Digital Business 2014 report[43] highlighted this gap and called it a "digital strategy execution crisis". Data from its poll of almost 2,000 senior business leaders in the UK and US in early 2014 showed that only one in five business leaders had a meaningful vision for business model innovation associated with digital transformation, and that a majority of organizations had a "bolt-on" approach where existing practices were simply augmented with new digital technology delivery channels.

How Not to be Innovative

Through our work with a range of organizations across several sectors, we have discovered that while each organization sets out with the best intentions, they have found success elusive or impossible to maintain. In particular, we discovered five innovation failure patterns, or 'anti-patterns', that offer important warnings for other organizations looking to achieve innovation in their digital transformation.

Innovation theatre

Cultural change in mature organizations is notoriously difficult to achieve, requiring determination, persistence, and clear communication. These characteristics are particularly important in digital transformation efforts, as many workers feel disoriented and displaced when digital technologies augment or replace the tasks they previously carried out. It is important, therefore, to celebrate new ideas and promote successful change initiatives. Unfortunately, such efforts can become separated from the broader experiences across the organization. Pronouncements about how agile and innovative an organization is could ring hollow to those without access to the latest technologies or who are struggling with bureaucratic processes. Attention must be paid to broader working practices. Showcasing innovation projects that benefit one part of the business must be balanced with the daily context of workers in the rest of the organization.

An example we observed recently was of a large insurance company engaged in a substantial digital transformation program to revolutionize its business practices. Unfortunately, the organization was plagued with leaked employee emails describing its inefficient and uninspiring working practices in core parts of its business. This was despite the press releases the company had issued to highlight the investments made in hackathons, innovation challenges, and incubator programs designed to create new product lines.

Innovation tourism

Across the world there are inspiring examples of organizations succeeding in increasing the flow of innovative ideas into practice. Case studies, from new digital natives such as Facebook and Airbnb to mature industry enterprises such as GE and 3M, offer insights into how to drive business, adapt to new challenges, and introduce new products and services into production. Learning about these digital transformation success stories is important for any organization wanting to succeed in a digital economy.

Consequently, visits and information sharing with such digitally enabled organizations are frequently high on the agenda for many senior managers looking for ways to improve. Unfortunately, such visits too often end up as 'innovation tourism'. Senior management teams' expensive tours to California's Silicon Valley, London's Tech City, and Tel Aviv's digital product incubators are meant to inspire and drive change but often end up as a collection of high-level meetings without clear purpose. Lack of preparation and follow-up leads to insufficient attention to gathering insights, poor analysis of how best practices can be applied, and inadequate resourcing for any resulting transformation efforts.

Our recent discussions with two different organizations highlighted the difference between innovation tourism and a well-planned investigation of the lessons learnt from innovation leaders. In the first case, the organization sent a team of five high-level managers to visit Silicon Valley giants such as Google and Apple. However, the organization, a 100-year-old clothing retailer, had a cultural and organizational structure wildly different from those visited, and the excitement from the visits soon petered out when faced with the company's day-to-day reality. In the second case, a large food retailer arranged for a team of senior IT managers to visit several innovative start-ups in Tel Aviv. Before the visit the team discussed the organization's current challenges and areas where new thinking would be welcomed. The companies they visited were chosen to provoke ideas and inspire discussion around those themes. Following the visit, the organization formed partnerships and invested in two of the companies visited, leading to the transfer of significant new capabilities into its IT team.

Innovation inquisition

The innovator's dilemma explored by Christensen neatly summarizes how organizations often continue pursuing the activities that made them successful long beyond the point where they are useful.[44] Metrics and mechanisms across organizations tend to become focused on current ways of working, disadvantaging change. To overcome this, encouraging innovation in a mature organization requires changes to the management and introduction of targeted incentive models to reward those willing to try new ideas. When appropriately applied, individuals and teams are then challenged to take risks by investigating new ways of working.

Too frequently, however, objectives encouraged in one part of the organization are thwarted by the competing goals of another. Consider a situation where high-level managers encourage innovation by requiring employees to document their involvement with new ideas as part of their annual objectives. Operational measures and weekly project reviews must also be aligned with these goals; otherwise those who invest their time trying out new ideas, many of which could fail, will be viewed as lower productivity contributors and will subsequently revert to conventional ways of working.

The ultimate example of this syndrome is when organizations seek to encourage new thinking with slogans such as "fail fast, fail early!". The intent is to give people permission to try out ideas in a safe environment and focus on maximizing the learning from these experiences. Yet, in practice, individuals looking to advance their careers find they are criticized and disadvantaged when they have such activities documented as part of their achievement record.

Innovation ghetto

Adopting changes within an existing organizational environment can be complex. The structures, processes, and mechanisms in place often seem to fight against changes in favor of the status quo. To reduce the likelihood of new ideas being suffocated by the prevailing culture, many organizations set up separate units where new ideas can be piloted. This provides the space necessary for such innovation groups to thrive without the need to conform to the organizational culture.

While such separation can encourage divergent thinking, it can also isolate those teams from the commercial and cultural reality of the organization. Without care, the organization can find itself torn apart by opposing views clouding strategic decision-making. Antagonism may grow to the point of destruction.

In a recent digital transformation initiative we examined, the organization had set up a 'digital innovation center' to investigate new online service delivery approaches to augment the bricks-and-mortar retail activities that formed the heart of its business. The new unit was set up in a fashionable part of London with an expensive design concept, a team of highly-paid data scientists and software engineers, and a high-profile marketing campaign celebrating its launch. This new initiative was intended to inspire the organization; the reality was that the innovation team was ostracized by the rest of the company.

Innovation fatigue

Digital technology is not only driving fast-paced change; it is also influencing innovation practices and encouraging experimentation in how organizations define, evolve, and support new products and services. As a consequence, organizations must constantly review these practices to decide which are appropriate for their environment, and monitor them to ensure they are providing the desired outcomes.

Unfortunately, for some organizations this results in a plethora of innovation activities being undertaken at any one time. While one part of the organization may be encouraging open innovation practices to obtain input from stakeholder communities, others may be investing in hackathons, trialing new ideas via crowdsourcing, and creating separate disruptive business units. Such a range of activities can offer the organization broad lessons to help define its forward-looking strategy. However, it may also result in a cacophony of uncoordinated initiatives confusing employees, partners, and customers alike.

Large technology-based organizations are particularly prone to such excesses. We have observed a multi-national software and services organization that was testing so many new ideas that those in the company would joke that at any point in time they "had more pilots than British Airways" and no way to realistically assess the contribution made by each of them.

Lessons and Observations

Having explored a number of different principles underlying innovation, we now look at key lessons for organizations aiming for digital transformation.

Lesson 1: Adopt a clear, structured approach to innovation aligned with the organization's strategy

Organizations have historically treated innovation as a separate activity undertaken by a few people isolated from the day-to-day activities of the broader business. While this can free an innovation team from some of the constraints restricting its work, it also can lead to a lack of discipline in the way ideas are surfaced, explored, validated, and pursued. As a result, many organizations celebrated for their entrepreneurial approaches are employing structured techniques to support their innovation activities. These are aimed at reinforcing the inspirational actions of individuals with a discipline of innovation across the organization. Such an approach has several critical elements, including the following:

- **Approach innovation as a disciplined activity.** Encouraging new thinking that challenges orthodoxy is important, but it is sustainable only if there are clear pathways through which new ideas can be supported to overcome the resistance to change inherent in mature organizations.

- **Invest in a comprehensive innovation support infrastructure.** Many new tools and techniques can help organizations capture, share, and manage innovative activities. For example, collaborative ideas management and support systems such as Wazoku and BrightIdeas engage with individuals and teams to share their ideas in an open, accessible way. Such systems not only support these ideas in their innovation journey, but also demonstrate the company's commitment to innovation to the entire organization.
- **Devote serious effort to looking for new ideas, even when they may threaten current business activities.** Innovation arises in many ways from a wide variety of sources, but it is all too easy for organizations to look in the same places for the same kinds of innovative ideas aimed at reinforcing existing ways of working. Many new ideas may be seen as destructive, with potentially negative impact on the organization. It is therefore important to encourage diversity of thinking as part of an organized, systematic, and continual search for new opportunities.
- **View innovation as an opportunity for everyone in the organization.** Often, organizations focus their attention on specialized teams aimed at providing new ideas for the company's future. This segregation of innovation as something outside of day-to-day business activity can be detrimental. New ideas can come from anywhere in the organization, often from the most unlikely sources. A culture of initiative and innovation is best encouraged when it involves everyone in the organization.
- **Evaluate innovation activities based on the outcomes they enable with the organization and its customers.** As organizations mature they frequently become internally focused, spending large amounts of time designing structures and procedures to enable them to operate as effectively as possible under changing conditions. This is essential for continued success. However, it also may remove emphasis on the broader objective: understanding and meeting customer needs. Innovation activities should focus on outcomes for stakeholders in the business, with particular focus on their customers.

In summary, creating a disciplined approach to innovation must be a purposeful activity central to an organization's strategy.

Lesson 2: Business model innovation requires a clear focus on business differentiation and maturity

The continued development of new digital technologies is driving a great deal of uncertainty and unpredictability in many sectors. However, digital transformation is only possible when such new technology is linked to an emerging market need.[45] Interesting digital technology advances, from the Internet to new media formats and machine learning algorithms, only became commercially viable when business models emerged to employ these technologies to solve problems, in ways that would compel people to spend time and money to apply them in their current lives and workplaces.

Organizations involved in digital transformation are recognizing the need to strike the right balance between technology and business model innovations. They also find many aspects of this struggle informative, and their experiences indicate that successful business model innovation needs to focus on the following areas:[46]

- **Personalization.** It has become critical for businesses to create products and services that can better meet consumers' specific needs. Customers now demand greater recognition and understanding of their circumstances, and are likely to reject offerings that do not adequately take account of these needs.
- **Circular economy.** Companies must assess their product development and delivery approaches to ensure they are using resources efficiently. Traditional models of product development and disposal are now being overtaken by more socially accepted approaches to product reuse and recycling.
- **Asset sharing.** Consumption models are moving from private ownership to shared value models that prioritize access to assets. In sectors as diverse as transportation, entertainment, retail, and energy delivery, industries are reacting to changes in both supply and consumption, with more interactive ecosystems emerging.
- **Value in use.** Real-time access to product and service usage data is moving pricing models away from traditional value-in-exchange models toward value-in-use.[47] Consequently, organizations are beginning to experiment with new approaches to understand and share the value provided and received with any offering.
- **Platform-based ecosystem.** The governance and control around traditional supply and value chains are moving toward platform-based models that create networked ecosystems. The dynamics governing such multi-sided

marketplaces provide new opportunities to review the behaviors of both providers and consumers. In many industries the rise of dominant platform owners has redefined how businesses must compete to create and capture value.

— **Agile decision-making.** Consumers place high value on new products and services that increase knowledge or facilitate decision-making. In several situations, traditional product providers have recognized that their value in a digital economy lies not in the product itself, but in the information they can gather on the product in use. Consequently, they have optimized their business model toward curating and delivering that data to create new sources of value.

The fast-paced development of digital technologies requires organizations to view their business model not as a static, long-term blueprint, but rather as a snapshot of current thinking to be challenged and evolved. Two different forms of evolution must be addressed.

The first is based on the observation that organizations disrupted by new digital technologies must differentiate between two distinct phases: discovering a viable business model and executing that model. According to Steve Blank, the challenge for many organizations whose innovation is in the start-up phase is to find a successful business model for their current environment, one that must be able to solve the problem they face in an effective and sustainable way.[48] Therefore, in order to make progress, a great deal of experimentation will be required to gain a better understanding of the business model. In this search for the right business model, the goal must be speed of action and to maximize learning, while recognizing that many ideas will not be viable. Once a business model looks promising, there is a switch to the execution phase where the focus is on rapid scalability to exploit the model for maximum benefit to the organization, its ecosystem, and its clients. Much of failure in innovation, Blank explained, is due to the lack of understanding about the differences between these two phases, and a failure to transition between them.

The second observation relates to the evolving priority of business model innovation as a market matures. With swift digital technology adoption, the life cycle for ideas may be short-lived. Even so, it is important to recognize that the focus for business model activity will shift throughout that time. Christensen[49] saw this as three distinct stages of a business model's journey:

- **Creation.** The initial stage during which the business model is created emphasizes development of the value proposition as well as an understanding of the resources required to deliver it. The questions asked at this stage seek to deepen knowledge about the "jobs to be done" and the information flows that surround them.[50]
- **Sustaining innovation.** Moving to a sustaining innovation brings the need for processes to manage customer activities, to understand priorities for improvement, and to compete in evolving marketplaces.
- **Efficiency focused.** This final stage highlights the business model's efficiency and optimization where strong revenue and profit motives must be addressed. Data on the business's operational aspects may be emphasized, guiding decision-making toward continued delivery of value where new offerings may become more dominant.

In summary, business model innovation is a core of successful digital transformation activities. While the digital journey requires emphasis on key areas where digital technologies provide particular advantages, there must be ongoing, careful review of all business model aspects.

Lesson 3: Support innovation by adapting strategy and planning activities to introduce greater flexibility

Organizations need to be flexible and adaptable, but this does not remove the obligation for strategy and planning activities. All organizations require some form of short-, medium-, and long-term vision for coordinating future actions. In a world of uncertainty and rapid change, however, it is essential that they are able to ensure an appropriate balance between conflicting demands.

Consider, for example, broad approaches to structuring strategic initiatives such as horizon planning.[51] This has three distinct phases. Horizon 1 focuses on near-time activities aimed at maintaining core business capabilities, extending critical services when necessary. Horizon 2 looks to build adjacent markets and leverage core strengths into these new areas of opportunity. Horizon 3 explores how new capabilities, markets, and clients can be created with longer-term disruptive potential. Many organizations use this framework as a basis for planning, and typically invest 70% of budgets in Horizon 1 activities, 20% in Horizon 2, and 10% in Horizon 3. Such rules-of-thumb for strategic investment are helpful but will require adaptation and reinterpretation in an age of digital transformation. In particular, it is helpful to consider horizon planning in relation to more agile approaches exemplified by lean start-up techniques.[52]

The lean start-up methodology also considers distinct phases: start-up, scale-up, and enterprise. In the start-up phase the organization is searching for an appropriate business model, in scale-up the focus is on validating and scaling the identified business model, and in the enterprise phase it is the business model's efficient execution that is emphasized. Bringing these ideas together, there is a clear mapping between Horizon 1 and the enterprise phase business model execution, between Horizon 2 and scale-up phase improvements to the business model, and between Horizon 3 with the start-up phase's search for new business models. This alignment, although requiring deeper analysis for practical application, provides a promising starting point for organizations considering the adaptability of planning processes for increased agility. Less clear, however, is the balance of investment across the three horizons in a digital transformation scenario. While significant effort is still required to manage and evolve existing core business opportunities, it can be argued that greater emphasis should be provided to the more disruptive investigations previously confined to Horizon 3.[53] In fact, successful digital companies such as Google and Facebook claim to have shifted this balance substantially.[54]

In summary, organizations with traditional strategy and planning approaches must seek to introduce increased flexibility to make them more relevant in the digital economy with its uncertainties. However, initial experiences with more agile approaches, such as lean start-up, fuel optimism that an alignment can be found in practice.

Lesson 4: Innovation requires a team, so pay careful attention to team dynamics

Innovation is too often viewed as the purview of a lone genius; an individual with the insight and tenacity to succeed against all odds. Ask for exemplars of innovation leadership and you would hear about the likes of Richard Branson, Steve Jobs, and James Dyson. However, this stereotype of personal triumph is at odds with the experiences of many organizations. More typically, teams are required to succeed. The extensive life cycle and pressured execution necessary for innovation demands a broad set of skills to take ideas from insight to implementation.

Much has been written about team formation, dynamics, and execution in creating high-performance groups capable of successfully driving change.[55] In terms of digital transformation, we emphasize two particular areas of importance: team capabilities and distributed team interaction.

With team capabilities, it is recognized that a wide set of skills may be required for success in innovation.[56] Innovation activities will require approaches to understand problems that matter to end users, marshal the skills and resources to address them, communicate effectively with stakeholders, and overcome barriers in execution. It is critical that these approaches are carried out together to ensure success, and rare that the necessary skills are found in a single person. Consequently, a team of people with a blend of capabilities is usually needed. Kelley describes three particular capabilities essential to a team:

- **Learning.** Understanding more about the problem domain and potential solutions often requires significant learning. This may be achieved with an anthropological approach through study and analysis of behaviors in situ, an experimental approach by proposing hypotheses and trying out new ideas to gain new insights, or by translating between different environments and domains to adapt ideas from one area to another.
- **Organizing.** Solutions require the management of individuals, schedules, and activities. In particular, it may be necessary to find ways to overcome financial and political barriers blocking progress, bring disparate resources together around common goals, or drive people forward within a shared framework of tools and practices.
- **Building.** Constructing a solution may go beyond the technologies and mechanics of problem-solving to include broader elements essential to success. Delivery may include shaping solutions to meet stakeholders' needs, adapting solution concepts to the consumers' experiences and usage contexts, or creating compelling messages to communicate the impact and value of a solution.

As for distributed team interaction, a particular challenge for innovation in digital transformation scenarios is to ensure appropriate coordination in contexts where quick decision-making and action is necessary. Building on experiences in agile software development teams[57], successful projects typically use co-located teams with small numbers of skilled workers to create tightly-managed, cross-functional units. However, increasing diversity and complexity in the operating environment frequently forces teams to address additional concerns, including:

- Larger team sizes requiring more coordination and transparency into planning and progress.
- Distributed teams supported by remote access, outsourced partnerships, and varied access to artifacts and system knowledge.
- Complex or mission-critical applications requiring more attention to analysis, architecture, and testing procedures.
- Multi-platform deployment environments often requiring more extensive and rigorous testing, management of multiple variants, and enhanced support mechanisms.

Each of these concerns can introduce friction and delay, and must be addressed to support continued progress. Very large team sizes, teams of teams, and more complex management structures require more coordination and management. At this level there is an increasing need to standardize best practices to avoid reinvention and miscommunication across artifacts and processes.

In summary, innovation most frequently requires teams that offer a range of skills and capabilities. Complexity issues across innovation teams can have significant impact on their progress. Innovation mechanisms must be evaluated, tailored, and perhaps combined with traditional approaches to suit the specific context.

Lesson 5: Manage innovation activities as a change program

Adoption of any innovation in practice requires explicit attention to cultural change and transition activities. In particular, a key consideration for any digital transformation is to plan that change within the confines of the organization's need to continue its day-to-day operations while adopting new practices. Much of existing academic literature and best practice in managing successful technology transitions can be applied to digital transformation.[58] However, the experiences of large-scale digital transformations highlight the need to focus on several specific areas where innovation has a deep impact on existing ways of working. Effecting change requires an approach that focuses on early success and builds incrementally toward broader institutionalization of those changes. As such, two techniques are particularly important for innovation to succeed.

The first technique is to structure change in 'streams' and to deliver that change in 'waves'. That is, identify areas where improvement can address explicit, known concerns and make measurable incremental improvements that demonstrate value to key stakeholders. For example, when introducing a new digital technology in an organization we may choose to focus on areas such as education, core business processes, tooling, and infrastructure as they relate to the digital transformation taking place. Each area may have different levels of maturity as well as needs. Hence, we consider these the 'streams of effort', and we plan change as a series of 'waves of change' that package a number of activities in each stream aimed at increasing the capabilities and maturity in these areas.

The second technique is to define a customized piloting scheme for rolling out the change to optimize early success and provide a clear focus on major organizational characteristics. For example, in one recent digital transformation roll-out we created a questionnaire that captured pilot project selection criteria in a simple, usable form. This was the basis for prioritizing potential projects to be included in those pilot activities based on the organization's needs and context. As well as focusing on characteristics such as project size and scope, the questionnaire paid particular attention to areas believed to be high risk for broader roll-out and delivery. This ensured the activities provided insight into areas of particular concern for the organization. The selection criteria included:

- At least one pilot project with some degree of globally-distributed team members.
- At least one pilot project with multiple teams in a team-of-teams structure.
- At least one pilot project involving cooperation with one or more internal or external vendors.
- Pilot projects that addressed different platform technologies in use across the organization.
- Pilot projects that addressed different kinds of project styles (e.g., new development, extension of existing systems, business improvement tasks, maintenance and fixes, etc.).

In summary, innovation brings significant change to an organization. Hence, disciplined change management processes must be considered to establish confidence in and support for rolling out the changes in a disciplined manner.

Examples and Illustrations

While many existing organizations were preoccupied with moving online to multi-channel operations,[59] other forms of digital organizations were emerging elsewhere. These organizations use new business models and operating approaches to take advantage of opportunities created by increasingly available high-speed connectivity, access to huge amounts of real-time information, and the convenience of digital media delivery models. However, the word 'digital' risks becoming meaningless through overuse, abuse, and misunderstanding. It is essential, therefore, to gain an operational view of digital transformation and how it is realized in practice.

UK Government Digital Service

As a useful illustration, consider the UK Government's digital transformation experiences over the past decade, where much emphasis has been placed on enhancing community interaction across a platform of public services. Using Weil and Woerner's business model framework[60] discussed earlier, we can readily apply the content, customer experience, and platform activities to the transformation of the UK government's service delivery. This was achieved through the work of the Government Digital Service (GDS), established in 2011 following agreement within the Cabinet Office on a new public sector IT approach based on progressive adoption of open standards.[61] Responding to the need for a tight central core to consolidate and agree standards across government, GDS had two primary thrusts.

First, GDS pushed for the adoption of a new central publishing platform (website) across the UK government, consolidating a diverse web estate into a single site: GOV.UK. In parallel, championed by GDS, the UK government began a program to open up public data sources (available at data.gov.uk) to offer content in new ways and to encourage a variety of user experience scenarios. For instance, the portal and dashboards presented at GOV.UK offer a unified customer experience for the websites of all government departments, and many other public bodies and agencies. At GOV.UK, web visitors can view all UK government policies, announcements, publications, statistics, and consultations. In addition, a restructuring of the underlying infrastructure is taking place to enable greater transparency in the way the public sector operates, and to support flexibility in how the content is made available for consumption. This is widely discussed and debated online through forums such as the GDS blogs.[62]

Second, GDS began turning to issues of architectural consolidation within government IT systems, identifying 25 government organizations with whom they have worked to transform legacy processes using principles based around simplification and reuse. In designing public services, GDS particularly highlighted the use of open architectures to design for variety, enabled by standard components, selected and configured locally using consistent thinking. Explicit attention to the tension between standardization at component level, and enormous innovation and variety at service level, lies at the heart of this digital transformation in practice. Lessons from these 25 demonstrators (both positive and negative in nature) have been used to refine the on-going approach, pace, and governance practices of GDS.[63]

IBM product delivery process

Large technology-focused organizations such as IBM rely on new product innovation for their success, and hence invest significantly in R&D activities of many forms to maintain their market leadership. In spite of their focus on innovation and encouraging entrepreneurial activities to advance the state-of-the-art, many of their most difficult challenges in delivering rapid business change lie in the roles and tasks that coordinate and support product delivery. Here, the energy and enthusiasm of the most innovative engineers meet the pragmatic realism of project and product managers. In many cases this is unfortunately not a happy marriage. In many software-intensive businesses, current approaches to software product delivery stifle innovation and suppress agility.[64]

Illustrated in Figure 6.3 are the main activities and flow in IBM's Integrated Product Delivery (IPD) process from 2010. The center of this figure shows a typical filter process that takes ideas from concept to launch, governed by a series of 'gates' that allow an idea to progress from one phase to the next based on formal reviews. This process brings together many different interested parties (including customer support, finance, legal, and marketing) to be part of the decision-making process at each 'gate' to ensure a rounded view is taken before an idea progresses.

While the IPD process depicted in Figure 6.3 has much to commend it in terms of rigorous governance and control, it also suffers from a number of issues with respect to the need for flexibility, openness, and speed of innovation. In particular, typical issues in this form of IPD process can include:
- Closed nature of the process to internal thinking only.
- High overheads in process management and administration.

- Unclear ownership, responsibility, and authority in decision-making.
- Difficulty of balancing viewpoints and reviewing competing priorities of each stakeholder.
- Lengthy time period from idea to its first delivery to the potential customer.
- Limited input and slow reactions to external needs for change, new opinions, and revised market insights.

Integrated Product Delivery (IPD) Process

Key Stakeholders Include:
- Customer Service and Support
- Finance
- Integrated Supply Management
- Legal
- Marketing
- Hardware and Support Service

Fig. 6.3: The IBM Integrated Product Delivery process, circa 2010

Hence, the balance between the 'need for speed' in innovation is often overwhelmed by 'organizational inertia' of the governance mechanisms that dominate the product delivery process. As a result, IBM embarked on a substantial review to redesign this process, resulting in a much more collaborative approach to new product and service creation.[65]

Summary and Conclusions

Digital transformation is bringing many organizations into a battleground they never expected to enter: combining core IT skills required for managing the core business processes with rapid delivery of capabilities to meet consumers' demands. Greater flexibility and time to market are driving many organizations toward practices that optimize their team interactions and their connection with stakeholders. The resulting innovation management approaches are widely discussed and are seeing broad adoption across many kinds of organizations. However, the results have been mixed.

In this chapter we have provided a broad view of innovation as it applies to digital transformation initiatives. In particular, we have focused on how innovation at scale can be realized, and have provided practical guidance on accelerating innovation in complex mature organizations.

References

1 Tucker, R.B. (2008). *Driving Growth Through Innovation: How Leading Firms Are Transforming Their Futures, 2nd Edition.* Berrett-Koehler Publishers.

2 PwC (2015). *Lessons from Digital Leaders: 10 Attributes Driving Stronger Performance.* PwC 2015 Global Digital IQ Survey, September. Available at: https://www.pwc.com/gx/en/advisory-services/digital-iq-survey-2015/campaign-site/digital-iq-survey-2015.pdf

3 Baden-Fuller, C. and Haefliger, S. (2013). Business Models and Technological Innovation. *Long Range Planning,* 46(6):419–426.

4 Prahalad, C.K. and Krishnan, M.S. (2008). *The New Age of Innovation: Driving Co-Created Value through Global Networks.* McGraw-Hill.

5 Levie, J. and Hart, M. (2011). *Global Entrepreneurship Monitor: UK 2011 Monitoring Report.* University of Strathclyde. Available at: http://www.strath.ac.uk/media/departments/huntercentre/research/gem/GEM_UK_2011.pdf

6 Augustine, N.R. (2007). *Is America Falling Off the Flat Earth?* National Academies Press.

7 Harvard Business Review (2013). *HBR's 10 Must Reads on Innovation.* Harvard Business Review Press.

8 Drucker, P. (2007). *Management Challenges for the 21st Century* (Classic Drucker Collection). Routledge.

9 Schumpeter, J. (1934). *The Theory of Economic Development.* Transaction Publishers.

10 Drucker, P.F. (1985). *Innovation and Entrepreneurship.* Butterworth Heineman.

11 Christensen, C. (1997). *The Innovator's Dilemma: When New Technologies Cause Great Firms to Fail.* Harvard Business School Press.

12 Tidd, J. and Bessant, J. (2009). *Managing Innovation: Integrating Technological, Market, And Organizational Change, 4th Edition.* John Wiley.

13 https://trendwatching.com/freepublications/

14 Schrage, M. (2016). R&D, Meet E&S (Experiment & Scale), MIT Sloan Management Review, May.

15 Chesbrough, H. (2006). *Open Business Models: How to Thrive in the New Innovation Landscape.* Harvard Business School Press.

16 See for example: http://www.forbes.com/sites/perryrotella/2012/07/06/cio-chief-innovation-officer/

17 https://kickbox.adobe.com/

18 https://www.centrica.com/news/centrica-launches-new-innovations-venture

19 https://wayra.co.uk/

20 Baden-Fuller, C. and Haefliger, S. (2013). Business Models and Technological Innovation. *Long Range Planning*, 46(6): 419–426.

21 Magretta, J. (2002.) *Why Business Models Matter?* Harvard Business Review, May.

22 Al-Debei M.M. and Avison D. (2010). Developing a Unified Framework of the Business Model Concept. *European Journal of Information Systems*, 19(3): 359-376.

23 Osterwalder, A., Pigneur, Y. and Tucci, C. (2005). Clarifying Business Models: Origins, Present, and Future of the Concept. *Communications of the Association for Information Systems*, 16.

24 Baden-Fuller, C. and Mangematin, V. (eds.) (2015). *Business Models and Modelling, Advances in Strategic Management,* Vol 33. Emerald Press.

25 Amit R. and Zott C. (2001). Value Creation in e-Business. *Strategic Management Journal*, 22(6-7): 493-520.

26 Al-Debei M.M. and Avison D. (2010). Developing a Unified Framework of the Business Model Concept. *European Journal of Information Systems*, 19(3): 359-376.

27 Doganova L. and Eyquem-Renault M. (2009). What Do Business Models Do? Innovation Devices in Technology Entrepreneurship. *Research Policy* , 38(10): 1559-1570.

28 Baden-Fuller C. and Morgan M.S. (2010). Business Models as Models. *Long Range Planning*, 43: 156-171.

29 Sabatier, V., Mangematin, V., and Rouselle, T. (2010). From Recipe to Dinner: Business Model Portfolios in the European Biopharmaceutical Industry. *Long Range Planning* 43(2): 431-447.

30 Teece D.J. (2010). Business Models, Business Strategy and Innovation. *Long Range Planning*, 43: 172-194.

31 Magretta, J. (2002). *Why Business Models Matter?* Harvard Business Review, May.

32 Rayna, T. and Striukova, L. (2016). From Rapid Prototyping to Home Fabrication: How 3D Printing is Changing Business Model Innovation. *Technological Forecasting and Social Change*, 102, 214-224.

33 Arend, R.J. (2013). The Business Model: Present and Future—Beyond a Skeumorph. *Strategic Organization*, 11(4): 390-402.

34 Rayna, T. and Striukova, L. (2016). From Rapid Prototyping to Home Fabrication: How 3D Printing is Changing Business Model Innovation. *Technological Forecasting and Social Change*, 102, 214-224.

35 Teece D.J. (2010). Business Models, Business Strategy and Innovation. *Long Range Planning*, 43: 172-194.

36 Marx, K. (1987). *Theory of Surplus Value, Part 1. Reprint edition.* Lawrence and Wishhart Ltd.

37 Jacobides, M.G., Knudsen, T., and Augier, M. (2006). Benefiting from Innovation: Value Creation, Value Appropriation and the Role of Industry Architectures. *Research Policy*, 35:1200-1221.

38 Ng, I. (2014). *Creating New Markets in the Digital Economy: Value and Worth.* Cambridge University Press.

39 Dunleavy, P. and Margetts, H. (2008). *Digital Era Governance: IT Corporations, the State, and E-Government.* Oxford University Press.

40 Doganova, L. and Eyquem-Renault, M. (2009). What Do Business Models Do? Innovation Devices in Technology Entrepreneurship. *Research Policy*, 38(10): 1559-1570.

41 Weill, P. and Woerner, S. (2013). *Optimizing Your Business Model.* Sloan Management Review, March.

42 Baden-Fuller, C. and Mangematin, V. (eds.) (2015). *Business Models and Modelling, Advances in Strategic Management, Vol 33.* Emerald Press.

43 Fenwick, N., Burris, P., Gill, M. and Wang, N. (2014). *The State of Digital Business 2014*. Forrester. Available at: https://www.forrester.com/The+State+Of+Digital+Business+2014/fulltext/-/E-RES113962

44 Christensen, C. (1997). *The Innovator's Dilemma: When New Technologies Cause Great Firms to Fail*. Harvard Business School Press.

45 Kavadias, S., Ladas, K., and Loch, C. (2016). *The Transformative Business Model*. Harvard Business Review, October.

46 ibid.

47 Ng, I., Smith, L.A., and Vargo, S.L. (2012). An Integrative Framework of Value. *Proceedings of the 12th International Research Conference on Service Management*, July.

48 Blank, S. (2012). *LSearch versus Execute*. SteveBlank.com. Available at: https://steveblank.com/2012/03/05/search-versus-execute/

49 Christensen, C. (1997). *The Innovator's Dilemma: When New Technologies Cause Great Firms to Fail*. Harvard Business School Press.

50 https://hbr.org/ideacast/2016/12/the-jobs-to-be-done-theory-of-innovation.html

51 McKinsey (2009). *Enduring Ideas: The Three Horizons of Growth*. McKinsey Quarterly. Available at: https://www.mckinsey.com/business-functions/strategy-and-corporate-finance/our-insights/enduring-ideas-the-three-horizons-of-growth

52 Blank, S. (2015). *Lean Innovation Management – Making Corporate Innovation Work*. SteveBlank.com. Available at: http://steveblank.com/2015/06/26/lean-innovation-management-making-corporate-innovation-work/

53 Oomen, J. (2019). *The 3 Horizons in Lean Innovation Portfolio Management*. Pimcy. Available at: https://www.pimcy.nl/en/3-horizons-in-lean-innovation-portfoliomanagement/

54 Bean, J. (2016). *Facebook's 3 Horizons*. Jonobean.com. Available at: https://jonobean.com/2016/04/12/facebooks-3-horizons/

55 Marquete, L.D. (2015). *Turn the Ship Around!* Penguin.

56 Kelley, T. (2016). *The 10 Faces of Innovation: Strategies for Heightening Creativity*. Profile Books.

57 Schmidt, C. (2016). *Agile Software Development Teams*. Springer.

58 Wahab, S.A., Rose, R.C., Jegak, U. and Abdullah, H. (2009). A Review on the Technology Transfer Models, Knowledge-Based and Organizational Learning Models on Technology Transfer. *European Journal of Social Science*, 10(4). Available at SSRN: https://ssrn.com/abstract=1949149

59 Janowski, T. (2015). *From Electronic Governance to Policy-Driven Electronic Governance-Evolution of Technology Use in Government*. In: J. A. Danowski & L. Cantoni (Eds.), *Communication and Technology*. Walter de Gruyter. pp. 425-439.

60 Weill, P. and Woerner, S. (2013). *Optimizing Your Business Model*. Sloan Management Review, March.

61 http://www.gov.uk/gds

62 http://gds.blog.gov.uk

63 National Audit Office (2017). *Digital Transformation in Government*. HC 1059, Session 2016-17, 30 March. Available at: https://www.nao.org.uk/wp-content/uploads/2017/03/Digital-transformation-in-government.pdf

64 Dikert, K., Paasivaara, M. and Lassenius, C. (2012). Challenges and Success Factors for Large-Scale Agile Transformations: A Systematic Literature Review. *Journal of Systems and Software*, 119, September: 87-108.

65 Brown, A.W. (2012). *Enterprise Software Delivery: Bringing Agility and Efficiency to the Global Software Supply Chain*, Addison Wesley.

7 Management

Introduction

Driving innovation in a well-established organization is critical for the success of its digital transformation. However, lessons from the agile software delivery domain have taught us that it is fatal for an organization to become overly-obsessed with digital technology's new capabilities, or to be carried away by the excitement of experimental practices in the company's delivery methods. To achieve success, organizations need to have a disciplined approach to change, supported by innovation management practices that yield results, and grounded in techniques that address the most common failure points. Speed and flexibility without appropriate discipline leads to chaos.

Hence, success in digital transformation requires a disciplined approach to management aligned with the characteristics of such efforts. Defining and executing a digital transformation strategy is neither straightforward nor without risk. Many organizations have taken their first limited steps on this journey by adopting digital technologies for interacting with customers, engaging in pilot projects built with commercial or open technology stacks, and by updating parts of their back office with lighter-weight technology infrastructure consumed as a service. Focused on technological shifts, these digitization efforts have yielded useful results, but they have had limited impact without significant attempts to manage the disruption they create.

Through our experiences with organizations undergoing digital transformation, we found that the most successful ones demonstrate three clear traits:
- They encourage an experimental mindset based around lean principles.
- They actively explore digital business model alternatives.
- They assist their people to become more change ready.

These traits bring to the organization the agility and flexibility necessary to embrace digital transformation. They surround the deployment of digital technology with the management structures and discipline essential to success.

Furthermore, such transformation cannot take place in isolation, within a closed, sterile environment. Consider as an example, one of the most complex areas for digital transformation: the US government. Former US Chief Technology Officer Aneesh Chopra has described[1] how a focus on open innovation has been essential, and how the disciplined introduction of new digital technologies can realize Tim O'Reilly's vision for Government-as-a-Platform.[2] To support his discussion, Chopra provided a wide range of examples to illustrate how a digital transformation mindset can revolutionize service delivery in government.

A primary inspiration for Chopra is Henry Chesbrough's pioneering work on open innovation practices.[3] Chesbrough's seminal work on understanding open approaches to innovation in the private sector is well known, but he also has applied his work to public institutions such as US government agencies. Government's role, according to Chesbrough, is to "do enough to liberate or harness the energies of the private sector" and use this to drive the public and private sectors closer together. Chopra has worked to realize this approach in several government agencies, with some notable successes in management of the Veterans' Affairs, coordination of tax refunds, and several others.

Notably, Chopra emphasized that progress depended upon a clear focus on the change in culture that is necessary to open up thinking around the options available to policymakers to provide more effective public services in a more collaborative way, and to do so as efficiently as possible. He specifically highlighted four key elements for achieving this:

- **Open data.** To enable public access to more of the information currently closed to external scrutiny and inaccessible to new service delivery opportunities.
- **Impatient convening.** To drive the private and public sectors toward the necessary open standards that increase competition and open up markets to suppliers of all sizes.
- **Challenges and prizes.** As incentives to focus potential providers of services on the issues critical to government, and to change the procurement processes from long-term risk avoidance to shorter-term value creation.
- **Attracting talent into the public sector.** By specifically recruiting private sector entrepreneurs into public sector roles, and by inspiring a new generation of digitally aware public sector employees.

This example reveals a great deal about the promises and pitfalls of digital transformation, and the management challenges that must be addressed. In the rest of this chapter we examine some of these in further detail. Following a discussion of how the characteristics of digital transformation relate to today's prevalent management practices, we consider more radical management approaches and their adoption. We then review the broader cultural challenges that face organizations going through rapid change and conclude with a set of leadership and management lessons for successfully navigating the choppy waters of any digital transformation initiative.

Toward Radical Management

All organizations require a management discipline that focuses on setting directions and marshaling the workforce within a strategy aimed at achieving both near- and longer-term goals. While management theory and practice is replete with approaches for leading and running organizations at all stages in their life cycle, few take account of fast-paced change. In particular, organizations facing digital transformation must adopt a management approach aimed at addressing three critical questions:

- **How do we change fast enough to stay relevant in a turbulent world?**
  The VUCA (volatility, uncertainty, complexity, and ambiguity) characteristics of the digital age place pressure on an organization's ability not only to deal with change, but to recognize that constant change is the new norm.[45] Such change is an anathema to existing management practices focused on stable structures that regulate and rationalize processes. Adoption of approaches highlighting flexibility and adaptability is essential.

- **How do we innovate boldly enough to stay ahead of our competition, and to meet growing user expectations?**
  The dilemma facing most organizations is how to invest more in evolving existing products and services while at the same time exploring radical and potentially disruptive avenues for future offerings. As Christensen elegantly summarized,[6] organizations tend to keep doing the things that made them successful, even to the point where those things begin to harm their future prospects. Making bold choices is difficult due to the constraints imposed by established organizational structures and decision-making dynamics. Such reticence is reinforced by the cultural inertia inherent in all human-centred activities.

- **How do we create an organization where people are able and willing to do their best work?**
  Great ideas need to be enacted through a strategy aligned to meeting market needs. Establishing an appropriate pace of change is critical. Without the skilled workforce capable of delivering that change, however, an organization falls into the trap where "vision without execution is no more than hallucination".[7] Successful organizations must establish a working environ-

ment that attracts the best talent, engages them effectively, grows their capabilities, and retains their services in a highly competitive marketplace for digital skills.

These challenges, while straightforward to define, are acutely difficult to address. This is particularly so for more mature organizations with a heritage of products and services to manage, an extensive list of urgent demands from customers, tremendous pressure from shareholders to meet short-term financial expectations, and a myriad of other concerns based on the complexity of the organization's current working practices, assets, and locations. Despite these barriers, however, most organizations have begun to adopt new management practices that address these issues. Two main elements underlie that move.

First, digital technologies have resulted in an abundance of data concerning all aspects of business. From instrumentation of the manufacturing process and production line status, to in-home sensors reporting on consumer product use, companies can now rapidly access new kinds of information potentially relevant to their strategy, planning, and operations. Organizations have been learning how to source relevant data, build meaningful models informed by data-based insights, and update working practices to leverage data effectively. Historically, these insights have been based on data captured in ERP products such as SAP, Microsoft Dynamics, and Salesforce.com.[8] While there have been efficiency and management successes, the complexity of these systems and the rigid manual processes required to enter data continues to be a significant barrier to their wider use. Too often their adoption is limited and fails to deeply embed data-driven practices in the organizational culture so that the company leaders can routinely rely on recorded information to make better, more timely decisions.

Second, by introducing aspects of agility into their working practices, organizations are encouraging innovation across their product and service delivery cycle and enhancing worker engagement by empowering individuals and teams with increased autonomy supported by outcome-related incentives. Agile practices widely adopted in software delivery contexts emphasize flexibility in working styles through short, time-boxed iterations delivering a stream of validated client outcomes. The main impact of agile approaches is a rethink of the balance between opportunism and stability in making progress in environments with significant unpredictability or requiring incremental learning to overcome unknowns. One way many organizations are managing the incentives for individuals and teams is by setting up a program of shared Objectives and Key Results (OKRs).[9] An OKR approach, popularized through its use at Google,[10] creates a network of impact measures across the organization to govern decision-making and to guide an individual's behavior.

This dual focus presents an obvious starting point for organizations seeking to improve their management flexibility in adopting digital technologies. However, elaborating on and implementing these changes can be much more challenging in practice without the adoption of radical management principles tuned to rapid decision-making. This requires individuals and teams to evolve within their existing organizational culture and context. Leading industry experts such as Steve Denning and Gary Hamel view the drive for data-powered organizational agility as a major challenge to traditional management practices.[11] They believe it requires quite a different approach to how organizations set goals, support managers in achieving them, coordinate their organizational supply chain, set incentives for individuals and teams, and create alignment within and across the organization and the extended partner ecosystem. Denning and Hamel's experiences in advising major corporations undergoing digital transformation highlight that top-down autocratic management styles must be replaced by more radical approaches based on peer-driven meritocracy and emphasizing shared responsibilities across multi-disciplinary teams.

As illustrated in Figure 7.1, Denning's radical management approach points to a shift in an organization's high-level focus in several significant ways; it places emphasis on the outcomes achieved, and measures impact through feedback from clients and broader stakeholders. Client-driven iterations are executed to deliver a stream of incremental value to clients via teams that self-organize around the opportunities being addressed. Flexibility is enhanced by flattening management hierarchies and adopting a more open, transparent culture.

Denning's radical management framework directly draws its inspiration from the agile software delivery movement of the early 21st century, which has been extensively discussed in Chapter 5.

	Traditional Management	Radical Management
Purpose of the firm	Produce goods and services	Delight clients and stakeholders
How work is structured	Bureaucracy & hierarchy	Self-organising teams
How work is organised	Single big plan	Client-driven iterations
Transparency	Tell people what they need to know	Radical transparency
How managers communicate	Top down: tell people what to do	Interactive: stories, questions, conversations
Impact	Only 20% fully engaged	High productivity & continuous innovation
	Things	**People**

Fig. 7.1: Radical Management for Digital Transformation

Adhocracy and the search for management flexibility

Management approaches that support greater flexibility have attempted to provide insights into the constant struggle between the need for rigor and stability and for flexible adaptation to a changing environment. The management style that exemplifies this approach most clearly is described as adhocracy,[12] an organizational design whose structure is highly flexible, loosely coupled, and amenable to frequent change.

Given prominence by Alvin Toffler in 1970,[13] adhocracy arises out of the need for organizations to recognize, understand, and solve problems in highly complex and turbulent environments. Any organization adopting this philosophy moves away from traditional hierarchical structures and decision-making to emphasize creative thinking, experimentation, and team-based problem-solving.

Critical to its use in volatile contexts, adhocracy supports a strong emphasis on speed of decisions over formal authority. This extends to a bias toward intuitive action rather than being stalled by waiting for outcomes from extensive data-driven knowledge exchanges. However, such an approach can raise several concerns. For example, adhocracy is sometimes viewed as a lack of discipline where the choice of a particular option is not fully assessed in advance, and trade-offs among alternatives are poorly reviewed. There is a need, therefore, to extend adhocracy to introducing new forms of governance appropriate for digital transformation initiatives.

In response to these concerns, there is now a refined notion of adhocracy aimed at making this approach more effective in a digital economy. As redefined by Julian Birkinshaw and Jonas Ridderstrale,[14] adhocracy focuses on actions essential to gain knowledge where there is significant uncertainty about the future. It also encourages an outward-facing perspective, insisting that those actions are prioritized based on external opportunities. Employees are empowered by the outcomes they see in relation to external stakeholders. Discipline is provided by ensuring that externally-focused activities are undertaken in small steps, frequently reviewed to assess their impact, and used to guide subsequent actions to form a clear, measured approach to progress. Critically, Birkinshaw and Ridderstrale placed significant emphasis on contextualizing the situations where adhocracy is appropriate, believing that most organizations naturally execute a blend of management approaches suitable for their circumstances.

Specifically, adhocracy is viewed as one of three management styles, each of which has strengths and weaknesses in delivering successful outcomes for an organization:
- **Bureaucracy** achieves coordination through a set of defined roles; decisions are made through strict enforcement of a hierarchy; workers are motivated by extrinsic rewards.
- **Meritocracy** addresses coordination through mutual consent; decision-making is achieved through assessing the most logical argument; workers view opportunities to enhance personal mastery as the primary reward.
- **Adhocracy** ensures coordination occurs around emerging opportunities; decisions are made incrementally though learning-based experimentation; workers consider the achievement of meaningful outcomes as the ultimate reward.

Hence, most organizations will gravitate toward a dominant style of management based on their sector and operational maturity. However, key aspects of their business may require different styles to be successful. For example, knowledge-intensive domains such as those dominated by software development activities may more naturally be comfortable with meritocracies, while central aspects of the business aimed at IT and business efficiency may be better structured as hierarchies.

Managing change

Regardless of the context, introducing more radical approaches to management must be undertaken with care. As many of their principles and practices depart significantly from what is commonly employed in most organizations, the approach and pace of their adoption requires planning and investment. However, as John Kotter forcefully describes it,[15]

> An organization that's facing a real threat or eyeing a new opportunity tries—and fails—to cram through some sort of major transformation using a change process that worked in the past. But the old ways of setting and implementing strategy are failing us.

Organizations are moving away from multi-year strategic upgrade programs and toward a constant set of adjustments to changing environmental conditions. However, this cannot occur as a series of reactive activities in response to actions by others. It is necessary that an organization predicts future directions and interpolates future trends by being fully aware of their current position in relation to those around them.

Hence, a dual approach is recommended. As well as the existing management mechanisms aimed at gradual, measured improvement, Kotter promotes the idea that organizations require a second additional set of change management practices that are agile, efficient, and focus on experimental, predictive actions. These 'accelerators' continuously monitor and adjust the organization's operating processes, require broad involvement from individuals across all parts of the business, and take advantage of loosely defined networks of communities to ensure agility in execution. The combination of systematic long-range change processes supported with these more dynamic accelerators leads to what Kotter refers to as a "continuous and holistic strategic change function".

This dual approach encourages an ambidextrous organizational approach supporting both incremental and more radical forms of change management.[16] The management discipline required in times of constant change involves a strong core set of incremental change mechanisms while acknowledging that more radical shifts are in play. Creating an appropriate balance between these two often competing forces is critical to success.

Digital Culture

As organizations adopt digital technologies to improve their operating processes, they also look to make more fundamental changes across all their business practices. By encouraging a more disciplined approach to digital transformation, they seek longer-term systemic change aimed at revolutionizing the organization's structure, strategy, and execution. They encourage their employees toward a vision of engagement enhanced through the transparency and interaction offered by digital technologies and optimized by digitizing inefficient processes. Surrounded by the instability and uncertainty prevalent in many sectors in the digital economy, organizations are forced to accept that an ability to recognize and manage change is essential.

To a large degree, all management is change management.[17] It can be argued that the heart of any management task is the need to define and enact a change within the organization and its environment. However, traditional change management often considers change as being detached from 'normal' management tasks, treating it as a separate process that takes the organization from one stable state to another.[18] In digital transformation where change is constant, it must be considered the essence of management, with implications on all the organization's activities.

Becoming comfortable with constant change means that an organization must have a strong understanding of its own culture. From both practical and academic perspectives, issues of culture have long been an area of concern.[19] In broad terms, an organization's culture consists of the patterns of behaving, feeling, thinking, and believing that pervade its activities and actions. Many studies from eminent scholars such as Peter Drucker,[20] Gary Hamel,[21] and John Kotter[22] have highlighted the importance of culture in accelerating or dampening change activities. The overwhelming evidence from their work, supported by a variety of practical studies, is that an organization's culture plays a key role in change activities from two perspectives: alignment of culture to the organization's overall strategy, and the extent to which the culture supports and encourages change. Misalignment in either of these raises significant challenges to initiating change if it is perceived as increasing operational risk, and to motivating employees to support change when it involves personal risk.

A Booz and Company analysis undertaken in 2011 highlights the challenges in overcoming cultural barriers for organizations undergoing digital transformation.[23] Their interviews with over 600 executives from the world's most innovative companies concluded that:

> The role of culture had a larger impact on innovation than innovation strategy, overall business strategy, deep customer insight, great talent, and the right set of execution capabilities.

It is therefore essential to consider the critical attributes of a digital culture as organizations undergo digital transformation. This understanding will help assess the priorities driving strategy and change. Our experience with such projects over the past decade enables us to make some important observations.

One fundamental conclusion is that cultural change within mature organizations will always be slower and more complex than the technological changes driving them. In a majority of cases the processes and practices in place, supported by organizational structures and governance mechanisms, are designed to emphasize stability over change. As a result, technology replacement is typically undertaken through well-defined paths following market analysis, proofs of concept, and roll-out into production. Operating procedures are adjusted to the capabilities of the new technology. It is much more complex, however, if these technologies force deeper questions to be addressed concerning the redesign of processes, reassignment of roles, or bring into question longstanding value propositions.

Our analysis, in line with other studies,[24] highlights five focus areas for creating a successful digital culture:
- **Organizing work.** In digitally driven projects with tight deadlines and fast-learning cycles, the decomposition of tasks into work items requires careful consideration. Coordinating and organizing teams around these work items creates a more dynamic delivery environment optimized to the outcomes delivered.
- **Strategic planning.** The balance between short-term flexibility and long-term planning must be reconsidered in digital transformation projects. New

approaches acknowledge uncertainties in the planning process and encourage more transparency to allow plans to be adapted to changing conditions.

- **Exploring new ideas.** The dynamic nature of the digital economy creates conditions where there is a constant stream of new insights and opportunities that influence all aspects of business. A more experimental approach to test new ideas is essential to increase the organization's capacity and accelerate the rate at which new ideas can be explored.
- **Attracting and retaining talent.** The lack of skilled workers in emerging digital technologies has become a major inhibitor for many organizations. In a highly-competitive environment, attracting and retaining talent is becoming a determining factor for success. Mature organizations also face the need to constantly upskill existing employees with relevant capabilities.
- **Maintaining leadership.** Sustaining momentum in digitally disrupted markets is critical for existing companies as they look to build on previous successes to ensure continued growth. The fundamental characteristics of leadership in a digital economy are shifting toward a more complex relationship between operational excellence, market-driven insights, and rapid exploitation of emerging opportunities.

Here we take a closer look at these five areas to provide deeper observations.

Organizing work

One of the most interesting observations from the experiences of large software development organizations is that you "ship your organization".[25] That is, the products and services an organization develops are invariably architected as mirror images of the organizational structure that produced them. In fact, this phenomenon is now known as "Conway's law"; in as early as 1968, computer scientist Mel Conway noted that:

> Organizations which design systems ... are constrained to produce designs which are copies of the communication structures of these organizations.

We often see how organizational silos typical of many companies have a critical impact on the way they operate. For obvious management reasons, large workforces are divided into separate groups based on role or function. These groups frequently become independent silos with a narrow self-centered view of their responsibilities, and a lack of communication and cooperation with other groups. Inevitably, the company's processes and operational practices become optimized to this siloed structure. Teams become segregated, and in the worst cases duplicate effort, diverge in strategic direction, and view their own objectives to be beyond those of the organization itself. This has a detrimental impact on the organization's ability to work collectively toward the outcomes necessary for success.

For many digital transformation efforts, misalignment between operating unit silos and the organization's broader goals has a critical impact. In fact, internal competition between departmental silos is the most significant barrier to digital transformation, according to 43% of organizations with a mature digital strategy surveyed by Forrester in 2015.[26] This is because digital transformation activities focus on client outcomes above internal structural needs, as they use digital technologies to expose gaps and overlaps in how value-creating actions are delivered, reduce waste and inefficiencies through automation, and highlight early insight through experimentation. Such needs encourage different organizational models that challenge the prevailing culture.

Digital transformation initiatives often require interdisciplinary, cross-functional teams that draw upon the skills and experiences of individuals previously separated into different siloed departments. Many of these activities combine the data analytics skills brought by data scientists, the architecture and design skills of software engineers, the user-centered design skills of user experience designers, and the deep domain knowledge of solution engineers. Bringing together teams and empowering them to focus on client outcomes connects different solution elements to smoothen the customer journey in using products and services, and to encourage a diversity of thinking that sparks innovation and creativity in problem-solving.

Strategic planning

Organizations have always had to deal with the challenge of having to focus on short-term needs while preparing for a longer-term future. This dilemma is somewhat exacerbated in digitally disrupted environments where there is increasing pressure on current needs, and uncertainties at every level mean widely varying predictions for the future. Three specific challenges lie at the heart of organizations' current strategic planning:

Digital technologies have enabled a new wave of competitors by dramatically reducing barriers to entry in many markets. New companies have the ability to create highly scalable digital products and services via cloud-based technologies. Moreover, they can operate without building expensive back-office infrastructure, and use third-party distribution channels to extend their market reach. More mature organizations are often at a disadvantage as they must manage and evolve their existing infrastructure while investing for the future. Furthermore, increased transparency offers potential competitors insights into market dynamics, cost models, pricing policies, and variations across market niches. Armed with this information they are more effective in targeting and timing their market interventions.

Digitization of processes fueled by increasing digital capabilities at ultra-low cost has accelerated the disaggregation of supply chains. This has relentlessly eroded the power that mature organizations hold to protect access to valued customers through their bundled collections of products and services. While unable to compete on size and scale, new start-ups are targeting narrow, high-value aspects of the supply chain with novel value propositions designed for disruption. This has driven down prices and margins in areas where mature organizations traditionally looked for profitability.

Greater availability of large private and public data sets tied to increasingly effective machine learning algorithms are driving automation into many elements of business strategy. From capacity planning to currency trading, the role and influence of automation is evident. Where once experience and insight offered mature organizations strategic advantage, software-enabled decision-making is now creating a much more level playing field. New providers of products and services have equal access to predictive algorithms, and without legacy structures to overcome they are often more agile in responding to the signals they receive.

In summary, the digital disruption across many industries is reshaping the competitive landscape, with new players rising quickly and with purpose. Traditional strategy and planning approaches are struggling to keep up, and recognizing this, most organizations are already making adjustments with well-known approaches such as horizon planning[27] (as discussed in Chapter 6) being reinterpreted for the digital age. For example, in Steve Blank's work with mature organizations he combines horizon planning techniques with lean start-up thinking to reshape the planning process, enabling organizations to distinguish between near- and long-term strategies by viewing sustaining and disruptive innovation as separate threads.[28]

New planning approaches for digital transformation are also beginning to emerge. Building on experiences in agile software development, more flexible approaches are using a combination of vision mapping and improvised action planning.[29] Through sprint-based planning exercises, future scenarios are envisaged as motivating images to guide near-term decisions. Medium-term milestones are sketched out to act as guideposts for establishing appropriate directions of travel. Such techniques help break 'analysis paralysis' cycles typical of planning in the uncertainty that digital disruption brings.

Exploring new ideas

The need to deal with the VUCA inherent in digitally disrupted domains has led to a surge of interest in how to bring greater flexibility into the early stages of product design and delivery. Experiences of agile software development has led to experimental processes that focus on rapid 'hypothesize-build-measure-reflect' cycles. As exemplified in Eric Reis's Lean Start-up techniques, they emphasize early market testing of ideas.[30] The basis for much excitement around lean start-up is Reis's liberating view of what he means by a "start-up": any group of people delivering new products or services in situations of massive uncertainty. This inclusive definition covers a wide swathe of activities in the digital economy.

Consequently, many mature organizations facing digital transformation are embracing the experimental approaches described by Reis. Typically, small teams are empowered to explore potentially disruptive ideas, creating prototypes and minimum viable products to test in the market. Initiatives such as ideation sessions, problem-focused hackathons, and week-long sprints have become fixtures in many corporate calendars. While such activities can be useful in challenging existing cultural norms and encouraging wider participation in innovation-centric activities, two important aspects help move these activities from the fringe to the mainstream of the organization:

- **Customer co-creation.** Explicit involvement of customers and broader stakeholders in experimental approaches raises their value in the eyes of many parts of the organization. Whether through direct secondment into projects or via more indirect means, customers bring insights and legitimacy to experiments.

- **Follow-thru funding.** Too often experiments create initial excitement, only to falter when the initiatives require the organization to adopt broader support and funding. Clear paths from idea to deployment are essential to avoid the frustration of partially completed efforts languishing without a corporate sponsor.

More recently, the focus in many organizations is to explore experimental approaches outside of products and services in the design of new business and operating models. By redefining supply and value chains, digital transformation initiatives are opening up competition to new players who can move at speed to exploit opportunities as they arise. Deploying technologies such as advanced software-based simulation suites, low-code development platforms, and 3D printing is helping many organizations revolutionize their business practices by placing new customized capabilities in consumers' hands faster than previously possible, building one-off solutions to address the 'long tail' of product demand, and restructuring their role in complex supply chains to simplify processes or bring in client-led insights.

Attracting and retaining talent

Organizations with experience in digital transformation are realizing that one of the most critical aspects of turning digital strategies into reality is the investment needed to ensure they have the right people with the right mix of skills. Core digital competencies command a premium, given the well-documented shortages of computer scientists, data scientists, and design specialists.[31] A 2017 survey undertaken by Tech Nation found that the lack of talent supply was the number one challenge facing the UK tech industry.[32] Just as important to organizations, however, is creating an environment capable of leveraging the skills and energy necessary for sustaining success in a digital culture.

Shortage of key skills has meant that many organizations are keenly interested in how to attract digitally trained workers in today's highly competitive market. As discussed in Chapter 4, authors Dan Pink and Dan Tapscott have highlighted how millennials look for different attainments in their work life compared to previous generations. While it is dangerous to overgeneralize, Pink and Tapscott's studies on what attracts and motivates digitally skilled employees emphasize that beyond material attractions of pay and bonuses, millennials want to be challenged by their work so they can improve their skills, have greater autonomy in the activities they undertake, and feel engaged through a sense of mission in their activities. It is not just the major digital platform companies that can offer such an environment. Projects with a social value in the public sector are also able to hire some of the best people, as seen with the UK's Government Digital Service (GDS) and initiatives such as the US government's "Code for America".[33]

As a result, many organizations are acquiring and retaining skilled individuals through enhanced talent management capabilities. The primary aim is to define processes for the "systematic attraction, identification, development, and deployment of individuals with high potential who are of particular value to an organization."[34] In a digitally focused culture, such practices must not only take account of the needs of millennials entering the workforce; they must also ensure that all workers are encouraged and supported to increase their digital capabilities and work habits. Many published surveys identify significant challenges in this regard. For example, a Fujitsu report based on discussions with over 1,600 executives in 2017 found that 70% believed their organization lacked the digital skills necessary for success.[35] Almost a third of those interviewed thought that not having the right skills in the organization was the greatest inhibitor to digital transformation success.

More fundamentally, however, organizations are finding that the definition of who is involved in projects and activities is being stretched. Traditional notions of workers and employees may no longer apply to digitally transformed organizations. For example, emerging graduates from top colleges are now more interested in much more flexible relationships with employers, preferring to divide their time to working on several tasks or to move between projects that excite them regardless of the employer. Their views on longer-term career development are based on the autonomy necessary to choose the quality of the teams they join, and the outcomes they achieve. Such thinking is exemplified in the growing number of freelance or flexible workers, with reports estimating that this "gig economy" now represents over 30% of the US workforce and is expected to rise to over 40% by 2020.[36]

Responding to these trends, most organizations are redesigning their talent management practices to draw the best talent from multiple sources including non-traditional ones such as coding clubs and open-source communities. They are building teams optimized around opportunities as they arise, and offering incentives beyond traditional transaction models of payment and bonuses. Hence, organizations' talent management role has moved away from a more transactional approach based on matching people to jobs, toward a flexible orchestration of diverse workforces that evolve to cope with near-term priorities, balancing permanent and temporary staff to ensure costs elasticity, and adapting to unpredictable market conditions.

Fundamental to retaining talent in organizations is the fostering of a culture that supports and encourages the dynamic nature of digital transformation. High-profile images of workplaces with beanbags and foosball tables may be useful for public relations, but behind the hype is a recognition that workers in digitally disrupted domains are dedicated, creative, curious, and collaborative. They look for working conditions where they will flourish. This has led to some creative measures, including organizations that encourage workers to engage with community-based projects, pursue personal entrepreneurial activities, and create their own start-up companies sponsored by the parent organization.[37]

Maintaining leadership

Leading organizations through complex and unpredictable digital transformation initiatives is a major challenge. As digital technologies create disruption, the boundaries between traditional business domains become blurred, driving new business models that require organizations to protect incumbent positions and adapt quickly to opportunities as they arise. In such circumstances, the practices and characteristics of leadership require significant attention. There are three pertinent questions that must be addressed:

What does it mean to lead in a digital economy?
Current management theories and practices are being reassessed in light of the changing parameters within which businesses operate. Renowned management experts are raising the prospect that management theories of the 20th century are inadequate to deal with the 21st century digital economy. In his book *What Matters Now*, Gary Hamel made a strong case to rethink fundamental assumptions about management, the meaning of work, and day-to-day operations.[38] He argued that the principles and values upon which businesses are based must be challenged. Birkinshaw and Ridderstrale pushed this further by insisting that the very basis on which organizations are structured and make decisions needs

to be redefined when success is contingent upon the speed at which an organization can marshal its resources around emerging opportunities.[39] The conclusion is that all companies must invest in challenging its organizational structures and expanding the basis for leadership in digitally disrupted markets.

What leadership characteristics are important in senior executives?

In leading any organization there are important personal characteristics and capabilities that are essential to success. From clarity of vision to communication skills, leaders must be able to describe a future state for the organization and to motivate those around them to make it happen. However, digital transformation raises significant challenges in achieving that future. Uncertainty and unpredictability can undermine the endurance of any strategic direction. Lack of the right skills in the right role can derail carefully considered plans. New sources of competition and redefined market boundaries can render even the most experienced domain knowledge redundant. Hence, enabling and encouraging new forms of leadership within an organization is essential.

When workers in a recent study were asked about the most important skill for leaders to succeed in a digital environment, only 18% of respondents mentioned technological skills. Instead, they highlighted managerial attributes such as having a transformative vision, being a forward thinker, having a change-oriented mindset, or other leadership and collaborative skills. Other studies go further by emphasizing the importance of leaders who operate well in conditions of extreme uncertainty,[40] with leadership and management approaches that focus on iterative and emergent strategies requiring extensive collaboration across diverse teams both within and outside the organization. Leaders in such circumstances are orchestrators where there is no explicit score to follow. Critically, they are able to recognize themes that arise in the cacophony of noise and can redirect resources to optimize opportunities as they emerge.

Who leads digital transformation in an organization?

Over the past decade, the gradual adoption of digital technologies has led to various digital initiatives throughout an organization. Such activities, created by distinct operating units for different goals, frequently lack central oversight and governance. They also take idiosyncratic approaches to overcome critical challenges typical of cultures that resist change (for example, bypassing internal IT infrastructure services in favor of external cloud services). They often compete between themselves for scarce skills in limited resource pools, and encounter conflict in their plans to open up legacy systems and structures that reduce the pace of delivering new capabilities.

Recognizing these challenges and the opportunities raised by digital disruption, many companies have brought together disparate responsibilities across the organization into a single executive role. A PwC study in 2016 looked at the growing trend of appointing chief digital officers (CDOs) in many organizations.[41] It found that 19% of the world's 2,500 largest public companies had designated an executive to lead their digital agenda, up from 6% in the previous year. In fact, the 2016 study revealed that 60% of the digital leaders identified had only been in their positions since 2015. The CDO has two distinct roles: addressing internal considerations for how digital technologies can make operating practices more efficient, and accelerating the organization's external interactions with customers, partners, and other stakeholders.

In summary, culture is a notoriously difficult concept to define in theory,[42] and to examine in practice.[43] Changing and evolving an organization's culture is equally difficult.[44] Embodied in a set of attitudes, values, beliefs, and behaviors shared by those within an organization, the characteristics of a culture play an important role in accelerating or dampening the organization's ability to operate and undergo change.

For organizations involved in significant digital transformation, assessing and understanding its cultural characteristics is essential. The digital transformation journey challenges many elements of that culture, often requiring a significant shift in existing values and working practices. Crucially, there is the need to re-examine aspects as diverse as leadership, talent management, and organizational decision-making in an era dominated by uncertainty and unpredictability, where management theories that have informed practice for much of the 20th century are now deemed impractical and irrelevant.

How Not to be Disciplined

Changing management approaches requires a great deal of care. As organizations adjust their leadership, structure, and practices, they risk destabilizing many of the core elements that make them successful. We consider three aspects known to derail digital transformation efforts: building up debt, breaking key processes and practices, and failing to address core cultural impediments.

Creating debt

Much of digital transformation efforts is directed at increasing flexibility and driving the pace of change. Great store is placed on an organization's ability to accelerate the speed at which it can identify new opportunities, coordinate individuals and teams around them, and drive new products and services to market. This has led to oft-quoted mantras such as "fail fast, fail often".

However, the urge to move quickly leads organizations to frequently take shortcuts, and to intentionally or unintentionally implement sub-optimal solutions that offer short-term gains for the sake of getting to the next stage of the project. Too often, such decisions leave behind the seeds of longer-term problems that must be addressed eventually. This can be described as introducing a 'debt' to be repaid. They can include:

— **Technical debt.** Organizations create technical debt when designing and implementing solutions without sufficient attention to the architectural decisions that can constrain the system's future evolution. Widely examined,[45] technical debt occurs due to the pressure to release new capabilities quickly and without a clear understanding of future needs.

— **Organizational debt.** Cultural change driven by rapid growth or restructuring can render organizational structures and practices inadequate for supporting future needs. To maintain momentum, however, many companies avoid the difficult questions of people, power, and processes. Such situations must eventually be addressed to align cultural and structural aspects with the execution of short- and long-term strategies.

— **Skills debt.** It is critical for organizations to sustain a staff of digitally enabled workers, but a lack of focus on training and education would greatly inhibit success in digital transformation. This skills debt requires future investment to bring in new hires with the necessary background and to refresh the skills of existing workers.

— **Financial debt.** Most frequently, the concept of debt is associated with financial matters. In most organizations, particularly those in the start-up phase, accumulating financial debt is necessary to support investment and growth. Unfortunately, most start-ups fail mainly due to their inability to address this debt effectively, leading to unsustainable negative cashflow.[46]

Debt can be overcome by explicit action, including refactoring and restructuring more robust solutions appropriate to the specific contexts. Unfortunately, in the excitement and turmoil of digital transformation, too many organizations pay insufficient attention to the forms of debt they have accumulated, and avoid planning for the time when such debts need to be repaid.

Failure to recognize common patterns of breakages

Our experience with many digital transformation initiatives enables us to identify common failure patterns that must be avoided. In particular, the 'boiling frog syndrome' that underlies many of these failures: slowly unravelling initiatives affecting multiple levels in the organization that are left unaddressed until the initiative becomes unsustainable.

This syndrome is quite common and presents a recurrent challenge to successful digital initiatives. Richard Durnall, a principal analyst with leading global digital transformation organization Thoughtworks, observed that the substantive culture change inherent in digital transformation faces a common order of failures, often in the following sequence:[47]

1. **The people break.** Resistance to change is common with any new way of working. Agile, open team practices can deeply affect existing culture and values and result in strong pushback from disorientated individuals.
2. **The tools break.** Most business processes are not targeted at rapid delivery cycles and extensive experimentation in creating new products and services. Tooling can severely inhibit agile ways of operating if not aligned with innovative practices.
3. **The governance breaks.** The measures and metrics used to govern assume a traditional view of project progress and success. Adjustments are required to provide a balance between governed progress and the need for fast-learning cycles.
4. **The customer breaks.** Any rapid delivery cycle demands more frequent feedback from customers and other stakeholders. Getting the input needed to learn is essential. Yet many consumer-supplier relationships do not readily support such interactions that when introduced, place added pressure on fragile customer relationships.
5. **The financial controls break.** Product funding cycles are frequently based on progress through various stage-gates such as 'design complete', and 'first customer shipment'. In more agile delivery cycles, progress may be less directly measured, with flexibility required to continue funding activities with different risk profiles delivering functionality in small slices.

6. **The organizational structure breaks.** Eventually the organization's management structure becomes stressed when empowered teams interact directly with consumers in rapid iterations of new product features. The command-and-control view of decision-making can be directly at odds with the shifting, priority-based delivery model of agile teams.

Focusing on details without addressing core cultural themes

Any digital transformation initiative must address the different aspects of organizational change, as the scale and impact of such activities can be rather overwhelming. Faced with this, the temptation is to dive into the details by applying complex project planning and management techniques aimed at coordinating each key task, assigning resources to projects, and introducing new governance processes. While many of these well-intentioned actions are useful, there is a danger of the organization losing sight of the bigger picture; the cultural and structural change necessary for success. Rather than improving creativity and productivity, enabling the workforce with new digital technologies and empowering them with more flexible team-based processes can risk the organization going out of control.

Leaders in digital transformation projects must resist becoming obsessed with the transformation details, so that they are able to continually focus on the primary inhibitors they face. In particular, it is essential that leaders 'walk the talk' by clearly demonstrating the values they tell the rest of the organization are essential to their digital future: transparency, honest interactions, and encouraging risk-taking. In company cultures, there are five areas of particular concern that can hinder digital transformation:[48]

– **Slow or stalled decision-making.** Often, the broad rhetoric of moving quickly and avoiding long decision-making cycles is not backed by the management teams leading the organization. Whether this is due to internal politics, competing priorities, or attempts to reach consensus, it can leave those within the organization confused about whether they are truly empowered for local decision-making. Without management support they would typically avoid taking the initiative for action and revert to hierarchical behaviors.

– **Inability to prove business value.** The risk-averse culture prevalent in many organizations leads to a lack of initiative when faced with decisions without clear near-term impact. In a digital economy there is often a more subtle set of indicators that must be employed. If leaders in the organization insist on traditional return on investment calculations, the resulting lack of senior management sponsorship risks choking the stream of new ideas.

— **Too much focus on technology.** Management discussions on digital transformation without clear ownership of their activities too often end up as IT-led initiatives based on technology refreshment. Leaders of organizations must be willing to address the deep cultural and operational changes necessary to shift how people think and work in a digital age.

— **Lack of understanding of operational issues.** The importance of digital technologies to business today means new skills and capabilities are required. Leaders often do not invest sufficient personal time and energy to understanding digital technologies and their implications for business operations. A high-level understanding of digital transformation is insufficient for effective decision-making; leaders must be able to navigate from digital theory to practice.

— **Fear of losing control.** Opening up organizations through greater transparency and improved knowledge-sharing is at the heart of digital transformation. Yet many leaders and managers struggle in practice when they realize that often they will not be the center point for information and decision-making. Encouraging workers to take initiative also requires leaders who trust them to make the right judgements and support them in understanding the opportunities and responsibilities this brings.

Lessons and Observations

Digitally driven disruption and the uncertainties they bring has placed many mature organizations at a disadvantage when they face the new generation of challengers that has sprung up since the start of the 21st century, with operating models and capabilities to exploit digital technologies, delivering products and services as 'born digital' organizations. This new generation, competing in new ways to deliver value to their customers, has compelled management theorists and practitioners to reconsider how businesses work and what is required for them to sustain success.

The disorientation experienced by many established organizations can be attributed to the reshaping of the principles on which their business activities are based. One of their most challenging aspects is the need to rebalance several levers of business. Consequently, engaging in any digital transformation requires organizations to address a series of fundamental paradoxes. Here we highlight five that summarize the profound challenge to management thinking.

Paradox 1: Being comfortable with being uncomfortable

The primary feature of the digital economy is a lack of clarity about the nature and depth of the disruption faced by individuals, companies, and society as a whole. All we can assert with any confidence is that the VUCA nature of digital transformation requires organizations to accept this uncertainty and invest in recognizing the signals that may indicate the onset of substantial changes in their business environment.

The emphasis, therefore, is on adopting leadership and management approaches optimized for situations of massive uncertainty. Processes and techniques that have been successful in the past may not be sufficient. Where they could have been essential in situations that call for stability and certainty, they may now be inadequate when there is a lack of relevant experience, inconclusive data, and highly unreliable trends. A move toward greater flexibility based on experimentation is necessary to encourage a culture of continual learning.

Predicting the future is difficult, sufficiently so that some believe the best approach is not to wait, but "to invent the future for yourself".[49] More than simply an offhand remark, this statement is an appeal to organizations not to lose hope in thinking about future possibilities. Rather, it suggests the opposite: all organizations need to have a bold vision and to make projections about how it could be realized given current understanding and expectations. The goal must be to identify meaningful short-term actions that can help the organization increasingly understand the validity of that vision and the paths toward its attainment.

Paradox 2: Keeping control by owning less

Many questions are being asked about the appropriate shape and form of an organization fit for a digital economy. At its most simplistic, it has been argued that the advantages of a larger organization's scale and reach are outweighed in a digital economy by a smaller organization's flexibility and speed of change.[50]

Operational agility is not just a function of size. Questions can also be raised about an organization's assets. Many organizations operate successfully without owning physical assets such as warehouses, trucks, stores and computing infrastructure. Acquiring these capabilities 'as services' to be consumed as and when required can bring operational elasticity without sacrificing control. If these capabilities are not considered essential to differentiating a company from its competition, then the investment and resources allocated to owning them may be better directed elsewhere.

Such thinking extends to a company's workforce. Organizations can adopt a similarly flexible approach to building skills and capabilities. Many companies, for example, source their critical digital talent from third-party service providers, or use temporary flexible contracts to fulfil needs on an ad hoc basis.

To operate successfully in such an environment requires that the organization acquires new skills to assemble a viable ecosystem, curate services that meet its needs, and manage their performance. The future of organizations may well be smaller core teams but with the support of much wider networks of associates and partners working together through a variety of means, coordinated dynamically around opportunities as they arise, and encouraged with novel, mutually beneficial incentive mechanisms.

Paradox 3: Strengthening the organization through exposing weaknesses

A key part of successful digital transformation activities is bringing together previously siloed groups through improved communication and transparency. There are many positive consequences of individuals and teams working together more closely, cooperating more effectively, and synchronizing tasks to avoid duplication and confusion. However, many organizations recognize that the transparency provided by this open approach also exposes a number of shortcomings in their processes, management, and operations.

Typically, the siloed nature of many organizations is a response to a natural, explicit decision to cluster tasks with common aims, and to ensure that teams have local control over all aspects of their tasks. Locally made decisions are optimized for the constrained environment in which the team operates. The breaking of these silos due to digital transformation will often shed light upon existing differences in structure, processes, and performance. While there is opportunity to promote best practices, greater attention is also directed at problematic areas. The organization must have a certain level of resilience to deal with such access and provide measures to contextualize the information so that it does not distract from the progress being made.

These internal challenges are also seen externally. Digital transformation often involves efforts to connect more closely with customers, engage in co-creative tasks, and share much more information with partners and other stakeholders. Greater stakeholder access to the company's day-to-day activities establishes a relationship of trust, creating a stronger bond across the organizational ecosystem and increasing the company's core capabilities.

However, many of those in leadership may find this move to greater openness challenging. At its worst they may see it as a threat to their competitive position, and an unnecessary step that exposes internal organizational detail best kept under lock and key.

Paradox 4: Ensuring a future by ignoring the plan

The planning process is a central element of many organizations. A great deal of effort and attention is directed toward prioritizing outstanding requests, determining how a problem will be addressed, decomposing it into tasks that must be carried out, allocating resources, monitoring each task's progress, and performing the interventions necessary to adjust those tasks to ensure successful completion. The focus is to create plans that act as blueprints for the organization's future.

Varied in form and detail, these plans are an essential artifact for many organizations. They are often high-profile documents, produced as the centerpiece of elaborate multi-year activity cycles. However, for many organizations the plans can become straightjackets restricting their ability to adjust to changing circumstances. Deviation from the plan is considered a failure. Digital transformation initiatives, however, recognize that the unpredictability of the environment in which plans are created deeply influences their value and utility. So much so that in highly volatile situations, some organizations believe that any plan is likely to be misleading.

Digitally disrupted domains face the challenge of adapting to unpredictable environments. The resulting agile methods have a reputation for increasing flexibility, but often at the cost of adding significant unpredictability into the planning process. Much of the debate around their adoption and scaling centers on how this flexibility can be maintained while adding greater governance.

How do you plan for a future you are struggling to predict? Addressing this question is the basis for planning approaches that encourage greater experimentation within a rigorous framework for using the results obtained to determine next steps. Short time-boxed investigations allow the organization to learn quickly, adjusting frequently as the journey proceeds. Progress is determined by increasing the speed and depth of learning at the lowest possible cost.[51]

Balancing short- and long-term success in digital transformation is essential, and it is important to recognize that plans and the planning process must not be abandoned. However, their role and significance should be reviewed. While a plan may have tremendous importance as a short-term operational artifact, in most cases the planning process is more significant as a longer-term cultural and structural ritual that engages and informs everyone in the organization about the relevant priorities and perspectives.

Paradox 5: Maintaining stability while embracing change

Organizational structures have a significant impact on the way an organization communicates, makes decisions, architects products and services, and on how it is perceived by its customers. From a cultural perspective, structure both reflects and determines many aspects of the day-to-day activities in which workers are employed. Digitally disrupted domains raise new challenges to understanding the appropriate organizational structures that can help balance the need for clear management and decision-making with the flexibility to adapt to varied and evolving contexts.

Emerging theories about radical management structures are making it possible to organize business activities around customer-facing opportunities driven by achieving outcomes that optimize customer satisfaction. Similarly, approaches such as "servant-leadership" are inverting traditional hierarchical styles to democratize key aspects of the management's role in recognizing how important collaboration and teamwork can be when an organization needs to move at speed to deliver successful solutions.[52] Building such flexibility into the organizational infrastructure ensures that it maintains relevance in complex changing circumstances.

Summary and Conclusions

Digital transformation is more than a mere technology upgrade. It encompasses the cultural and organizational changes required to adjust to digitally savvy consumers and embraces the use of new digital technologies to enable major improvements to user services, streamline operations, or create entirely new market offerings. The challenge then, for most large-scale organizations, is how best to plan and execute the strategic changes necessary to survive the disruption that digital transformation brings.[53]

Many organizations lack the structure and experience with digital technologies to make significant progress in this transformation, as evidenced in a recent study by MIT Sloan School.[54] Its analysis confirmed that approaches to digital transformation differ significantly depending on the organization's maturity with digital technology deployment. This analysis found that 79% of organizations can still be classed as low maturity in terms of digital transformation. They may have made efforts in adopting digital technologies but have done so without considering the broader transformational implications of such a move.

Here we have considered digital transformation in terms of an organization's structure, the key principles on which management and leadership are based, and the cultural implications for change when undertaking the digital transformation journey. This requires a combination of technology and business model innovation, and a major change in operating models. If organizations are to relieve growing internal and external pressures to accelerate delivery of new products and services, they need to rethink, redesign and optimize their approach, and place the client at the center of their activities. They need to move rapidly and effectively away from outdated business models, management approaches, cultures, and processes inherited from earlier eras, to increase flexibility and adaptability necessary for a digital age.

References

1 Chopra, A. (2016). *Innovative State: How New Technologies Can Transform Government*. Grove Press.

2 O'Reilly, T. (2010). *Government-as-a-Platform*. Innovations 6(1). Available at: https:// www. mitpressjournals.org/doi/pdfplus/10.1162/INOV_a_00056

3 Chesbrough, H. (2006). *Open Innovation: The New Imperative for Creating and Profiting from Technology*. Harvard Business Press.

4 Anthony, S.D. (2009). *Constant Transformation is the New Normal*. Harvard Business Review. Available at: https://hbr.org/2009/10/constant-change-is-the-new-nor

5 Prahalad, D. and Bagrodia, K. (2012). *Leading Change in the "New Normal"*. Harvard Business Review. Available at: https://hbr.org/2012/01/leading-change-in-the-new-norm

6 Christensen, C. (1997). *The Innovator's Dilemma: When New Technologies Cause Great Firms to Fail*. Harvard Business School Press.

7 A favorite saying of technology entrepreneurs, credited to Thomas Edison.

8 Plant, R. and Willcocks, L. (2007). Critical Success Factors in International ERP Implementations: A Case Research Approach, *Journal of Computer Information Systems*, 47: 60-70.

9 Doerr, J. (2017). *Measure What Matters: OKRs – the Simple Idea that Drives 10x Growth*. Google Books.

10 https://rework.withgoogle.com/guides/set-goals-with-okrs/steps/introduction/

11 Denning, S. (2010). *The Leaders Guide to Radical Management*. Jossey-Bass.

12 https://en.wikipedia.org/wiki/Adhocracy

13 Toffler, A. (1973). *Future Shock*. Pan Books.

14 Birkinshaw, J. and Ridderstrale, J. (2017). *Fast/Forward: Make Your Company Fit for the Future*. Stanford Business Books.

15 Kotter, J.P. (2012). *Accelerate!* Harvard Business Review, November.

16 Tushman, M.L., and O'Reilly, C.A. (1996). Ambidextrous Organizations: Managing Evolutionary and Revolutionary Change, *California Management Review*, 38(4): 8-29.

17 Schaffer, R. (2017). *All Management is Change Management*. Harvard Business Review, October.

18 Kotter, J.P. (2014). *Accelerate: Building Strategic Agility for a Faster-Moving World*. Harvard Business School Press.

19 Cameron, K., and Quinn, R. (2011). *Diagnosing and Changing Organizational Culture*. Jossey-Bass.

20 Drucker, P. (2007). *Management Challenges for the 21st Century* (Classic Drucker Collection). Routledge.

21 G. Hamel (2012). *What Matters Now? Josey*-Bass.

22 Kotter, J.P. (2014). *Accelerate: Building Strategic Agility for a Faster-Moving World*. Harvard Business School Press.

23 Jaruzelski, B., Loehr, J. and Holman, H. (2011). *The Global Innovation 1000: Why Culture is Key*. Strategy + Business, Winter, Issue 65. Available at: https://www.strategy-business.com/article/11404?gko=62080

24 Kane, G.C. et al., (2017). *Achieving Digital Maturity. Sloan Management Review*, July 13. Available at: https://sloanreview.mit.edu/projects/achieving-digital-maturity/

25 Brooks, F. (1995). *The Mythical Man-Month: Essays on Software Engineering, Anniversary Edition*. Addison Wesley.

26 Forrester (2016). *Leading Digital Business Transformation Report*, March.

27 McKinsey (2009). *Enduring Ideas: The Three Horizons of Growth*. McKinsey Quarterly. Available at: https://www.mckinsey.com/business-functions/strategy-and-corporate-finance/our-insights/enduring-ideas-the-three-horizons-of-growth

28 Blank, S. (2015). *Lean Innovation Management – Making Corporate Innovation Work*. SteveBlank.com. Available at: http://steveblank.com/2015/06/26/lean-innovation-management-making-corporate-innovation-work/

29 Leberecht, T. (2016). *Make Your Strategy More Agile*. Harvard Business Review, October.

30 Ries, E. (2017). *The Startup Way: How Entrepreneurial Management Transforms Culture and Drives Growth*. Penguin.

31 Consultancy.uk (2018). *Digital Skills Gap Could Cost UK £141 Billion in GDP Growth*. Consultancy.uk. Available at: https://www.consultancy.uk/news/18895/digital-skills-gap-could-cost-uk-1415-billion-in-gdp-growth

32 https://technation.techcityuk.com/digital-skills-jobs/digital-skills-shortage/

33 https://gds.blog.gov.uk/about/ and https://www.codeforamerica.org/

34 Tansley, C. and Sempik, A. (2008). *Talent Management: Design, Implementation and Evaluation*. CIPD.

35 Fujitsu (2017). The Digital Transformation PACT Report. Available at: https://www.fujitsu.com/global/microsite/digital-cocreation/insight/pact/

36 Gillespie, P. (2017). *Intuit: Gig Economy is 34% of US Workforce*. CNN Business. Available at: http://money.cnn.com/2017/05/24/news/economy/gig-economy-intuit

37 Dery, K., Sebastian, I.M.., and van der Meulen, N. (2017). The Digital Workplace Is Key to Digital Innovation. *MIS Quarterly Executive,* 16(2): 135-152.

38 Hamel, G. (2012). *What Matters Now*. Josey Bass.

39 Birkinshaw, J. and Ridderstrale, J. (2017). *Fast/Forward: Make Your Company Fit for the Future*. Stanford Business Books

40 Perkin, P. and Abraham, P. (2017). *Building the Agile Business Through Digital Transformation*. Kogan Page.

41 Péladeau, P., Herzog, M.and Acker, O. (2017). *The New Class of Digital Leaders. Strategy + Business,* Autumn (88). Available at: https://www.strategy-business.com/article/The-New-Class-of-Digital-Leaders

42 Hofstede, G. (1991). *Cultures and Organizations: Software of the Mind*. London, UK: McGraw-Hill.

43 Schein, E.H. (2010). *Organizational Culture and Leadership*. Jossey-Bass.

44 Burke, W.W. (2017). *Organizational Change: Theory and Practice, 5th Edition,* Jossey Boss.

45 See, for example, https://www.sei.cmu.edu/architecture/research/arch_tech_debt

46 For example, http://time.com/money/3888448/cash-flow-small-business-startups/

47 Smith, D. (2016). *Agile Adoption Patterns*. Medium. Available at: https://medium.com/rootpath/agile-adoption-patterns-724fb921945f

48 McConnell, J. (2015). *The Company Cultures that Help (or Hinder) Digital Transformation*. Harvard Business Review, August.

49 A widely-used comment originally attributed to Alan Kay, https://www.forbes.com/sites/chunkamui/2017/04/04/7-steps-for-inventing-the-future

50 Mele, J. (2013). *The End of Big: How the Internet makes David the New Goliath*. St Martin's Press.

51 Ries, E. (2011). *The Lean Startup: How Constant Innovation Creates Radically Successful Businesses*. Penguin.

52 Greenleaf, R.K. (2002). *Servant Leadership: A Journey into the Nature of Legitimate Power and Greatness*. Paulist Press.

53 Janssen, M. and Estevez, E. (2013). Lean Government and Platform-Based Governance: Doing More with Less. *Government Information Quarterly*, 30(1): S1–S8.
54 See http://sloanreview.mit.edu/article/the-advantages-of-digital-maturity/

Part 3: **building for success**

8 A Case Study in Digital Transformation

Introduction

Digital transformation projects take many forms and exhibit diverse characteristics. In some situations, the priority may be to deliver operational efficiencies to reduce costs and improve flexibility. In others, there may be an urgent need to accelerate product delivery into a disrupted marketplace. Or the attention may be focused on redefining the products and services to satisfy an evolving set of stakeholder expectations. For many organizations however, the emphasis is on changing their attitudes and practices to be more responsive to the demands of the environment in which they operate, and to speed up all aspects of their business. Hence, agility is frequently the cornerstone of digital transformation.

As discussed in Chapter 5, organizations of all sizes are committing to agile approaches to improve speed of delivery and transform their decision-making processes to remain competitive in the digital economy. Already the preferred methodology for accelerated and risk-reduced software development, agile approaches are now used to improve project management and decision-making, even in areas unrelated to technology. However, data on the current state of agile adoption offers a mixed picture.

Organizations are seeing agile success primarily at the project level, according to the VersionOne Annual State of Agile Report,[1] the most comprehensive study into agile adoption. Now in its 12th year, the most recent edition highlights a number of important trends, including the fact that the scaling of agile approaches across multiple delivery teams and within an organization's broader management functions remains largely fragmented and inconsistent. A wide variety of approaches to scaling were reported, with the Scaled Agile Framework (SAFe) being the most frequently cited; 29% of respondents say that SAFe is the method they "follow most closely", with "scrums of scrums", Disciplined Agile Delivery (DaD), Large Scale Scrum (LeSS), and Nexus some way behind.

This poses a problem for organizations looking for best practices to build on their initial experiences of agile delivery. Although a great deal has been written about agile adoption, there are many idealizations and anecdotes but remarkably few detailed case studies and empirically based strategies (a notable exception being the Ericsson case study[2] discussed in Chapter 4). This is particularly true when scaling agile is not simply seen as increasing the number of agile delivery teams, but also as raising the profile and impact of agile practices across other management practices within a landscape of broader digital transformation activities.

To offer a deeper perspective, this chapter considers a digital transformation case study at DigiTran, a UK-based software and systems delivery organization in the transportation sector.[3] Due to its history and market position, focus was placed on the opportunities and challenges of adopting agile ways of working across several business units and management functions. Consequently, for this case study there is a strong emphasis on analyzing agile delivery at DigiTran. From this analysis, we deduce a series of principles for digital transformation through scaling agile delivery, and explore the implications for DigiTran's management and organizational structures. The chapter concludes with a summary of DigiTran's management and organizational journey in digital transformation.

Digital Transformation in Context

Like many organizations, DigiTran is not new to digital technologies; it is in fact well advanced in its digital transformation. This is particularly true with regard to its use of digital sensing and monitoring devices for dynamic capacity planning, process control, resource scheduling, and real-time conflict management. DigiTran has a successful history of creating and installing digitally powered control and monitoring solutions based on high availability software-intensive systems. Over several years, its software teams have successfully adopted methodologies that allow for continuous development, sprint-based working, and accelerated delivery processes. Long-standing members of these teams have moved to best-practice agile models, joined by new agile-first staff.

This has been quite some undertaking. DigiTran offers far from a traditional transaction-based software environment, and several important contextual characteristics have shaped its approach to agile adoption. Understanding these characteristics is at the heart of the challenges that DigiTran faces in accelerating its adoption of agile practices throughout the organization.

First, the majority of DigiTran's ongoing software development is in performing maintenance tasks. Systems have been created and deployed over extended periods of time, in a wide variety of technologies. They are embedded into contexts where systems have multi-year deployment horizons, may be difficult to access for maintenance and upgrade, and are managed through long safety-focused procedures largely out of DigiTran's direct control and authority. Hence, much of what DigiTran does is not easily amenable to agile practices, and this is unlikely to change in the near term, if at all.

Second, DigiTran is developing software-intensive systems where software, as a key part of a broader system, is embedded in complex hardware, integrated with a variety of existing systems of different heritage, and operated in a complicated socio-technical, human-centric environment that combines manual and automated activities. All of this supports a domain in which system performance, safety, dependability, and reliability is paramount. A systems engineering approach and culture pervades the organization.

Third, DigiTran operates principally in a waterfall-based, long-termist, slow-moving sector. Domains such as aerospace, defense, transportation, and industrial process control have a primary view of projects as being large, complex, multi-year construction efforts. Consequently, clients still rely on traditional models that involve rigid delivery dates, inflexible budgets and 'big release' expectations. Aligning with client expectations is critical to success. Therefore, for DigiTran to move toward more agile delivery models requires the client (and others in the supply chain) to also adjust their ways of working. Encouraging and aligning this shift in approach is far from straightforward.

In addition, there are considerable constraints playing upon DigiTran's offering: in a number of its main markets, industry is heavily-regulated, with state-owned or state-funded infrastructure, and with little appetite or incentives to adopt the 'fail-fast' fluency of agile. Beyond external constraints, DigiTran has its own structural opponents of rapidly scaling agile; it has a long history of waterfall delivery, a demanding set of client expectations, and is run by newcomers to the methodology. None of these factors are unusual, especially for the kinds of industry in which DigiTran operates, but they frequently dominate strategic decision-making and must be accommodated as expectations are set.

DigiTran's Digital Transformation Journey

As with all complex change projects, a variety of activities have taken place at DigiTran over a multi-year period. To gain a deeper understanding of DigiTran's digital transformation journey, four key dimensions must be explored: their restructuring of tasks around products rather than projects; introduction of outcome-based contracts; adoption of a risk-managed approach for decision-making; and restructuring of management from hierarchical command-and-control toward empowered teams.

Project to product

Perhaps DigiTran's most profound transformation is in recognizing the implications of a product focus on strategy and delivery. DigiTran's business operations are determined by the way it has historically created project teams to bid on requests for proposals and invitations to tender. A great deal of their operating model and business practices are centered around the rhythm and working practices associated with competing for these bids, delivering to contracts negotiated around the capabilities they describe, and supporting long-term maintenance of deployed systems. All aspects of delivery are evaluated and valued according to the project's contractually-agreed scope and delivery parameters.

In contrast, a product focus requires a different set of priorities and optimizations to be made by the delivery teams and the different stakeholders across the organization. Products have a life independent of the specific contracts for which they are supplied. Furthermore, products and product delivery teams may simultaneously support multiple delivery contexts. A new set of rules, compromises, and decision-making procedures is necessary; hence it was a priority for DigiTran to put this in place across the whole organization.

Consequently, DigiTran enacted three fundamental changes to support their focus on products. The first involved a reorganization of the group structures away from project teams and toward product teams. The second was to explicitly create a common product framework extracted from several previous project assets, maintained by a dedicated team and shared across several delivered product variants. The third was to reshape incentives to support the stability, quality, and utility of the products being delivered independent of specific deployment contracts.

Output to outcome

DigiTran began a process to change many of the metrics and measures it uses to define progress so that they are aimed more directly at understanding the impact of outcomes rather than on meeting poorly defined requirements. In support of this, they also have created extensive progress reporting tools focused on learning more about improvements to the outcomes achieved with their products in areas such as usability, understandability, and maintainability. Some of this change is driven by new kinds of contract arrangements that incorporate a shared set of rewards amongst stakeholders for achieving certain targets. Other drivers aimed at creating a product focus further define these success measures. Two particular challenges can, however, be observed with this move regarding incentives and product ownership.

At present, the behaviors of DigiTran's workers are not always well-aligned to these new incentive models. After many years of viewing their performance through traditional productivity measures, the company's workers need help in understanding how their activities contribute toward organizational goals and contract specifications. For example, developers on a project often see their role in heroic terms where their response to last-minute client requests for changes build credibility and enhance their position in the organization. 'The client is always right' means that success is closely bound to reaction to exceptions and a fire-fighting mentality. However, it may be more appropriate for individuals to say 'no' or 'not now' when moving to a product focus. Broader concerns come into play where the outcome desired by all parties must be taken into account. Support for strong product ownership and management is critical, while workers with the right mentality and skills is essential. The organization's culture must evolve to reflect this.

Strong product ownership brings further challenges to DigiTran. A focus on outcome rather than output means there may well be more ambiguity and uncertainty in day-to-day decisions, particularly with regard to delivery objectives. Historically, DigiTran has a small, experienced, strong leadership team driving decisions in a fairly dominant top-down style. This has resulted in a corporate culture where those at the lower ranks of the organization do not readily accept their own decision-making responsibilities and may feel their voices are not heard when they do step forward. They are hesitant and unsure of their leadership credentials. An outcome-based approach will only be successful if all those in the organization work together toward common goals and bring their experience and energy to maximize delivery.

Risk avoidance to risk management

Sectors that are dependable and safety-critical are generally risk-averse and hence tend to adopt a disciplined approach where all areas of risk are identified and removed. Agile practices, however, take a different approach to risk. Fundamental to an agile philosophy is that uncertainty and ambiguity cannot be avoided; they must be managed. Through a combination of empiricism and short, time-boxed iterations, an agile approach recognizes that there are many unknowns in any development activity which become better understood through a process of progressive disclosure.

At DigiTran, like many organizations rooted in an engineering culture, help will be required to educate all those involved in delivery activities on how to handle risk. Agile practices are disciplined and highly governed. Yet many traditional engineers believe the opposite: that agile is chaotic and avoids responsibility for managing risks. The only viable way forward has been to initiate honest, open dialogue around the discipline of agile practices to address these concerns. These discussions now involve all parties, both advocates and sceptics, in the hopes that they will lead to an acceptance of agile approaches, particularly in key areas of risk management.

Commanding to coordinating

As mentioned earlier, DigiTran practices a top-down, hierarchical management style. Much of the company's success has been a consequence of strong leadership, deep knowledge of the industry gained over many years, and a maniacal focus on meeting delivery specifications and timelines. These are characteristics to be applauded and celebrated. However, it is inevitable that over time, the disruption in digital technologies, business models, and working practices have rendered some of these characteristics obsolete. Guarding against the use of outdated management practices is essential. In defining one of the most well-cited innovation theories of the past decade, the innovator's dilemma, Clayton Christensen described how continuing to pursue the strategies that made an organization successful may eventually lead to its downfall.[4] This is particularly true with management styles and approaches in agile transformation.

Consequently, DigiTran is moving toward adopting a coordinating leadership approach where agile delivery teams are empowered to use their skills and experiences to self-organize around the problems and opportunities they face. As they are the ones deeply involved in delivery, they are encouraged to take responsibility for all aspects of it. The critical issue is to ensure that those in traditional management and leadership roles understand and evolve their responsibilities alongside those of the agile teams. If not, confusion and ill-will could derail progress. Many organizations undergoing agile transformation struggle not because they cannot build high-functioning agile teams, but because they do not establish leadership and management practices that are well adapted to an agile delivery philosophy. As a result, experienced leaders and managers feel disempowered, obsolete, and bypassed.

DigiTran's Principles of Digital Transformation

The digital transformation at DigiTran, while centered on agile practices, has provided insights into a broader set of principles for digital transformation that impact many aspects of the organization. By taking an incremental approach, DigiTran has found that bringing agility to an organization often begins with a small, contained project that adopts agile development practices within a limited set of teams. As the rhythm of delivery adapts to this approach, new teams are created, and the project is expanded to subsume related activities or capabilities. Frequently, however, this is where many organizations experience significant problems, as the scale of managing multiple agile teams overwhelms the organization's ability to coordinate its actions within the context of its broader constraints.

Far from being a problem of growing the agile teams (which naturally expand anyway), the main challenge lies with *aligning* those agile initiatives with the digital transformation affecting the whole of the organization. Similarly, organizational constraints, particularly those related to management, project investment, and prevailing client expectations, can stunt the growth of agile adoption. Critically, management practices aimed at governing and supporting traditional project teams are not well-matched to the agile delivery processes being introduced. Consequently, frustrations arise; from the agile development teams because they see the rest of the organization intent on dampening the energy and vitality they are injecting into the delivery process, and from the management team as they struggle to fit the new approaches into existing management practices, where the perceived lack of rigor and predictability is viewed as out of step with the rest of the organization.

DigiTran's experiences, echoing those of many other organizations undergoing digital transformation, confirm that undertaking significant efforts to adopt agile approaches beyond the software development and delivery functions require a varied approach with respect to pace, impact, and value. Hence, a set of important lessons can be extracted to guide those in similar circumstances.

Lesson 1: Principles of leadership must change

Classically organized hierarchical models of management are optimized for rigorous command-and-control; responsibilities and authority are largely held at higher levels and those lower in the hierarchy work within strict limits.

Agile practices require a *different form of governance* that tries to push more of the responsibility and authority into the teams doing the work. The flexibility of teams to self-organize around the problems they are solving requires the *whole organization* to review its understanding of values and principles to ensure that new forms of governance are understood, welcomed, and incorporated into its broader culture. In other words, *organizations need to change for agile to work.* At the very least, the barriers between clients, management and the agile workforce must be eliminated; even if they are not willing to change, clients and managers must be able to see what this change requires of them, and how the tensions that will be experienced can be addressed.

Hierarchical management structures frequently struggle in organizations adopting agile practices. This is because hierarchies work well when those in higher positions are the most experienced and informed about the tasks being carried out, but may not be the case for fast-moving, technically-demanding environments, where different forms of leadership style may be more appropriate.

For many agile organizations the concept of servant leadership is particularly helpful in understanding how to manage teams. In its purest form, the servant leader focuses on sharing power by putting the needs of others first, and by helping people develop and perform as effectively as possible. More practically, agile teams rely on leaders to be willing to encourage and empower those around them to accept responsibilities for shared problem-solving, delivery discipline, and knowledge-sharing. These skills, however, need time and support to flourish in many leaders.

On an operational level, many organizations face the challenge that their leadership teams too often believe that while agile thinking is required by *the rest* of the organization, it does not have material impact on the way the leadership team itself operates. In fact, agile transformation requires new ways of working across *all levels* in the organization. This is well summarized by Darrell Rigby, Jeff Sutherland, and Andy Noble:[5]

> When leaders haven't themselves understood and adopted agile approaches, they may try to scaleup agile the way they have attacked other change initiatives: through top-down plans and directives. The track record is better when they behave like an agile team. That means viewing various parts of the organization as their customers—people and groups whose needs differ, are probably misunderstood, and will evolve as agile takes hold. The executive team sets priorities and sequences opportunities to improve those customers' experiences and increase their success. Leaders plunge in to solve problems and remove constraints rather than delegate that work to subordinates. The agile leadership team, like any other agile team, has an "initiative owner" who is responsible for overall results and a facilitator who coaches team members and helps keep everyone actively engaged.

Lesson 2: The operating architecture must improve

The technical underpinnings for product delivery must be reshaped. Establishing a shared set of concepts for architecture and design is one of the most difficult aspects for organizations undergoing digital transformation. The heritage of many organizations lies in relatively static, centralized or layered architectural models. In contrast, recent approaches to software architecture focus heavily on orchestrations of microservices and the creation of externally accessible capabilities that can be dynamically knitted together via their APIs.

The principles of designing service-based solutions have been explored for years, and well-established practices are emerging to ensure such systems are secure, stable, and performant. However, the operational implications for organizations adopting service-based approaches are broader than software architecture. Systems created as networks of interacting services require significant new approaches to support how they are designed, tested, and evolved.

As monolithic software transitions from static, central coordination and control to a dynamic network of fluent, independent and interrelated microservices, centralized command-and-control organizations transition to networks of teams working transparently in the open. It is often found that there is a symbiotic relationship between the products being shipped and the structure of the organization responsible for them; sometimes referred to as Conway's Law.[6] For example, classical hierarchical structures align well where an Enterprise Service Bus (ESB) is used to hierarchically manage interactions between technology components. They do not work efficiently for systems where peer-to-peer services with collaboratively designed APIs are used. It is no accident that this architectural shift is occurring while there is also a transition from top-down hierarchical management to autonomous multi-disciplinary teams operating as meritocracies. The evolution of systems architecture and organizational structures are mutually reinforcing.

These changes present two different kinds of challenges to managers at companies such as DigiTran. First, most managers in engineering-based organizations have risen through the ranks and their current high-level position is due to their experience and demonstrated engineering skills over an extended period of time. Introducing a new architectural paradigm for systems engineering poses a challenge to their position. They frequently find themselves in an uncomfortable position where they are not the main expert in the room and cannot draw on their years of experience to identify and solve problems. In the worst cases, an intellectual battle takes place between those proposing the new paradigm and those who see it as undermining their position.

Second, the classic project team model may be less relevant for decentralized architectural models. Function-based organizational models typically in use (e.g., separate development and test teams) may also need to be reconsidered. Furthermore, a product focus to delivery may have significant impact on how new features are defined, prioritized, allocated, and funded. Agile team roles such as product owner assume responsibility beyond the development aspects of the product features to include tasks that are normally the purview of others across the organization. Such conflicts must be addressed to avoid confusion and frustration.

Lesson 3: Find the right talent

The speed and growth of many agile organizations are limited by their ability to attract and retain the right talent. For example, DigiTran opened a new office in central London with the intention to attract those with the right digital skills that it had been unable to recruit elsewhere. In digitally disrupted teams the influence of individuals with the right skills is amplified, and innovation and productivity can be very high when they are in place and appropriately supported. Conversely, when they are absent in teams, much of the energy and potential of agile, digital-first approaches is lost.

As a result, talent identification and management are paramount, and for HR departments, many of their talent development functions may require review; from incentive schemes, and learning and development, to progression and career development. Where there is a systemic risk to talent acquisition (which, for engineering organizations such as DigiTran, might be its primary locations far from major urban centres), *all options* must be considered.

We also must accept that with agile ways of working there is a greater need for continual coaching and mentoring across the organization. Training teams in agile delivery is important. But too many organizations expect those teams to be independently operational too quickly, especially in the context of legacy environments with deeply rooted cultures, technologies, and processes. Support from experienced coaches is hence critical to ensure that agile teams can gain experience in an optimal way. In fact, some organizations report that the availability of internal coaches is the critical success factor in their broader adoption of agile practices. As one digital transformation manager recently stated:[7]

> Speed wasn't the problem, but rather, that we didn't have enough internal coaches to support the teams after the initial launch. We had to reorganize and shift the mindset to successfully overcome the challenges our initial roll-out created.

Several management roles require particular attention for agile approaches to flourish in complex organizational environments. Three such roles are worth highlighting with respect to DigiTran:

Product owner. The product owner plays a pivotal role in any agile team. They are accountable for ensuring maximum value is delivered during each sprint. In this role, the focus on 'value' is critical. In the case of DigiTran this holds particular significance in two ways. First, the product owner acts as the intermediary between the agile delivery teams and others within the organization, and between the teams and external stakeholders. This requires the product owner to have significant communication skills, and a broad view of the organization's technical and non-technical success criteria for the product. What is valuable at any point in time must be determined by the product owner across this range of inputs and concerns. Second, the product owner will frequently lead negotiations on focus and priority for the delivery teams. Establishing the right balance and pace in delivery requires significant understanding of when and how to negotiate with diverse internal and external stakeholders. At the center of these negotiations is an understanding of the product's value proposition and its implications for everyone concerned. Consequently, product owners able to succeed in these circumstances are a rare breed.

IP/Contracts manager. Highly regulated industries with complex safety-critical characteristics come with their own particular set of challenges. One area of major concern is how various aspects of Intellectual Property (IP) and contracts are addressed. While such issues may at first glance appear to be rather esoteric and abstract, they frequently have deep implications for many legal and auditing functions that assume a critical role amongst key stakeholders. In situations where it is necessary to interpret whether product deliveries provide the expected capabilities, communicate ongoing progress, and assess the value of specific outcomes, agile approaches can challenge conventional thinking. For organizations used to extensive lists of requirements, multi-year Gantt charts, and shared risk registers, the discipline and governance associated with agile product management techniques are difficult to appreciate. Such problems are exacerbated where product delivery involves complex supply chains and multiple stakeholders. In such circumstances it is essential to ensure that a set of common principles is shared across all parties. This may require the delivery teams to educate the stakeholders on what is and isn't being monitored and reported as the product evolves.

Test/Release manager. Integral to agile approaches is the automation of test and release management, and its tight integration with agile teams. Moving at speed with a sprint-based philosophy will only be successful if the activities required to test and deploy new capabilities are minimized. This aspect of agile delivery is often especially difficult for organizations invested in substantial integration and acceptance test functions. It is essential that testing strategies and approaches take account of these concerns. For example, many organizations in safety-critical domains continue to set up independent testing teams outside of the agile delivery teams. Although from a purist view this goes against the agile principles of multi-disciplinary teams, it may nonetheless be the most practical way to proceed. The goal of this independent testing effort is not to duplicate testing already being carried out by the agile delivery teams, but to identify defects that may have been missed due to conflicts or gaps in the individual team-based testing. This independent test team focuses on investigative and exploratory testing scenarios, production-readiness testing, and addressing other critical use cases. Such approaches are particularly important for regulatory compliance and offer the organization an additional level of comfort and reassurance.

Lesson 4: Review planning phases and budgeting cycles

Sectors such as the aerospace, defense, and transportation industries have multi-year planning horizons, with annual budget reviews governing spending priorities and revenue targets. Key stakeholders in such industries will align around these plans and timeframes. As a result, organizations such as DigiTran will feel bound to operate within a strategic and budgeting framework that governs their activities and priorities in the context of these industry and stakeholder constraints.

Hence in budgetary terms, agility may be more of an aspiration than a reality. Budgeting processes that form the backbone of many organizations are frequently the straightjacket constraining innovation and flexibility when the organization is trying to increase agility. Investment cycles in particular are often damagingly rigid. To overcome these challenges, agile delivery organizations balance the broader strategic framework actions with shorter funding goals, and use an agile budgeting approach that has two different elements.

The first element is to **recognize and separate budgeting of discovery activities from delivery activities**. Steve Blank's lean start-up model[8] emphasizes that discovery should be managed in the style of a "time and materials" contract where the goal is to learn as much as possible about the problem and its potential solutions as efficiently as possible. Only once that understanding is validated (through broad stakeholder agreement) is it advisable to produce a realistic 'fixed price' estimate of the effort and costs required to deliver the agreed outcome. This separation creates an appropriate incentive for both producer and consumer stakeholders.

The second element is to **spread budgeted investment across several alternative solutions,** akin to the way a Venture Capital (VC) firm looks at its investment portfolio. Due to the high level of uncertainty, VC firms will typically invest by understanding the uncertainty and high risks involved, diversify their investment across many potential solutions, and use a well-defined process for quickly closing down those that do not show strong signs of meeting their objectives. This discipline encourages an agile budgeting approach and has been adopted in several organizations such as DigiTran that are delivering products where market needs and success criteria are unstable or ill-defined.

These elements make it possible for an organization's planning and budgeting approaches to become more effectively aligned with the agile delivery practices in place. They also force the organization into a more consistent, integrated strategy and delivery alliance, summarized in the UK Government's Digital Service mantra of "strategy is delivery".[9]

Lesson 5: Recognize and support a dual transformation strategy

Thriving organizations such as DigiTran usually find themselves with a legacy of multiple ongoing projects, client commitments, and multi-year delivery contracts. While these represent a steady revenue stream essential for business stability, it also means that the organization continues to use traditional approaches for its management, contracts, budgets, and delivery. This practice of existing ways of working, even while new activities focus on agile approaches to product delivery, can create a tension within the organization and potentially disrupt many aspects of the day-to-day running of its business. Hence, the need to recognize and maintain two distinct identities can be one of the most difficult strategic challenges facing organizations that are scaling agile practices.

To reconcile these two identities, organizations like DigiTran have attempted a wholesale reinvention of themselves around agile principles, but they are rarely successful.[10] Rather, what is needed is a more measured approach where new activities can aggressively adopt new practices while the organization's core evolves more slowly. Scott Anthony, Clark Gilbert, and Mark Johnson view the challenge as one of dual transformation.[11] It is not simply about creating something new to offer products to new markets; it simultaneously requires a repositioning of core business activities to address the current problems in new ways and ensure revenues are maintained. This combination encourages two different forms of transformation with different objectives, characteristics, and outcomes. Balancing these two objectives takes substantial care to be successful.

Summary and Conclusions

Digital transformation requires many changes to operating practices, processes, management structures, and decision-making. In situations such as DigiTran, where software development and delivery practices play such a large part of the solutions, significant adoption of agile practices are at the core of these changes. Development teams employ new approaches to delivery aimed at optimizing processes toward managing progress in short sprints, increasing visibility, and encouraging feedback and review. More substantially, however, these techniques also introduce a core set of values into the organization's culture: commitment, courage, focus, openness and respect,[12] as summarized by scrum.org, the leading proponent of agile methods. Far from a mechanistic process of introducing new technologies, digital transformation within an organization requires the embodiment of these values to change corporate culture.

DigiTran has continued its digital transformation journey by expanding its use of agile practices and has made significant progress in a relatively short time. This chapter has highlighted important elements of that journey, and extracted key lessons characterizing their experiences. While each digital transformation context will necessarily be different, these lessons provide useful insights to guide all organizations taking this road.

—————

References

1 http://stateofagile.versionone.com/

2 Paasivaara, M., Behm, B., Lassenius, C. and Hallikainen, M. (2018). Large-scale Agile Transformation at Ericsson: A Case Study. *Empirical Software Engineering*, 23(5): 2550-2596. Available at: https://doi.org/10.1007/s10664-017-9555-8

3 For commercial reasons, the name of this company has been anonymized and is referred to throughout as "DigiTran".

4 Christensen, C. (1997). *The Innovator's Dilemma: When New Technologies Cause Great Firms to Fail*. Harvard Business School Press.

5 Rigby, D., Sutherland, J., and Noble, A. (2018). *Agile at Scale*. Harvard Business Review, May-June.

6 https://en.wikipedia.org/wiki/Conway%27s_law

7 Personal communication.

8 Blank, S. (2013). *Why the Lean Startup Changes Everything*. Harvard Business Review.

9 Bracken, M. (2013). *Digital Transformation in 2013: The Strategy is Delivery. Again*. GOV.UK. Available at: https://gds.blog.gov.uk/2013/01/06/digital-transformation-in-2013-the-strategy-is-delivery-again/

10 The only exceptions that we are familiar with involve organizations facing an existential threat; where they find themselves in a "change or die" scenario.

11 Anthony, A., Gilbert, C., and Johnson, M. (2017). *Dual Transformation*. Harvard Business Review Press.

12 West, D. (2016). *Updates to the Scrum Guide: The 5 Scrum Values Take Center Stage*. Scrum.org. Available at: https://www.scrum.org/resources/blog/5-scrum-values-take-center-stage

9 Summary & A Look to the Future

Introduction

For most organizations, delivering digital transformation requires setting out on a journey with many unknowns, a path on which many twists and turns will be encountered. This book has provided a guide, offering insights into the key elements that shape and define the strategies and tactics fundamental to achieving measured progress along the way. In particular, the essential characteristics for digital transformation have been explored through three lenses: agility, innovation, and disciplined management.

While the preceding chapters have focused on the fundamental characteristics of digital transformation, it is important to recognize that this is a rapidly evolving landscape with many moving parts. A wide spectrum of advances across technology, business, and society is likely to have significant impact on how individuals and organizations address the challenges they face and plan for the future. It is appropriate therefore, to speculate on how this evolution will impact the digital transformation journey and make a few observations on the areas of greatest promise to our digital economy.

Before looking forward, however, here is a brief retrospective look at the current state of digital transformation organized around this book's three key themes of Agility, Innovation, and Disciplined Management.

Looking Back

The first two decades of the 21st century have seen a particular focus on the impact of digital technology on business and society. From initial investigations into technology's capabilities for speeding up back-office processes and increasing online channels to customers, organizations have taken steps to build deep knowledge to drive the delivery of digital products and services. The impact on many businesses has been extensive and dramatic.[1][2]

An interesting illustrative example is in the restaurant and food delivery services industry. The past few years has seen a phenomenal rise in personalized menu planning programs (such as HelloFresh, Gousto, and Blue Apron) and online ordering businesses (such as JustEat and Deliveroo). These are founded on digital platform business models that open up marketplaces to a variety of consumer tastes and food suppliers.[3] Similarly, traditional restaurant businesses such as Domino's Pizza have focused their strategies on digital technology deployment and invested significantly in sophisticated point of sales systems, mobile online ordering apps, and efficient digital supply chain management solutions to drive their competitiveness. Domino's Pizza former CEO Patrick Doyle went as far as to claim that the rise in Domino's Pizza's share price from $10 in 2010 to over $200 in 2018 was largely founded on their digital technology leadership.[4] Even pizza companies are claiming to be differentiated through digital technology!

It is tempting, therefore, for organizations to talk in broad terms about digital transformation as if it is a new phenomenon unconnected with previous management approaches. Dealing with uncertainty and change has, however, always been a major element of public and private sector life. The additional pressures being faced in a digital world are experienced at three distinct levels:

1. **New streams of technologies needed to be understood and adopted as part of any solution**. The speed at which these technologies have appeared and are evolving is leaving many organizations behind. Consequently, organizations are investing in innovation skills to become more aware of potential technology-driven disruption, and to accelerate their ability to quickly absorb the resulting changes.

2. **The tools for planning, organizing, managing and delivering large-scale projects have increasingly become digital**. Hence, the individuals, communities, and companies responsible for project execution are going through their own digital transformation. Business leadership in the digital era requires new skills unfamiliar to executives trained in 20th century management approaches. Many are struggling to adopt the new tools and techniques at sufficient pace, increasing the volatility of key management tasks.

3. **Expectations of stakeholders on all sides have massively increased due to high-profile, digitally powered organizations raising the bar in product and service delivery far above previous industry norms**. Consumers are becoming accustomed to high levels of service offered by companies with significant experience in digital ways of working. These include companies in technology (e.g., usage-based pricing models from Google, Amazon, and Microsoft), logistics and delivery (e.g., real-time tracking and planning capabilities from FedEx and UPS), retail (e.g., agile market sensing from retail groups Inditex and Net-a-Porter) and financial services (e.g., responsive customer service from digital-only UK banking start-ups such as

Monzo, Starling, and Tide). Regardless of the context, customers will make comparisons with these digital business leaders when they experience ineffective processes or substandard product performance.

As a result, several studies report that organizations undergoing business digital transformation are taking steps to embed digital technology, processes, and skills within their broader strategic planning and management activities.[5] [6] [7] Significantly, they are looking beyond the traditional home for digital programmes within the IT department, to insist that all aspects of the organization adjust to meet the challenges and opportunities that digital transformation brings. A practical starting point for many organizations has been to focus extensively on customer experience programmes aimed at enhancing their interactions with customers and broader stakeholders through a variety of online channels. More recently, this has been expanded to include an increasing focus on internal employee experience and to develop the organizational culture necessary to accelerate growth, change, and innovation. The success of such efforts is based on a deeper review of the disruptive nature of emerging digital technologies, and an investment in cross-functional, collaborative teams sponsored by senior leaders in the organization.

However, these studies also highlight that experiences in digital transformation have not been wholly positive, particularly within complex organizations and when associated with significant cultural change. In the public sector, for example, digital technology deployment and the transformation of processes to adopt them have come under scrutiny. In the UK, three of the largest digital transformation programmes; Universal Credit,[8] London Crossrail,[9] and the high-speed rail network HS2[10] have been heavily criticized for cost overruns, delays, and lack of transparency. Running large transformations of this scale is particularly challenging, especially when they are carried out with wide public review. Regardless of their digital component, the issues that need to be addressed are ones of scale, diversity, financial management, and politics. The execution of these programmes is notoriously difficult to manage, and widely commented upon. As a result, evidence of poor performance has been seized upon as causing broader damage to the UK's national reputation for managing large projects,[11] with the UK National Audit Office (NAO) viewing "weak management, ineffective control and poor governance"[12] as the root of many of these issues.

Each of these projects have very high digital technology components, as expected of any major infrastructure program in the 21st century. While beneficial in many ways, these components have been specifically highlighted as significantly adding to the risks inherent in those projects; they force new operating procedures and introduce untried, evolving technologies into complex arenas with unprecedented socio-technical challenges.

Such examples serve to highlight the importance of leadership in driving successful adoption of digital technologies in mainstream projects, something that appears to still be in short supply. This was highlighted in a 2018 survey of over 4,000 managers and leaders worldwide conducted by MIT's Sloan Management Review and Cognizant.[13] The survey found that only 12% of respondents strongly agreed that their organizations' leaders had the right mindset for digital transformation, and less than 10% strongly agreed that their leaders had the appropriate skills for success in the digital economy. A situation that must change over the next few years.

Looking Forward

There are many different views and opinions regarding the future of digital technology, digital business processes, and the digital transformation they bring. While there is a wide breadth of vision for the future, the consensus seems to be that we are only at the early stages of digital transformation in business and society; a great deal is yet to occur. Here we highlight three areas that we believe will play a significant role in accelerating or dampening the pace and direction of digital transformation over the next decade: supporting hyper-connectivity, understanding the value of data, and moving toward strong AI-based solutions.

Hyper-connectivity

Many more physical devices and everyday objects are being imbedded with sensors to capture data about their operation and environment. These Internet of Things (IoT) devices form widely distributed networks connecting frequently via the Internet, wireless, and cloud-based platforms to share information, interact, and take actions. They bring new insights and operating processes to many domains and sectors.

Underlying the growing number of interconnected devices is the communications infrastructure on which it is based. Increasing demands are being placed on that infrastructure as the number of devices and the applications that drive them has risen. Today's trends indicate up to 50 billion connected devices by 2025,[14] with zettabytes of data transferred between them.[15] Applications for connected devices in sectors such as healthcare, transportation, utilities, retail, and entertainment vary widely. Each brings different requirements in terms of data transfer rates, speed of operation, latency in data transfer, reliability and security of communications, geographic coverage, availability, and accuracy.

To support these growing needs, 5G, the latest generation of communications infrastructure, builds on previous technologies to offer not only faster speeds of data transmission, but to also improve the reliability and performance of communications between devices.[16] The continued focus on driving technological advances in all aspects of 5G is resulting in a stream of new announcements as the technical characteristics are defined and matured.[17] Wide-scale roll-out of 5G infrastructure is expected from 2020 onwards, although some significant issues remain to be addressed.[18]

5G and associated developments in satellite technologies promise to offer a leap forward in communications functionality. They come at a time when a confluence of social, economic, and technological developments is demanding dramatic improvements to existing levels of connectivity. Such trends include:

— Global population is predicted to increase from seven to almost nine billion by 2030, with emphasis on developing regions such as India and China. Such populations will need to be educated, fed, and cared for in new ways. At the same time, record levels of populations in developed countries will enter retirement, with associated healthcare and occupational needs. Advances in communications will play a key role in meeting such challenges on a global scale.

— Interconnected autonomous machines will populate our homes, cities, and factories. IoT is proving to be a key use case for mobile networks to support applications that take advantage of data streams delivered through the billions of devices containing sophisticated sensors. Ubiquitous networking will be required to connect such a massive deployment of devices.

— New supply patterns are displacing traditional manufacturing practices with the widespread adoption of 3D printing in areas as disparate as home construction, personalized retail, and body part replacement.[19] This could lead to substantial investment in local manufacturing approaches, as compared to current global sourcing practices. Furthermore, the distributed nature of the processes will drive increases in the computing power necessary for flexible manufacturing and associated robotics. Improved connectivity between local facilities and remote computer centers will be a critical success factor.

- The nature of work will continue to change and evolve, with typical employment patterns compressing in time from years to months. Most people in the developed world will be employed in units of 10 or less staff. Connectivity will be the essential glue that binds together such disparate work groups and enables hyper-scaling of winning products and services.
- At a personal level, data consumption will continue to rise. With almost four billion people connected to the Internet, use of social media and consumption of personal entertainment is quickly growing around the world.[20] Demand for high-quality data connectivity will increase significantly over the coming years.

The ability of improved communications infrastructure such as 5G to handle massive data volumes with high transaction rates from remote and mobile locations will have the biggest impact on business. For instance, to support IoT applications it is essential to have the ability to capture data from remote sensors, transfer it to large data centers, and apply both AI and machine learning techniques for near real-time analysis. Additionally, solutions such as 5G must offer far greater capacity and be faster, more energy-efficient and more cost-effective than any of their predecessors.

These macro trends offer a useful context within which to envisage possible future hyper-connected usage scenarios. As AI, augmented reality and IoT become mainstream in both business and consumer markets, we anticipate at least four new scenarios that will give rise to opportunities for future mobile communications:

- **'Everything as an experience'** that exploits advances in virtual and augmented reality to bring new forms of entertainment, education, healthcare, and other services to the rapidly growing global population.
- **'Pop-up enterprises'** that align with current trends in design thinking and agile delivery. In such a scenario, small teams of people from multiple locations connect temporarily to test new business ideas in days or weeks. Successful ideas can be hyper-scaled using universal digital platforms.
- **'Flexible manufacturing'** that combines advances such as 3D printing with robotics to transform factories and the workplace. Working in close cooperation with humans, such flexible production units may be small enough to

operate in or close to the home, with new possibilities for high street retailers to design and build items on demand.
- **'Digital twinning'** that enables integration between physical (e.g., white goods) and digital (e.g. data) assets. Value shifts toward understanding 'products in use' rather than 'products in exchange' (e.g., at the point of sale). Consequently, the ability to monitor products through the full life cycle is becoming a critical success factor for many suppliers.

Illustrative of the dynamic, always-connected environment we are now entering, these scenarios emphasize the central role that advanced connectivity such as 5G will play in enabling digital transformation. Such trends stretch current thinking about the extent and impact of digital technology and put pressure on all organizations to recognize the urgency for change.

Data value

Curation of digital data and online data management have long been critical areas. The massive shift in the last few years to online commerce, digital communications, and social interaction has heightened the concerns. In an increasingly online lifestyle, individuals and organizations have become more sensitized to managing the privacy and security of personal information such as credit card details, to the implications of companies reusing data such as browsing history and social media interactions for commercial gain, and to criminal attempts of stealing information through techniques such as hacking and phishing. News reports of high-profile hacks and computer failures have intensified the focus on the role that digital technologies play in our lives, and the need to protect online information.

Concerns have heightened recently based on several important advances:
- Many people are becoming more aware of the vulnerability of computer systems to sustained, well-organized attacks by groups with criminal, terrorist, or political motivations. Large-scale data exploitations at major banks, insurance companies, and public agencies have served as a wake-up call for individuals and organizations to rethink their use of digital technology; in particular, how they act to protect the data that is being stored.
- The increasingly pervasive nature of digital technologies is producing a stream of popular consumer devices such as personal wearables and interconnected IoT devices. For many people, these technologies are now of a

different realm; in near real time they can detect, analyze, and communicate information on what is happening inside our homes and our bodies. Some of our most personal and intimate data is now being recorded, transmitted, and analyzed.

— Improvements in AI and machine learning algorithms are creating new forms of analysis and predictive insights. Driven by an abundance of data, a new generation of algorithms is being trained to detect and predict with very high accuracy. The utility of these advances in areas such as medicine and crime detection cannot be overestimated. However, the increasing use of such techniques for identifying, profiling, targeting, and selecting individuals based on explicit and implicit data signals is challenging prevailing views on fairness, bias, and exploitation (a topic explored in more detail later in this chapter).

Spurred by these new sensitivities, a set of deeper questions is now being asked about data ownership, data rights, and especially about the value of data. Currently, companies that build the digital technologies and manage the applications that run on them are frequently the ones that store and protect personal data on our behalf. In a majority of cases, the companies making the devices that generate and process this data also assert that they own that data and control its use. They claim ownership of the data, and also bear the liability and responsibility for its use.

Balancing the opportunity and responsibility of data ownership is becoming a major debate within many organizations, as well as gaining the attention of regulators.[21] Recent initiatives such as the Global Data Protection Regulation (GDPR)[22] have forced adjustments to operating practices across all organizations, accompanied by a rapid inventory check to determine what data they hold and how it is being used. In many cases this has led to a realization that the data management practices in place are lacking. This, in turn, has driven significant changes to how data is collected, organized, managed, and governed in many organizations.

Associated with data governance issues is the growing interest in forcing fundamental change to the Internet by encouraging individuals to claim ownership of their data, enabling them to store and protect that data, and allowing them to reuse and re-share it whenever they wish. The aim is to give individuals greater agency over one of the primary reasons for the Internet: information sharing.

Research initiatives such as the Hub-of-All-Things (HAT)[23] have focused on these issues for some time. Their championing of personal data stores has been important and influential in shining a light on the power given to companies when they assemble large data sets created from personal data. In fact, increasing the profile of this work is the voice and actions of Sir Tim Berners-Lee, widely regarded as the 'inventor of the world wide web'. He has expressed his growing concern for private ownership of data and believes that it is time "to restore rightful ownership of data back to every Web user".[24]

Berners-Lee's initial focus is to regain control of "Social Linked Data", known as Solid.[25] In a blog post[26] he explained that "Solid is guided by the principle of 'personal empowerment through data', which we believe is fundamental to the success of the next era of the web". Through his work at MIT, Berners-Lee is building a new platform, model, and social movement aimed at redesigning the data-sharing architecture at the core of the Internet.

The next few years will see many emerging ideas and technologies around data ownership and governance. But at the heart of this activity remains some very big questions: What's my data worth? To whom? How do I assert ownership for it? And in what circumstances does it become more or less valuable? At present, there are no widely accepted answers to these questions. Furthermore, variation in the understanding and perception of data value is distorting many practical areas for data transformation where managing and transferring data across multiple parties is a key concern.

For example, one of the more interesting areas of personal data recently coming into widespread use involves the analysis of DNA through genome sequencing; the process of determining the complete DNA sequence of an organism's genome. In the last few years genome sequencing has moved from science fiction to reality, with costs falling rapidly. The use of genome sequencing in medicine has been prevalent over the past decade. Outside of their direct medical use, however, partial approaches are now routine. People are interested and excited to learn more about their genetic makeup. Companies such as AncestryDNA and 23AndMe offer DNA tests for home use at $99,[27] and together are said to have delivered more than 15 million tests. Such activities are fun and entertaining as part of personal family tree research or curiosity. Beyond that, however, is the scientific and commercial value of such information.

Obtaining such data raises many questions: Should I receive some sort of payment for providing DNA data to medical research, pharmaceutical or insurance companies? Can I trade it in isolation or in combination with others to create a marketplace for pools of coordinated data? Can I decide who gets to use it and how? A new set of companies such as LunaDNA[28] and Nebula[29] are addressing these questions with data-based business models that support personal ownership and empowerment around such data. LunaDNA, for example, assigns specific value to different pieces of data; for instance, shares worth **14 cents** are paid for **20** minutes of fitness tracker data, **$3.50** for a genome-wide microarray, and **$21** for a whole genome.

In summary, focus on the importance of data in digital transformation will continue to grow over the next few years. Consequently, a variety of initiatives will challenge our perceptions of data and propose new ways to think about our actions online and the data they generate. Organizations will be strongly influenced by the directions that this work will take, which will result in adjustments to technology infrastructure, business models, regulations, and public opinion. At the heart of the debate will be an increasing awareness of what data is worth, who decides its value, and who profits from its use.

AI and robotics

With increasing automation, the use of AI and robotics have been very important components of digital transformation in many organizations and sectors. These technologies have been deployed to support all aspects of business, with solutions such as Robotic Process Automation to automate repeatable high-volume tasks, industrial robots in manufacturing to improve productivity and quality in product assembly, and chatbots using conversational AI to enhance customer service.

However, these solutions represent just a starting point for AI and robotics. Developments in these fields are moving rapidly to provide innovative solutions in many areas, including the use of collaborative robots (cobots) that work more closely with humans to perform tasks, and 'strong AI' that brings greater human-like intelligence to systems. Such advances offer huge opportunities for digital transformation, but also raise important questions about their impact and appropriate use that will slow their adoption and dominate business strategy discussions in many organizations.

Cobots

The challenge and opportunity for greater adoption of AI and robotics are encapsulated in the current adoption of cobots. These represent an important trend for robotics by delivering complex machines specifically designed to support human beings in their tasks. In a collaborative work process, they support and relieve the human operator in conducting jobs that are dirty, dangerous, repetitive, and difficult.[30] Initially deployed in manufacturing scenarios such as production line assembly, they are beginning to be used outside of the factory environment, in sectors such as agriculture, healthcare, and retail where they encounter similar challenges.

Unlike industrial robots that tend to be large, fixed, and operate in a controlled, caged environment separated from people, cobots are devices that help humans by amplifying their cognitive processes, interacting with both customers and employees to extend human physical capabilities.[31] Increasing attention is turning to cobots due to their smaller size, mobility, lower cost, and ease of maintenance. Consequently, many new applications for such devices are currently being designed, typically in sectors where humans are unwilling or unable to perform tasks due to difficult environments, repetition, or expectations of high accuracy levels.

The cooperative role played by cobots is the critical advance: they interact with humans frequently and within both controlled and uncontrolled operational contexts. This brings important benefits (e.g., in healthcare and agricultural scenarios) but also many challenges with respect to safety and liability. A great deal of investment in their development is now taking place to address this, and the next few years will see cobots evolve to become quicker, cheaper, and safer.

As a result, it is predicted that robotic automated assistance will become a key element of digital transformation for many organizations. Loup Ventures estimates that the number of cobots deployed will rise from a few thousand in 2016 to almost half a million in 2025 at a compound annual growth rate (CAGR) of over 60%.[32]

Toward strong AI

Current commercial applications of AI operate within well-defined, pre-specified constraints. Even high-profile solutions such as DeepMind,[33] Google Translate,[34] and IBM's Watson[35] are targeted toward problems with defined boundaries and clear measures of success. The resulting Artificial Narrow Intelligence (ANI), also known as 'Weak AI', is designed to perform single tasks such as playing chess, translating between different spoken languages, analyzing medical images for signs of abnormality, highlighting situations such as unusual bank account activity, and examining email traffic to determine the sender's emotional state.

Trained on massive datasets and powered by brute force, the effectiveness and efficiency of ANI will continue to grow as computing capacity increases and machine learning algorithms improve. More substantially, however, the direction for AI is toward solutions that exhibit greater human-like intelligence, where reasoning is required to adapt to new circumstances or where judgement is necessary to deal with ambiguity in context or outcome. Artificial General Intelligence (AGI), also called 'Strong AI', uses deep learning and unsupervised learning techniques to function in situations it has not yet encountered. Hence, AGI is able to reason, solve problems, and make judgements under uncertainty. These give AGI the characteristics of creativity and adaptability. In fact, AGI's ultimate goal is to create the intelligence that mimics how humans think and understand.

While true AGI may be some way off (or perhaps ultimately unachievable[36]), the application of AI as it evolves will be critical to digital transformation in the coming years. Not only will AI supported by data science techniques become the backbone of business analytics, but the incorporation of greater intelligence into AI systems will bring new insights, open new business opportunities, and support greater efficiency in achieving an organization's goals.[37] Undoubtedly, an organization's ability to adopt AI and robotics technologies will be a determining factor of their success.

Beyond technology

It is unjustifiable to discuss the future implications of AI and robotics without highlighting their impact on business and society more broadly. Experience from early uses of these technologies, backed by a plethora of dystopian commentaries on their long-term role,[38] raise significant questions about how they will change our view of work, the workplace, and ourselves. Such discussions tend to address critical social issues in four main areas:[39]

Labor and automation. Increased automation from AI and robotics is affecting all domains. The breadth and scope of impact is increasing with greater amounts of data being generated to fuel more powerful algorithms exploited on faster computers. Many foresee a productivity boom as companies adopt these technologies. This is to be welcomed, particularly in the UK where low productivity has been highlighted as a critical national challenge.[40] The downside of increasing productivity through automation, however, is the displacement of employment. Wildly speculative estimates of job losses through automation in the coming years have increased concerns about the introduction of AI and robotics,[41] and in some cases led to an almost Luddite approach to resist their use.[42] Others see automation in terms of an employment shift toward new kinds of jobs, tasks, and work mobility patterns.[43] Furthermore, within some organizations the use of AI and robotics can also be perceived as de-humanizing the workplace. Rather than supporting humans by removing unwanted and dangerous tasks, some workers may see their role reduced to tending to the technology as they watch it replace them in the tasks they used to perform.[44]

Bias and inclusion. All technological advances suffer from the consequence that they tend to advantage a subset of society above others. Whether through a lack of access, insufficient skills, or geographic remoteness, the asymmetry of their adoption brings bias into their definition and may amplify the exclusion of certain groups in their use. More than simply an issue of 'fairness', the lack of diversity has operational implications for technologies such as AI and robotics. Significant errors have been reported, for example, where AI algorithms have been trained with narrow datasets,[45] and expensive legal claims have arisen when bias has been found in selecting and interpreting data.[46] More broadly, a widening gap and lack of diversity in digital technology deployment may only serve to exacerbate critical social challenges rather than help overcome them.

Rights and liberties. Application of AI and robots is leading society into unprecedented situations that often challenge existing legal frameworks.[47] While a wide set of issues must be addressed, underlying many concerns is the legal status of AI systems and robots. From a legal perspective, it is essential that the responsibilities and rights of these devices is determined in order to deal with issues as diverse as liability, security, and taxation. This is particularly complex in environments where responsibilities are shared across owners, designers, developers, and other stakeholders of deployed systems. Furthermore, if such systems will be making life-changing decisions (e.g., in some healthcare and automotive scenarios) responsibility must be clearly established, recorded, audited, and shared. This may imply, for example, that AI systems or robots might need to have a 'legal identity'; the term used to establish which entities have legal rights and obligations and can enter into contracts or be sued.

Ethics and governance. In using AI and robots, the speed of change is so rapid that questions of technical feasibility and legal precedent are subsumed by more profound concerns of ethics and governance. For example, when analyzing large datasets about smartphone use, AI-based algorithms may be able to detect patterns of inappropriate or illegal behavior from people's locations and movements. What should be done with those insights? Due to the interpretive and predictive nature of AI, deciding on such issues brings designers, owners, and users of those systems into conflict. This is particularly challenging from an ethical perspective when such systems embed AI that makes autonomous decisions on behalf of their users. For example, if the AI-based systems inside a car detect erratic driving patterns, should it flash a warning on the dashboard, limit the speed of the car, turn off the engine, or inform the police? Who should decide that? The ethical aspects of such situations are further complicated by the challenges of governing the design and deployment of these systems. Often it is very unclear how decisions are made by these devices: in most cases there is a complex chain of concerns regarding who designed the system, how it was tested, how the algorithms were trained, what behavior has been inferred through use, and much more. Even more worrying is that there is very little requirement for public transparency over each of these steps in the chain. Recognizing these concerns, regulators and national governments around the world are beginning to propose policies and practices that at least partially address these ethical and governance issues through initiatives such as the UK Centre for Data Ethics and Innovation[48] and the Ada Lovelace Institute.[49]

While the promise of AI and robotics is to increase employment and enhance productivity, many existing jobs across a wide spectrum of domains are susceptible to displacement or much-reduced roles. Furthermore, the introduction of these technologies will have unequal impact across different communities, sectors, and geographies. The impending danger over the next few years is that without careful management, vulnerable communities will be further disadvantaged. The opportunity in digital transformation is to recognize these concerns, and to ensure strategies take into account broader societal issues.

A Final Word

The strategies and approaches explored in this book are aimed at preparing, enabling, and supporting organizations to deliver digital transformation. However, to conclude, it is important to reiterate that digital transformation is not an end in itself. It is the means to an end: to growth, efficiency, innovation, and opportunity.

In our digital world, transforming organizations to be more efficient, responsive, and better aligned with stakeholder needs will drive the use of digital technologies and practices across many different dimensions. Success demands that everyone in the organization is digitally aware in the same way they understand fairness and diversity in recruitment, financial controls, marketplace innovation, and their role in driving corporate strategy. With the rapid evolution of digital technology, this will be an ongoing process of education, experimentation, and delivery. Looks like interesting times ahead!

References

1 Hamel, G. (2012). *What Matters Now*. John Wiley.
2 Friedman, T.L. (2017). *Thank You for Being Late*. Penguin.
3 Warner, J. (2018). *Just Eat and Deliveroo: What Has the Takeaway Delivery Market Got on the Menu?* IG.com. Available at: https://www.ig.com/uk/news-and-trade-ideas/shares-news/just-eat-and-deliveroo--what-has-the-takeaway-delivery-market-go-180622
4 Maze, J. (2018). *How Patrick Doyle Changed Domino's, and The Restaurant Industry*. Restaurant Business. Available at: https://www.restaurantbusinessonline.com/leadership/how-patrick-doyle-changed-dominos-restaurant-industry
5 Information Age (2019). *Digital Transformation Trends to Watch in 2019 and Beyond*. Information-age.com. Available at: https://www.information-age.com/digital-transformation-trends-to-watch-123477837/
6 Hushon, D. (2019). *6 Digital Trends to Accelerate Business Transformation in 2019*. DXC. technology. Available at: https://www.dxc.technology/innovation/insights/1457296_digital_trends_to_acce lerate_business_transformation_in_2019
7 https://www.adobe.com/uk/modal-offers/econsultancy_digital_trends_2018_report.html

8 https://www.gov.uk/universal-credit

9 http://www.crossrail.co.uk/

10 https://www.hs2.org.uk/

11 The Economist (2018). *Britain's Engineering Reputation Goes Down the Tube.* The Economist. Available at: https://www.economist.com/britain/2018/12/06/britains-engineering-reputation-goes-down-the-tube

12 Schraer, R. (2018). *What is Universal Credit - and What's the Problem?* BBC. Available at: https://www.bbc.co.uk/news/uk-41487126

13 https://sloanreview.mit.edu/big-ideas/future-of-leadership/

14 Nordrum, A. (2016). *Popular Internet of Things Forecast of 50 Billion Devices by 2020 is Outdated.* IEEE Spectrum. Available at:https://spectrum.ieee.org/tech-talk/telecom/internet/popular-internet-of-things-forecast-of-50-billion-devices-by-2020-is-outdated

15 Patrizio, A. (2018). *IDC: Expect 175 Zettabytes of Data Worldwide by 2025.* Network World. Available at: https://www.networkworld.com/article/3325397/idc-expect-175-zettabytes-of-data-world-wide-by-2025.html

16 https://futurenetworks.ieee.org/about/overview

17 https://5g.co.uk/

18 Webb, W. (2018). The 5G Myth: When Vision Decoupled from *Reality.* De Gruyter.

19 Reichental, A. (2018). *The Future of 3-D Printing.* Forbes. Available at: https://www.forbes. com/sites/forbestechcouncil/2018/01/23/the-future-of-3-d-printing/ #165a9d8665f6

20 Marr, B. (2018). *How Much Data Do We Create Every Day? The Mind-Blowing Stats Everyone Should Read.* Forbes. Available at: https://www.forbes.com/sites/bernardmarr/2018/05/21/how-much-data-do-we-create-every-day-the-mind-blowing-stats-everyone-should-read

21 https://www.futureagenda.org/insight/data-ownership

22 https://eugdpr.org/

23 https://www.hubofallthings.com/

24 Duraj, M. (2019). *Sir Tim Berners-Lee at Forefront of New Movement to Take Back Ownership of Our Data.* Vmvirtualmachine.com. Available at: https://vmvirtualmachine.com/sir-tim-berners-lee-at-forefront-of-new-movement-to-takeback-ownership-of-our-data/

25 https://solid.mit.edu/

26 Berners-Lee, T. (2018). *One Small Step for the Web...*Medium. Com. Available at: https://medium.com/@timberners_lee/one-small-step-for-the-web-87f92217d085

27 Ibrahim, B. (2019). *Your Ultimate Guide to DNA At-Home Testing Kits.* CNN Underscored. Available at: https://us.cnn.com/2018/09/18/cnn-underscored/dna-kit-guide-shop/index.html

28 https://www.lunadna.com/

29 https://nebula.org

30 Lloyds (2019). *Taking Control: Robots and Risk, Lloyds Register Emerging Risk Report,* April. Available at: https://www.lloyds.com/news-and-risk-insight/risk-reports/library/technology/taking-control

31 Daugherty, H.J. and Wilson, P. (2018). *Human + Machine: Reimagining Work in the Age of Auto-mation.* Harvard Business School Press.

32 Murphy, A. (2019). *Industrial: Robotics Outlook 2025.* Loup Ventures. Available at: https://loupventures.com/industrial-robotics-outlook-2025

33 https://deepmind.com/

34 https://translate.google.co.uk/

35 https://www.ibm.com/watson

36 Rodriguez, J. (2018). Gödel, Consciousness and the Weak vs. Strong AI Debate. Towards Data Science. Medium.com. Available at: https://towardsdatascience.com/g%C3%B6del-consciousness-and-the-weak-vs-strong-ai-debate-51e71a9189ca

37 Wilson, H.J., Daugherty, P.R. and Davenport, C. (2019). *The Future of AI will Be About Less Data, More Intelligence*. Harvard Business Review, January. Available at: https://hbr.org/2019/01/the-future-of-ai-will-be-about-less-data-not-more

38 Carr, N. (2011). *The Shallows: How the Internet is Changing the Way We Think and Remember*. Atlantic Books.

39 Campolo, A. et. al. (2017). *AI Now, The AI Now Report 2017*. AI Now Institute. Available at: https://ainowinstitute.org/AI_Now_2017_Report.pdf

40 Tetlow, G. (2018). The UK's Corporate Productivity Challenge, in Charts. *Financial Times*, February 21. Available at: https://www.ft.com/content/c78ff64c-fc7f-11e7-9bfc-052cbba03425

41 Garimella, K. (2018). Job Loss From AI? There's More To Fear! *Forbes*. Available at: https://www.forbes.com/sites/cognitiveworld/2018/08/07/job-loss-from-ai-theres-more-to-fear/#425b8ca423eb

42 Bartlett, J. (2018). Will 2018 be the Year of the Neo-Luddite? *The Guardian*, March 4. Available at: https://www.theguardian.com/technology/2018/mar/04/will-2018-be-the-year-of-the-neo-luddite

43 Frontier Economics (2018). *The Impact of Artificial Intelligence on Work: An Evidence Review Prepared for the Royal Society and the British Academy*. Available at: https://royalsociety.org/-/media/policy/projects/ai-and-work/frontier-review-the-impact-of-AI-on-work.pdf

44 Rotman, D. (2013). How Technology is Destroying Jobs. *MIT Technology Review*, June 12.

45 Hao, K. (2019). This is How AI Bias Really Happens – and Why it's So Hard to Fix. *MIT Technology Review*. February 4.

46 Villasenor, J. (2019). *AI and Bias: Four Key Challenges*. The Brookings Institute, January 3. Available at: https://www.brookings.edu/blog/techtank/2019/01/03/artificial-intelligence-and-bias-four-key-challenges/

47 Rissland, E.L., Ashley, K.D. and Loui, R.P. (2003). AI and Law. Artificial Intelligence, 150 (1–2), Nov: 1-346. Available at: https://www.sciencedirect.com/journal/artificial-intelligence/vol/150/issue/1

48 https://www.gov.uk/government/groups/centre-for-data-ethics-and-innovation-cdei

49 https://www.adalovelaceinstitute.org/

Index